I0810093

IMAGES
of America

MERCEDES

Map Showing Location of Mercedes, Texas

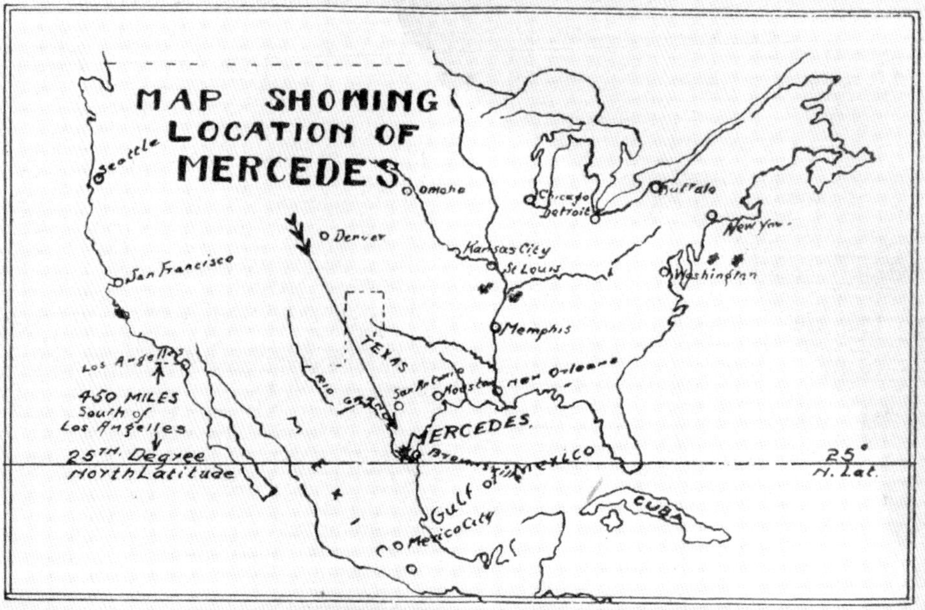

Excursion rates can be had to Mercedes for $25.00 to $30.00 from Northern points for the round trip, good for 25 days. Tickets are on sale every first and third Tuesday of each month. Have your ticket read direct to Mercedes; side trips may be taken from this point for one fare for the round trip.

This map was part of an accordion postcard from 1909 that showed a map of Mercedes's location and invited northerners to travel by train to visit and purchase land or start a business. The postcards were commissioned by the Mercedes Commercial Club, forerunner of the Mercedes Chamber of Commerce, as part of an aggressive marketing strategy. Mercedes is located in the southeast corner of Hidalgo County in South Texas, only five miles from the Rio Grande and the border with Mexico. (Courtesy of Vito Buenrostro.)

On the Cover: Mercedes celebrates its 25th anniversary on September 15, 1932, with a historic parade. The town was founded in 1907 to serve as the headquarters of the American Rio Grande Land and Irrigation Company. The first residences and businesses were railroad boxcars, tents, and shanties, but by 1932, prosperous shops lined the main street in town and the population had grown to more than 5,000 inhabitants. (Courtesy of the Margaret H. McAllen Memorial Archives, Museum of South Texas History.)

IMAGES
of America

MERCEDES

Beatrice de León Edwards, EdD

ARCADIA
PUBLISHING

ISBN 978-1-4671-3206-0

Published by Arcadia Publishing
Charleston, South Carolina

Printed in the United States of America

Library of Congress Control Number: 2014943728

For all general information, please contact Arcadia Publishing:
Telephone 843-853-2070
Fax 843-853-0044
E-mail sales@arcadiapublishing.com
For customer service and orders:
Toll-Free 1-888-313-2665

Visit us on the Internet at www.arcadiapublishing.com

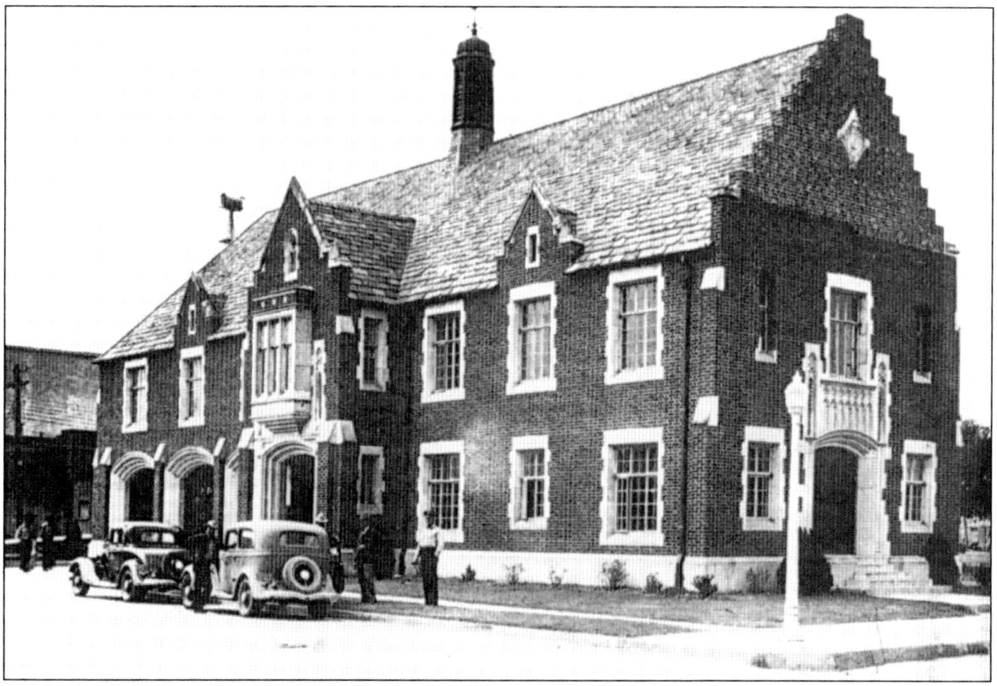

The Mercedes City Hall and Fire Station, built in 1928, was designed by architect Roscious Newell Waters. The first floor held city offices, and the second floor housed a firemen's dormitory and city meeting rooms. The building is in a Gothic style with red brick with the exception of the replacement bricks on the end from repairs after the hurricane of 1933. It features a copper cupola to hold the fire alarm. (Courtesy of the City of Mercedes.)

Contents

ACKNOWLEDGMENTS

Many heartfelt thanks go out to all of the individuals who so generously allowed me to scan their personal family photographs and postcard collections for use in this book, including Vito Buenrostro; Carolyn Crenshaw López; Irma Palacios; Rolando Hinojosa-Smith; Sylvia Arteaga Calles; the Riess family; the García family; Robert, Loretta, Kenneth, and Debbie Eilers; Rosendo Gonzales; Eddie Howell Sr.; Helen Vogel; and Delia de León. A very special thanks to Fran Isbell, whose in-depth knowledge of the Rio Grande Valley and its history were warmly shared with the author. Especially helpful also were the staff of the Weslaco Museum of Local History and Cultural Art; the members of the Hidalgo County Historical Commission; Janette García of the University of Texas-Pan American; and Phyllis Kinnison and Esteban Lomas of the Museum of South Texas History. All images from the Museum of South Texas History (MSTH) come from the Margaret H. McAllen Memorial Archives of the Museum of South Texas History in Edinburg, Texas. A special thanks to Olga Hinds and Clarissa Martínez of the *Mercedes Enterprise*; as well as the City of Mercedes; the members of the Mercedes Chamber of Commerce; Dr. Daniel Treviño Jr., superintendent of schools, Alicia Z. Vásquez, district librarian, and Debbie Winslow of the Mercedes Independent School District; Sam MaGee, general manager, and Adell Dufour, museum director, of the Rio Grande Valley Livestock Show; Our Lady of Mercy Catholic Church; the Rubén Hinojosa Congressional Office; and Marisol Vidales, library director at the Hector P. García Memorial Library of Mercedes, Texas. Also invaluable have been the publications and work by the Mercedes Centennial Book Project Committee. Special thanks to the Carrizo/Comecrudo Tribe of Texas for the use of its tribal seal. More information about this tribe is available at www.carrizocomecrudonation.com. Public domain images from the Library of Congress and the National Archives have also been used. Special thanks also go to Dr. Armando Alonzo, Borderlands historian at Texas A&M University, for reviewing text and making important recommendations. Heartfelt thanks for her patience and assistance go to my acquisitions editor, Stacia Bannerman; David Mandel, production coordinator; and Jennifer Sexton, sales manager, at Arcadia Publishing. Finally, thanks to all my family members for their love and encouragement on this project. Without these entities, this book would not have been possible.

INTRODUCTION

Mercedes, Texas, the "Queen City," is located in the southeastern corner of Hidalgo County only five miles from the Mexican border in South Texas in a geographic area known as the Lower Rio Grande Valley. The "Valley" is not a true valley, but a river delta formed as the Rio Grande empties into the Gulf of Mexico. Before the advent of river dams and levees, the Rio Grande flooded annually, much as the Nile did in Egypt, creating rich, fertile soil in a narrow band suitable for limited agriculture.

The earliest known inhabitants of this area were called Coahuiltecans by anthropologists who grouped all of the separate native indigenous groups together. Later studies of the copious annotations of Spanish *entradas*, or exploratory expeditions, to this area in the 1600s revealed that many different groupings existed, each with their own language and customs. These early explorations noted that there were numerous native settlements the Spanish called *rancherías*.

Under the leadership of José de Escandón, the Count of Sierra Gorda, Spanish colonists migrated in the mid-1700s to the northern reaches of Nueva España, or New Spain, to the region called *Nuevo Santander*, which reached from Tampico to the Nueces River. On both the southern and northern banks of the lower Rio Grande, Escandón established six villas or townships between 1749 and 1755, and numerous land grants called *porciones* were apportioned out. These *porciones* were narrow strips of land that each had access to the river to ensure that water was available to each landowner. Because of the climate, topography and soil composition, these Spanish colonists decided that ranching was best suited to the area, with some subsistence farming in selected areas near the river waters or the *resacas* through the use of *acequias*, or irrigation channels, that used gravity to move the water streams.

In 1778, Juan José Hinojosa, a captain and chief justice at the villa of Reynosa, petitioned the king of Spain for the Llano Grande land grant on the north side of the Rio Grande where the city of Mercedes is now located. This royal land grant contained 25 leagues of land with 15 miles of river frontage, or more than 100,000 acres. By the time the grant was approved in 1790, Hinojosa had died, and his grant was divided up amongst his eight heirs. Mercedes was later established on what were parts of shares five, six, and seven.

Mexico's separation from Spain in 1821 and the Texas Independence of 1836 disrupted the everyday business of the ranching communities, and many Mexican-heritage inhabitants of Texas began calling themselves Tejanos. The Mexican–American War in 1848 profoundly impacted the area when the original landowners, suddenly now US citizens, were forced to protect their land claims in land adjudication courts. Being land-rich but cash-poor, many were able to do so successfully but still lost land when they were forced to pay the American lawyers' fees and their property taxes with acreage.

During the Civil War, when the Rio Grande was the only waterway available to the Confederate cotton growers for shipping to market, the value of the river and the region was noted by northern venture capitalists. Many Anglos had come to the Valley during the Mexican–American War and the Civil War to make their fortunes, and many married Mexican heiresses. By 1865, northern eyes were set on the Rio Grande Valley and interest grew in developing international trade and commercialized agriculture in this region.

In July 1904, the Sam Fordyce Branch of the St. Louis, Brownsville and Mexico Railway reached Section 14 and established the stop that would later become Mercedes, declared the "Sweetheart of the Branch." Upon visiting the Valley, railroad magnate Benjamin F. Yoakum became convinced that commercialized agriculture was a viable venture in the Rio Grande Valley. Yoakum convinced a group of investors to form the American Rio Grande Land and Irrigation Company to purchase land and develop an irrigation system that would transform the Lower Rio Grande Valley into an area of profitable commercialized agriculture.

The American Rio Grande Land and Irrigation Company purchased land from the Capisallo Town and Improvement Company belonging to Lon C. Hill in 1907 with the intention of making the town its company headquarters. Hill had already platted a town and named it Capisallo, then later renamed it Lonsboro. The American Rio Grande Land and Irrigation Company then decided to move the site west about a mile to an area called the Pear Orchard. It was so named because of the abundance of cacti bearing prickly pear fruit in that location. Mercedes was officially founded on September 15, 1907.

By sheer force of manual labor, thousands of Mexican and Tejano laborers with pick, shovel, and hoe cleared the land, and the town was finally mapped out in its present location. The American Company directors decided to rename the town Díaz because they greatly admired Mexican president Porfirio Díaz but then changed it to Mercedes, somehow erroneously believing that President Díaz's wife's name was Mercedes. But Díaz's first wife was named Delfina, and his second wife was named Carmen, so the choice of name remains a mystery to this day. No known primary sources exist explaining the choice of name. Unfortunately, numerous published works since the early days have reported that the name Mercedes referred to President Díaz's wife, and the inaccuracy has been repeated many times.

It should be noted that the phrase *mercedes reales* means "royal grants" and *mercedes de tierra* means "land grants." It is possible that somehow, someone who heard these phrases mistakenly believed Mercedes to be a person; namely, President Díaz's wife. The phrase *mercedes reales* also gives a connection to the choice of the nickname "Queen City" for the town of Mercedes because "*real*" which means "royal" could have made someone think Mercedes referred to a royal person; namely, a queen. In reality, *mercedes reales* referred to the fact that the *porciones* and the larger land grant tracts such as the Llano Grande were royal gifts.

On March 8, 1909, Mercedes became incorporated and elected a mayor and city council. The town grew rapidly as the Mercedes Commercial Club, forerunner of the Mercedes Chamber of Commerce, aggressively promoted land development. The winter vegetable and citrus farms began producing immediately, and Mercedes became a major exporter of produce, citrus fruits, and cotton. In 1939, Mercedes promoted an annual agricultural and livestock show that became the Rio Grande Valley Livestock Show. In 2014, the Rio Grande Valley Livestock Show celebrated its 75th anniversary.

As did most Valley cities, Mercedes experienced growing pains with bandit troubles, the effects of World War I and II, influenza and smallpox epidemics, hurricanes, floods, droughts, freezes, and the Great Depression. Mercedes overcame these obstacles and continued to thrive. The town established many churches and businesses and an excellent school system. Mercedes has produced notable citizens in the fields of art, literature, music, business, education, government, athletics, and science among others; and although it has produced excellence, its noble work is not yet done.

One

The Early Settlers

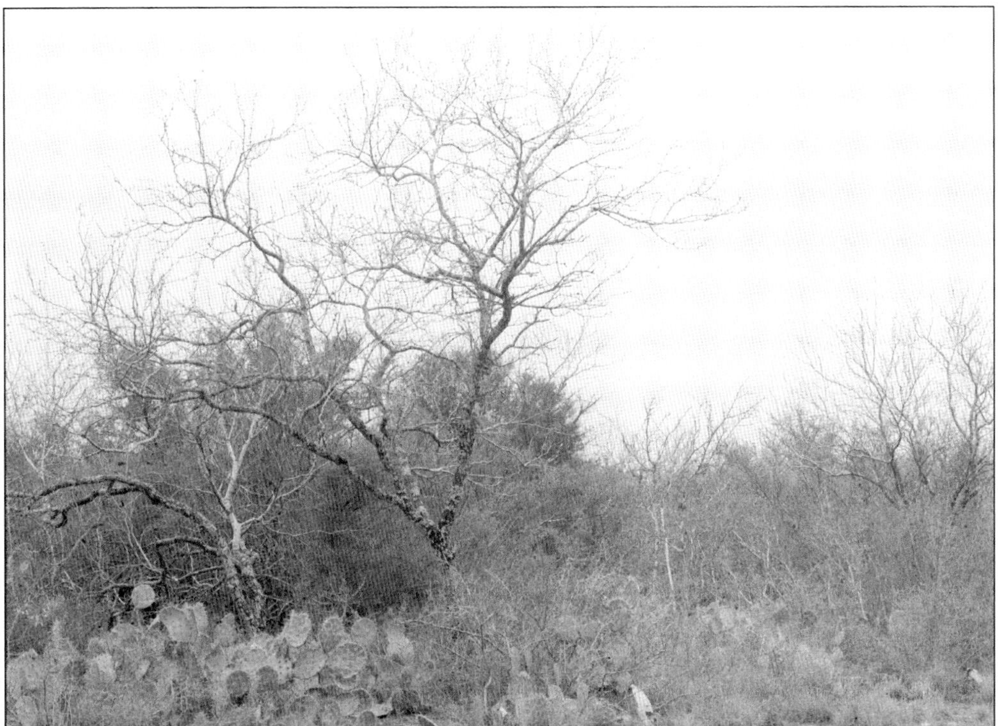

Spanish explorers first came to the area where Mercedes is now located in the 1600s. The expeditions found that the land was covered with heavy brush similar to that of this photograph. Mesquite, cactus, huisache, and other native plants covered the land thickly. When the Spanish colonists arrived in the 1700s, they decided to use the land for ranching with some subsistence farming where water was available. (MSTH.)

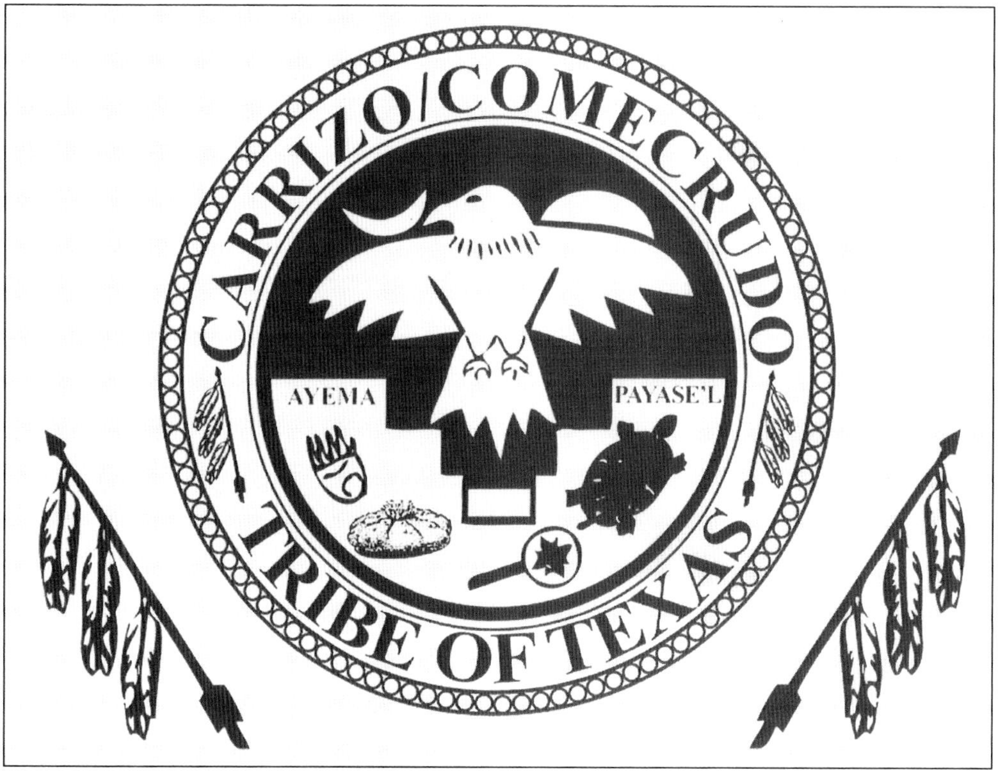

The Spanish made several expeditions or *entradas* into the Rio Grande Valley in the 17th century. They reported finding many *rancherías*, or settlements of nomadic bands that historians first called Coahuiltecans. After rereading Spanish chronicles, later historians discovered more than 50 different indigenous groups inhabited this region. The Carrizo/Comecrudo were most associated with the Rio Grande river delta. Once thought extinct, descendants have resurfaced although they were displaced to other Texas areas. (Carrizo/Comecrudo Tribe of Texas.)

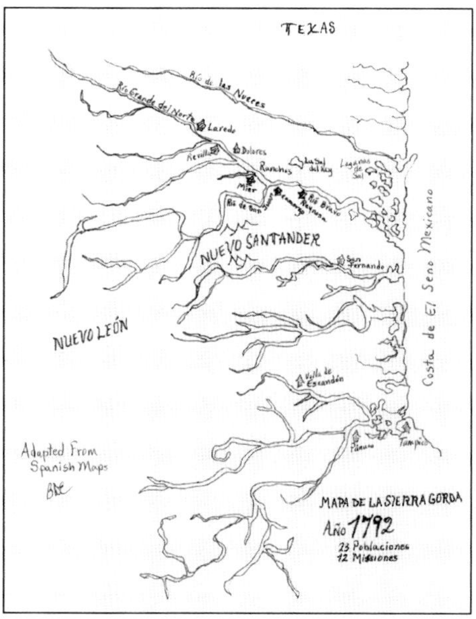

Spanish explorer Alonso de León led four expeditions between 1686 and 1689 to explore the area around the mouth of the Rio Grande, also known as the Rio Bravo. After finding the ruins of a French settlement on his fourth expedition, the Spanish king commanded that settlers be brought in to establish a more solid claim to this area. In 1746, José de Escandón, the Count of Sierra Gorda, was commissioned to explore the area between Tampico and the San Antonio River. The province of Nuevo Santander, which corresponds generally to the Mexican state of Tamaulipas and south Texas, is pictured in this adaptation of a 1792 Spanish map. (Courtesy University of Texas-Pan American.)

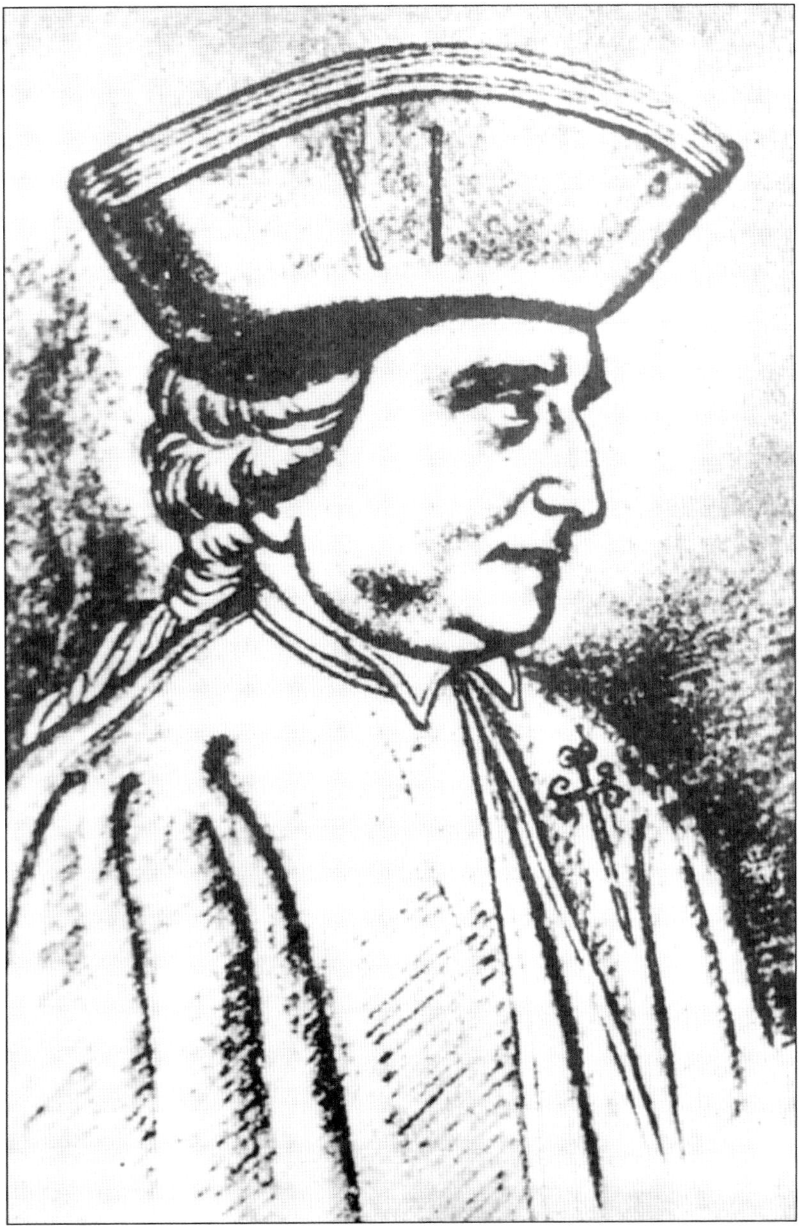

José de Escandón was a Spaniard who chose a military career and immigrated to New Spain in 1715. By 1740, he had risen through the ranks and was lieutenant captain general of the Sierra Gorda frontier. His successful strategies for pacification of the region while remaining fair-minded with all groups brought him the title of Count of Sierra Gorda as well as the charge of leading colonists to the Rio Grande region. After determining which areas were suitable for settlement and carefully choosing which colonists to take, Escandón brought in more than 400 families and founded Camargo, Reynosa, Mier, Revilla, Laredo, and Nuestra Señora de los Dolores on the banks of the lower Rio Grande. For this reason, he is often called the "father" of the lower Rio Grande Valley. Beginning in 1755 with the founding of Laredo, Spanish colonists began establishing ranching communities on the northern banks of the river, including the area where Mercedes is today. (University of Texas-Pan American.)

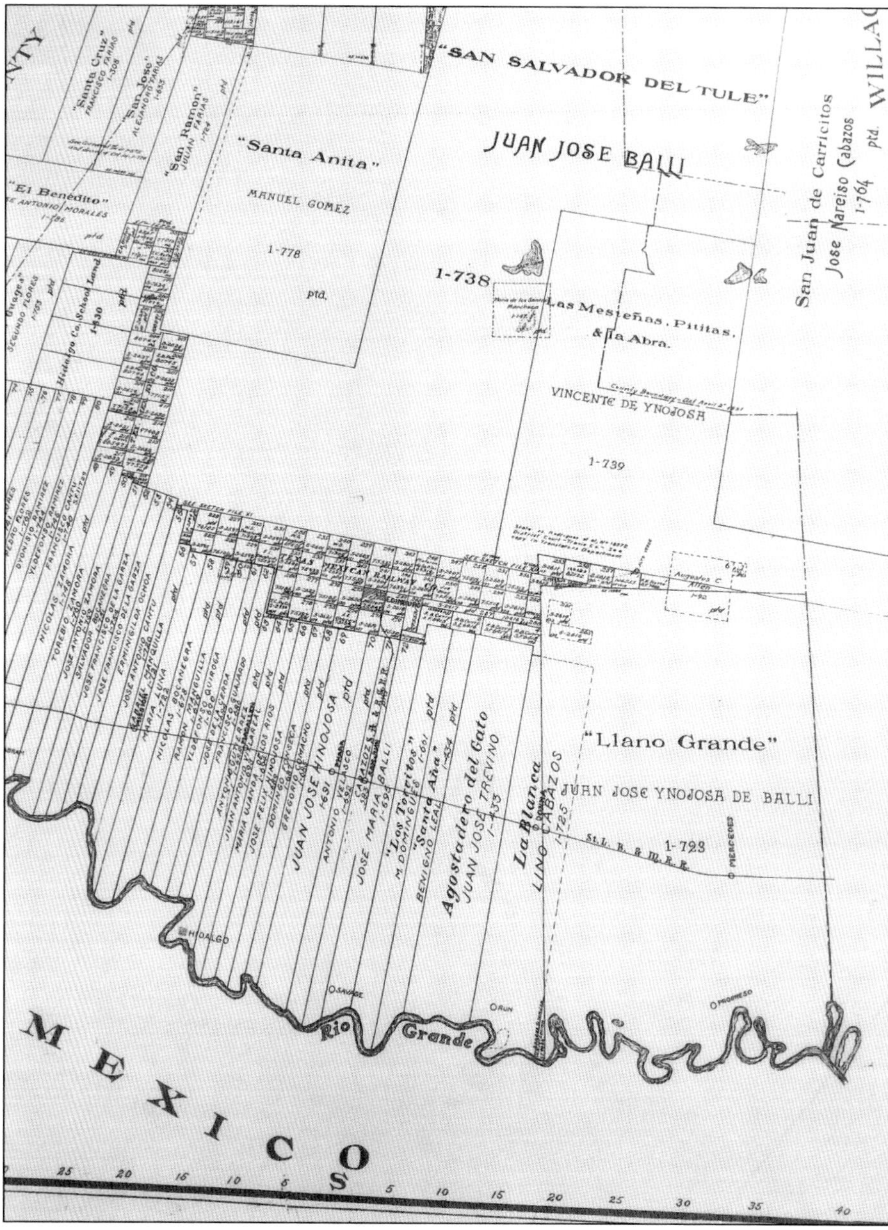

This map shows the *porciones*, or long narrow strips of land, and larger land grants owned by the original Spanish colonizers of southern Hidalgo County in the late 1800s. In 1778, Juan José Hinojosa, a captain and chief justice at the villa of Reynosa, petitioned the king of Spain for the Llano Grande grant where the city of Mercedes is now located. This grant contained 25 leagues of land with about 15 miles of river frontage. Hinojosa died before he was finally granted the land in 1790, and his children inherited the land in eight equal shares. Mexico's separation from Spain in 1821, the Texas Independence of 1836, and the Mexican–American War of 1846 created turmoil in the region. In 25 years, these first families' citizenships changed three times. At the end of the Mexican–American War, they were forced to prove their land ownership in Texas state courts. Although most of them retained title to their land grants, many lost acreage when they were forced to pay their attorneys and taxes in land. (Hidalgo County Historical Commission.)

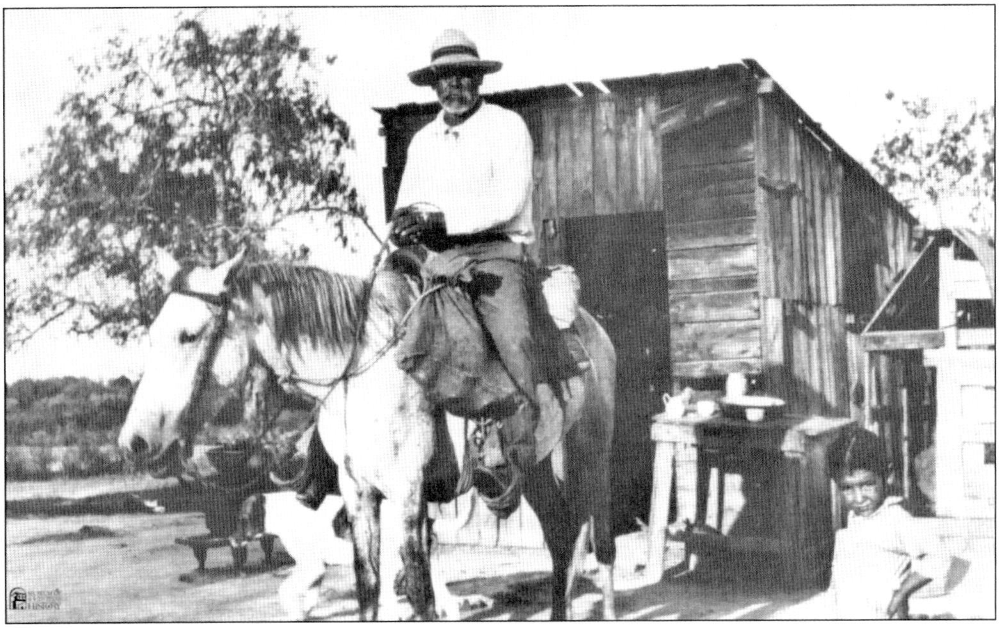

By the end of the 19th century, there were hundreds of ranches on the northern side of the Rio Grande. Although the brush land was thick with mesquite, cactus, huisache, and native grasses, the land was suitable for grazing cattle. Every ranch had access to water, either directly from the river or from the *resacas*, the old river channels of the Rio Grande. (MSTH.)

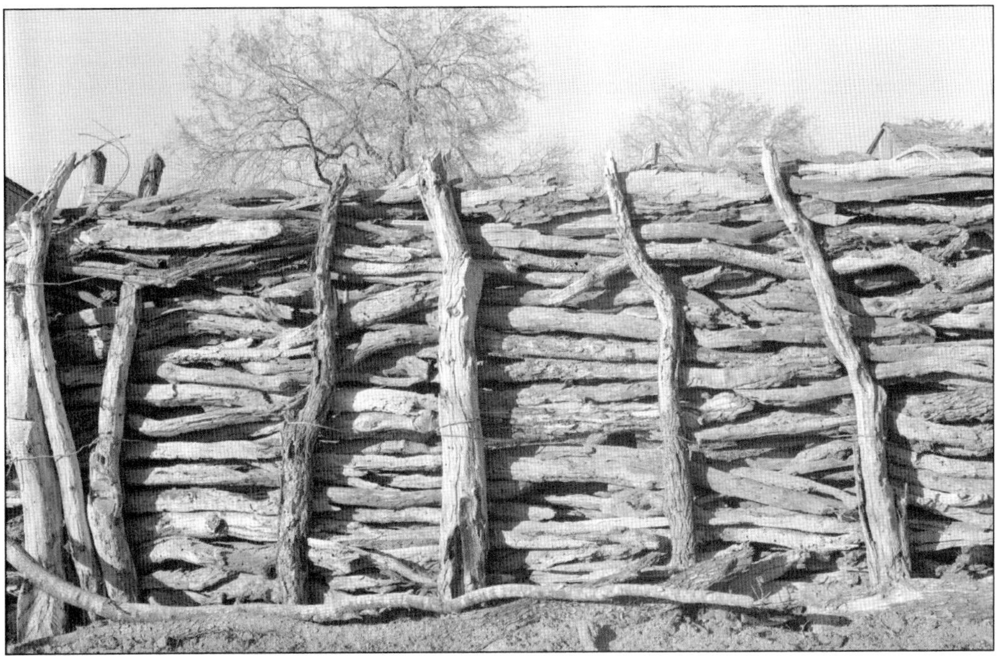

In the 19th century, the most obvious choice as a building material in the valley was mesquite wood. Even though it was twisted rather than straight, it was abundant, strong, and durable. The wood is so hard that it is sometimes called "Texas Ironwood." Corrals and fences made of mesquite such as the one seen here were common sights on valley ranches of that era and are still seen today. (National Archives.)

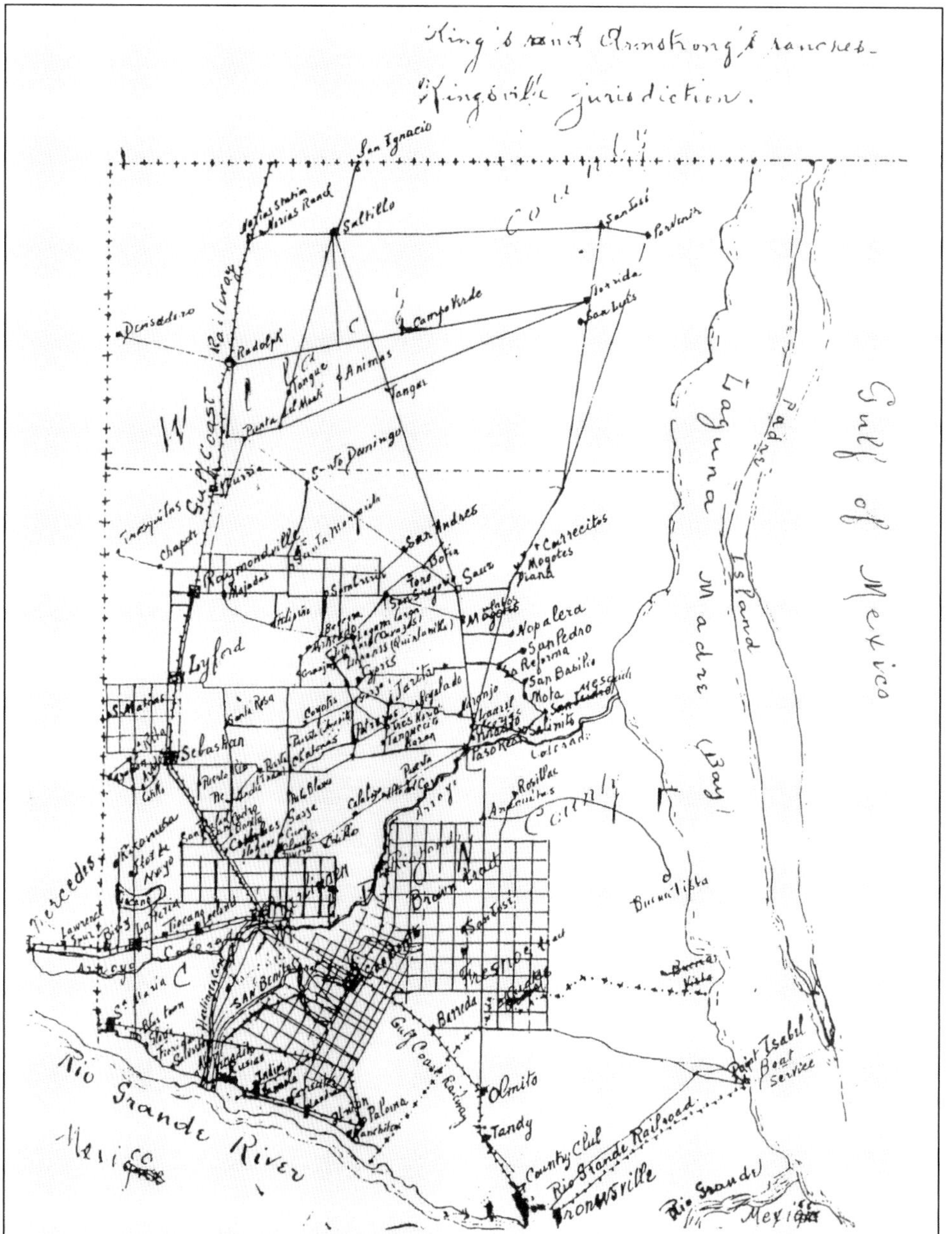

This map is a partial replica of one of the hand-drawn maps used by the Missionary Oblates of Mary Immaculate from around 1849 to serve the Catholics living on the scattered ranches of south Texas. These missionary priests had established headquarters in Brownsville before the advent of the railroad or even of paved roads. They traveled their lonely trails through the wild brush land alone, mounted on horseback. Their circuits usually lasted about six weeks during which time they traveled 100 miles or more. The Oblate Trail in the Rio Grande Valley stretched from Port Isabel and Brownsville up the river to Laredo, a distance of more than 200 miles. They also traveled north to service ranches and townsites farther away from the river. In 1949, the Brownsville Historical Association designated the trail by erecting road markers. (Hidalgo County Historical Commission.)

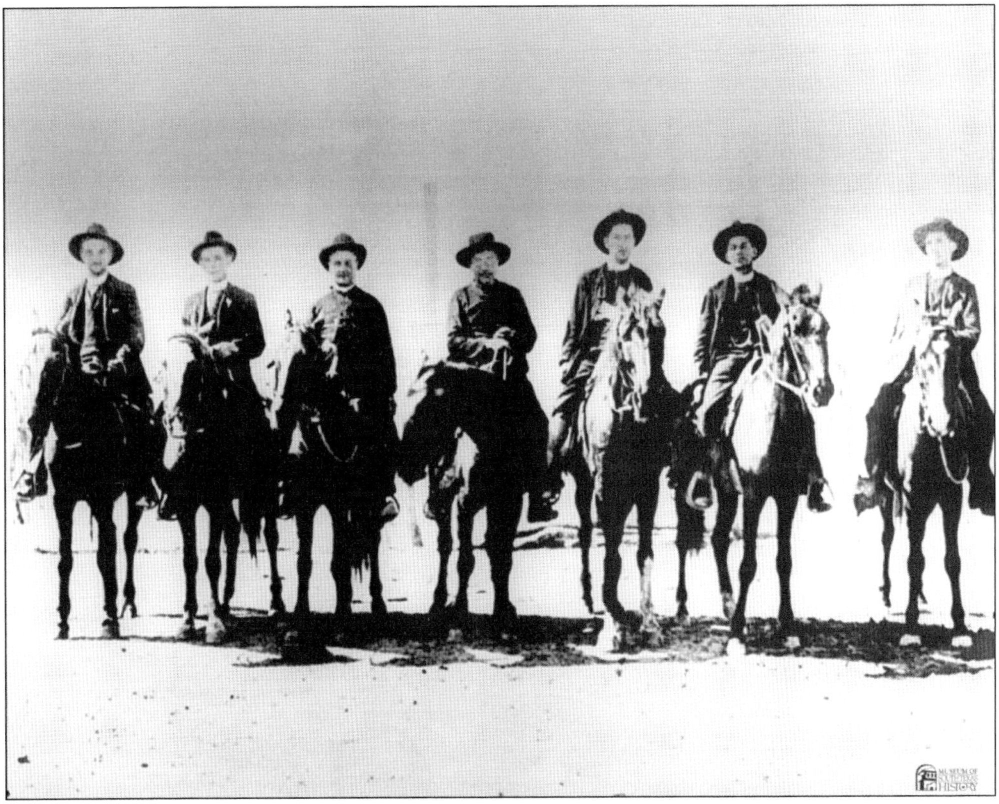

The Missionary Oblates of Mary Immaculate were founded in France in 1816 by Blessed Eugene de Mazenod. In south Texas, they were commonly known as the Cavalry of Christ because they served their parishioners as circuit-riders on horseback. Their black soutane habits, black rounded hats, and silver Oblate cross worn round their necks were widely recognized in the region. (MSTH.)

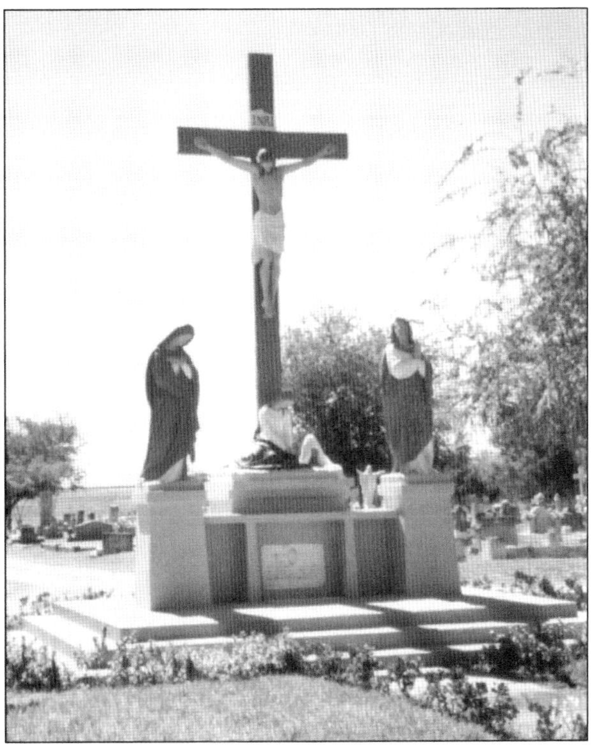

Fr. Pierre Yves Keralum was an Oblate priest who, despite his advanced age, continued to serve his people. In November 1872, he set out on his circuit and never returned, being last seen at a ranch north of Mercedes. His remains were found in 1882. In 1920, a memorial was erected to the much-loved Padre Pedrito at the Catholic cemetery in Mercedes. (Our Lady of Mercy Catholic Church.)

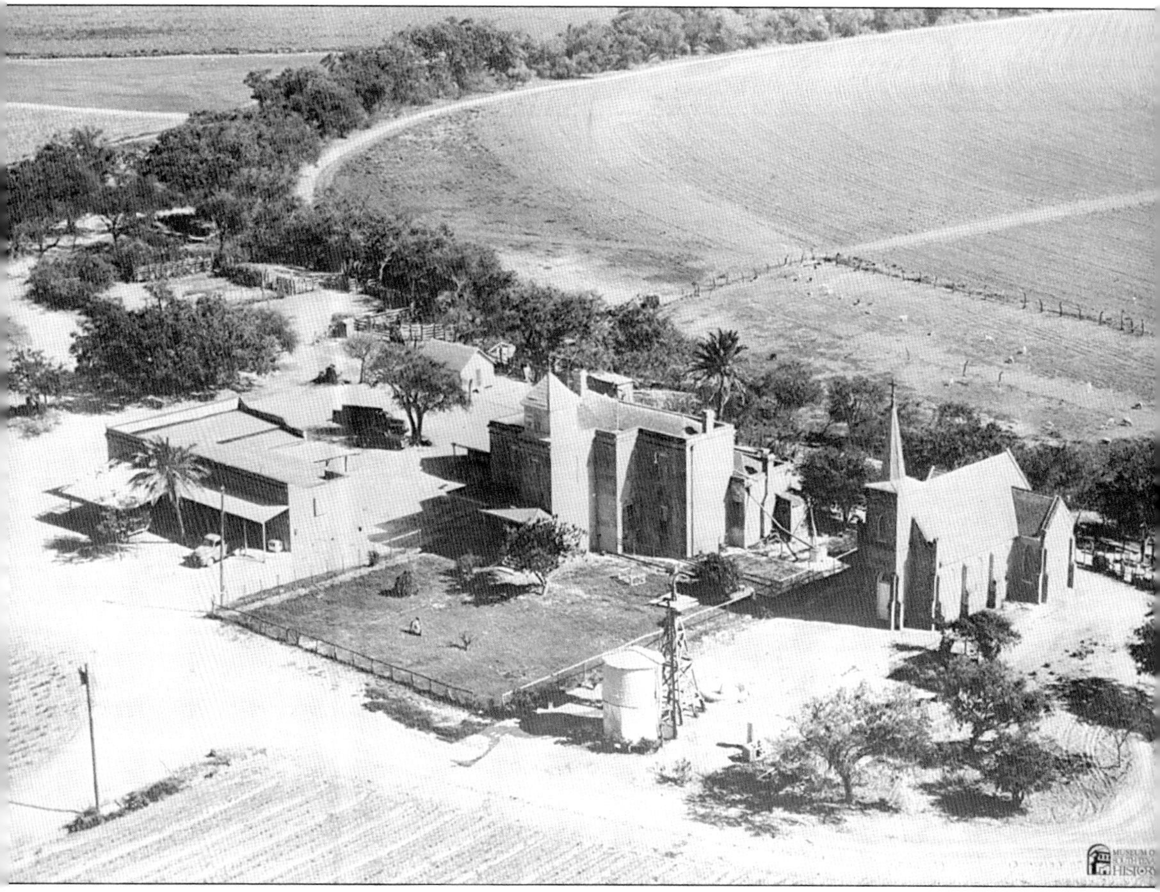

Before Mercedes was founded, many ranches were located in the area, including the Anacuitas (Anacahuitas), Los Burros or Guadalupe, Parajitos, Relámpago, Rosario, San José or Solises, Tampacuás (also known as Campacuás), and Toluca Ranches. This aerial view shows the Toluca Ranch, located about a mile south of US 281 (Military Highway) and a quarter mile east of Farm to Market Road 1015. It is remarkable for having survived almost intact until the present time and is a good model of what a *hacienda* ranch of the past century would have looked like with its main house, its chapel, a school, a store, the ranch hands' houses, work sheds, vegetable gardens, and corrals. At one time, Toluca Ranch had a post office from which mail was distributed to surrounding ranches by horseback, or farther away by stagecoach or steamboat. At its largest, Toluca Ranch had around 12,000 acres with river frontage and stretched northward 17 miles. (MSTH.)

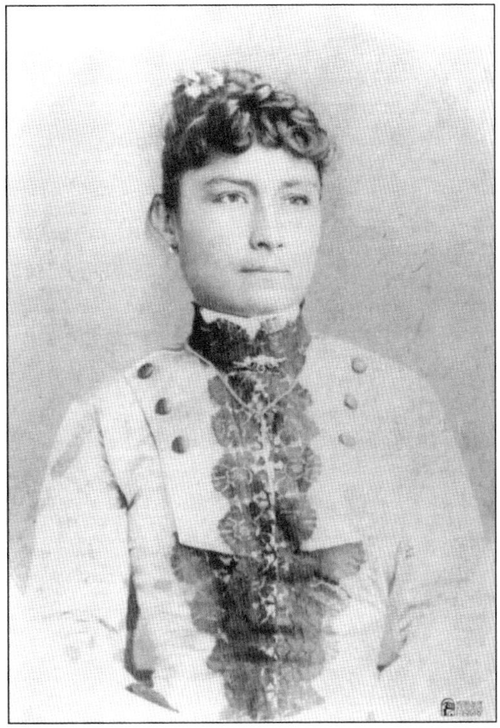

Pictured here are Sóstenes Cano (right) and Florencio Sáenz. After working for many years as a bookkeeper for don Antonio Cano of the Tampacuás Ranch, don Florencio Sáenz married Sóstenes Cano, youngest daughter of Antonio and Mauricia Fernández Cano. Don Antonio Cano of Reynosa had purchased acreage in 1862 from the descendants of Juan José Hinojosa of the Llano Grande land grant; specifically, from Cirildo Hinojosa's fifth share. As her inheritance, Sóstenes received a tract of land in the southern part of the Tampacuás Ranch that the couple named the Toluca Ranch. The name of the ranch is likely a reference to the town of Toluca in south-central Mexico. The word "Toluca" comes from the indigenous word "Tollocan," which means "place of the god Tolloh" in náhuatl, the language of the Aztecs. (Both, MSTH.)

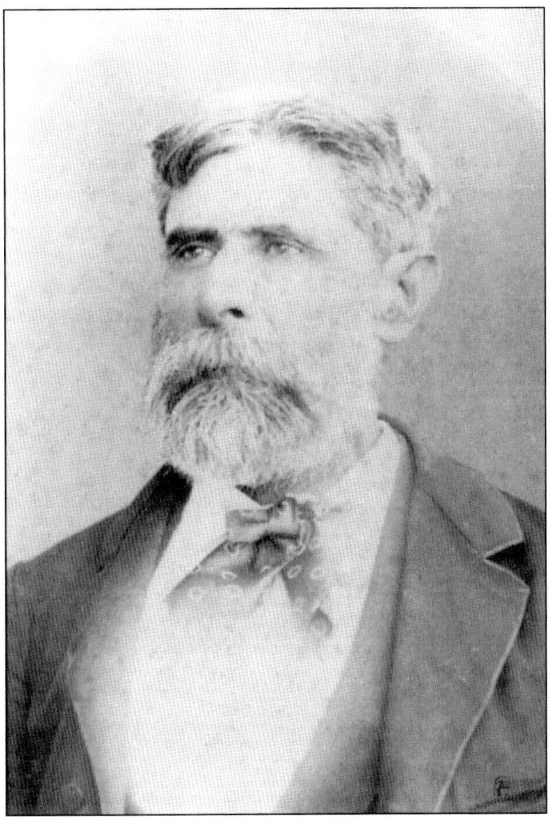

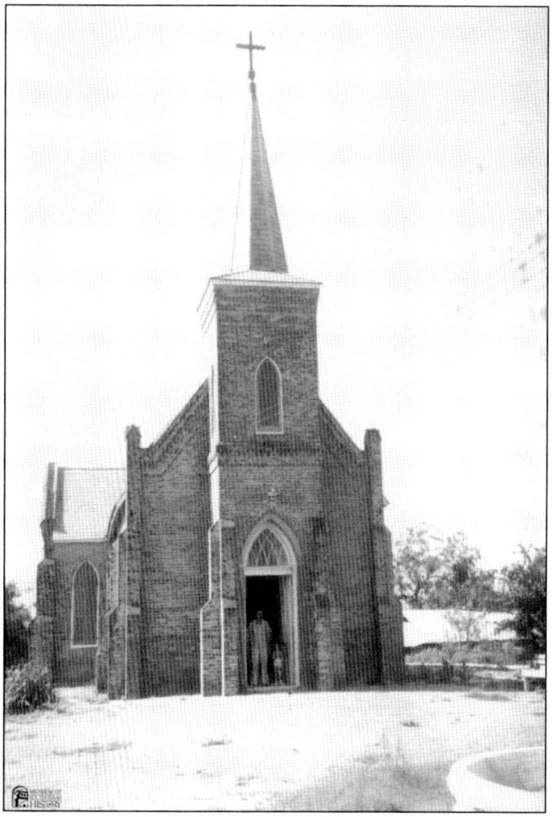

St. Joseph's Chapel was built in 1896 by don Florencio Sáenz in thanksgiving for when he was finally able to dig a well that yielded sweet, drinkable water. Many previous attempts had only yielded salty, brackish and undrinkable water. The chapel was designed by the Oblate priest Pierre Keralum. The pews accommodate 85 people. Don Florencio's grandson Santiago Fernández and his great-granddaughter Florence stand in the doorway in this photograph taken in 1951. (MSTH.)

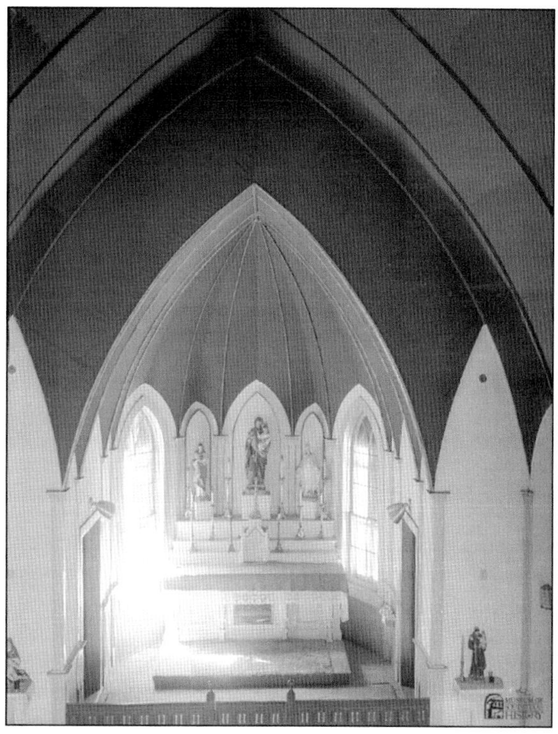

The interior of St. Joseph's Chapel is decorated with statues purchased in Spain by the Sáenz-Fernández family. Some of the statues were donated to Our Lady of Mercy Catholic Church in the town of Mercedes in 1947 in thanksgiving after doña Manuela Fernández's five sons all returned safely from World War II. (MSTH.)

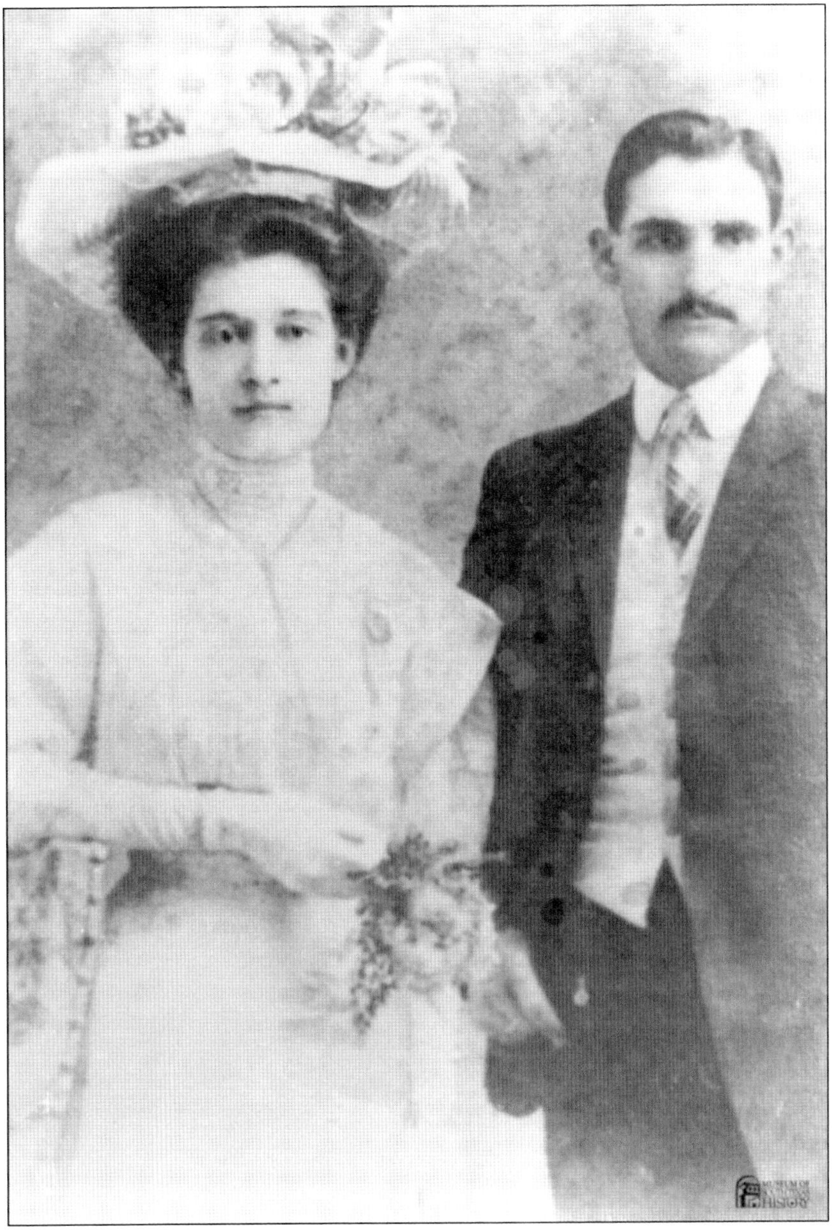

This is the wedding portrait of Manuela Cano Champion (left) and Amador Fernández, a Spanish émigré. Don Florencio and doña Sóstenes Sáenz were unable to have any children, so they decided in 1882 to adopt their three-month-old niece Manuela Cano Champion, daughter of Pedro and Gumecinda Cano Champion. Manuela met and married Amador Fernández in 1908. They eventually had eight children: José Florencio, José Augustín, Guadalupe Anastasio, Joaquín Jorge, Ernesto Mónico, Santiago "Jimmy," Manuela Lourdes, and Amador Tomás. All the children were well educated and several participated in Mercedes city and school district positions. Some of the children and grandchildren continue living in Toluca Ranch to this day. Toluca Ranch was well known for having a brick factory that supplied bricks for many buildings in Mercedes and for a ferry landing where steamboats stopped to load farm and ranch products and unload supplies. (MSTH.)

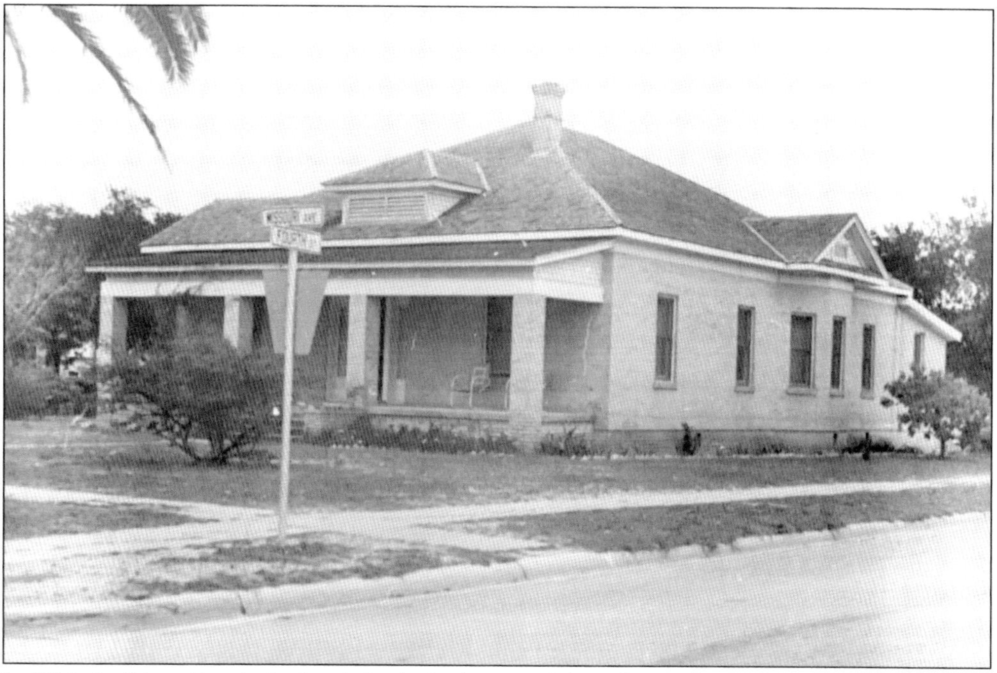

In 1914, the Sáenz-Fernández family built this home in Mercedes on the corner of Missouri Avenue and Fourth Street. They were forced to move to town after their Toluca Ranch was attacked four different times by roving bands of Mexican revolutionaries. The spillover violence of the Mexican Revolution, which lasted from 1910 to 1920, greatly affected the lower Rio Grande Valley region. (Carolyn C. López.)

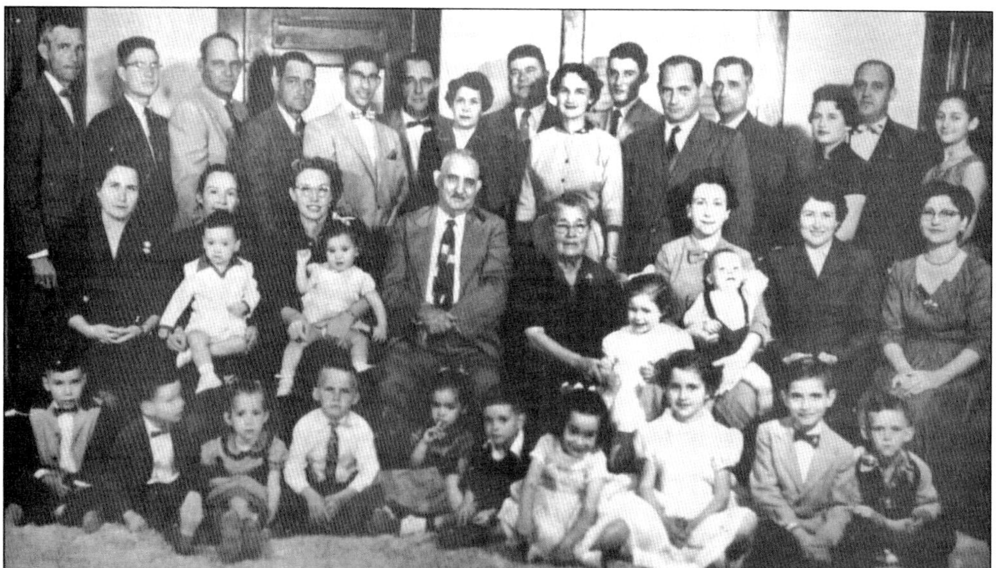

The Fernández family is depicted in this reunion photograph taken in the early 1950s. Amador and Manuela Fernández are seated in the center with their eight children, sons-in-law, daughters-in-law, and grandchildren surrounding them. In the early 1900s when Mercedes was still young, Amador Fernández had a dry goods store just opposite the First National Bank on Texas Avenue. (*Mercedes Enterprise.*)

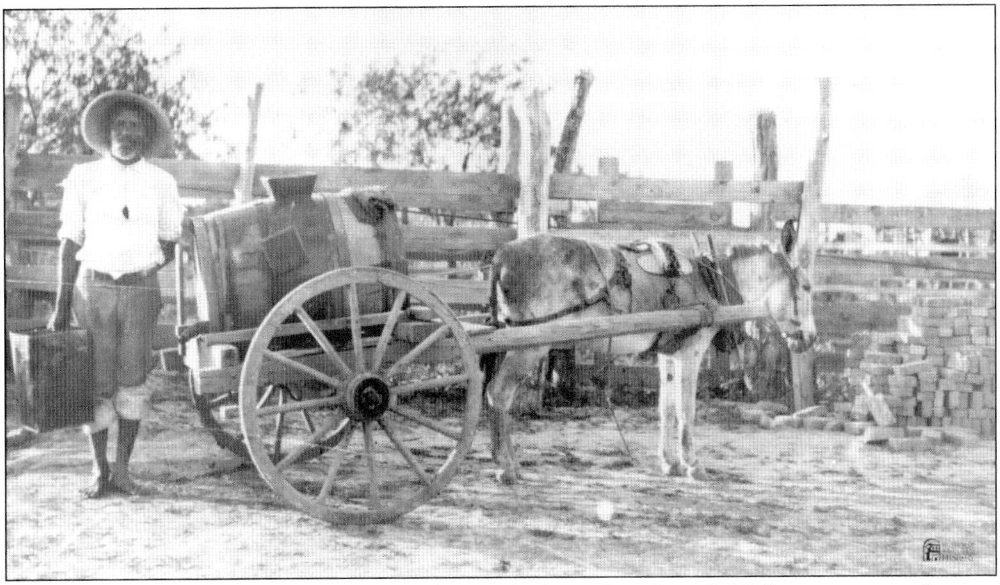

Water has always been a precious commodity in the lower Rio Grande Valley since its settlement in the 18th century. In areas where there was no access to river water or lakes, wells had to be dug but these often produced brackish or salty water. Frequently, communities had to rely on water sellers such as this one who brought water in barrels to sell. (MSTH.)

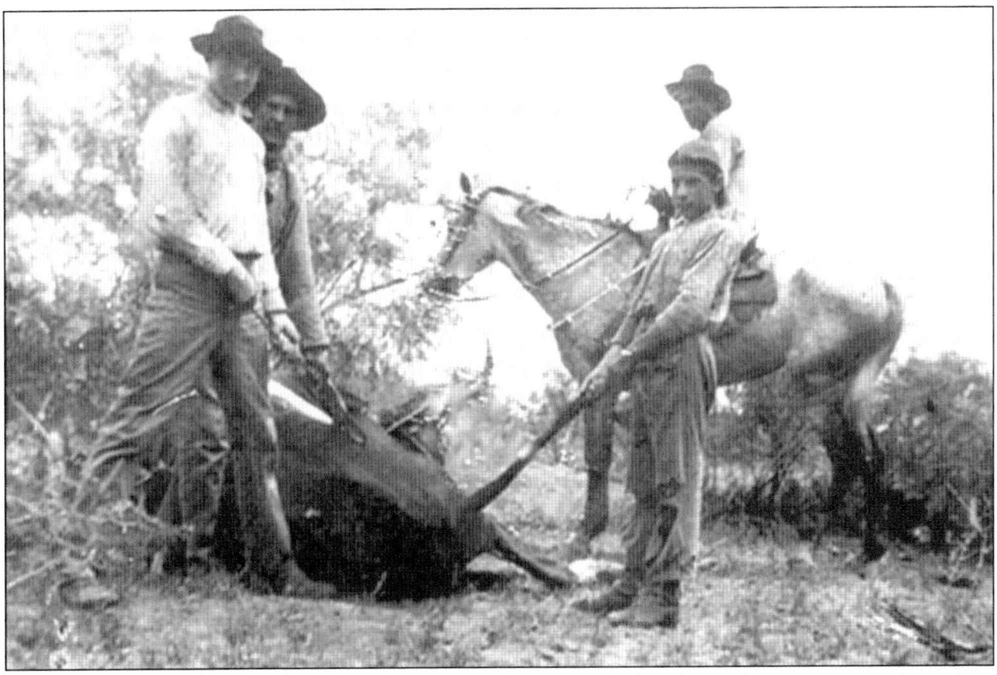

Most ranches had developed into small communities by the end of the 19th century. Ranch workers and their families also lived on the ranch. Workers included vaqueros, or cowboys, blacksmiths, cooks, storekeepers, brick makers, carpenters, and masons among others. When Mercedes was founded, there were several ranches in the surrounding areas including among others: Toluca, Tampacuás, Los Burros, Anacuitas (Anacahuitas), Relámpago, Parajitos, Los Ebanos, and El Fuste. (National Archives.)

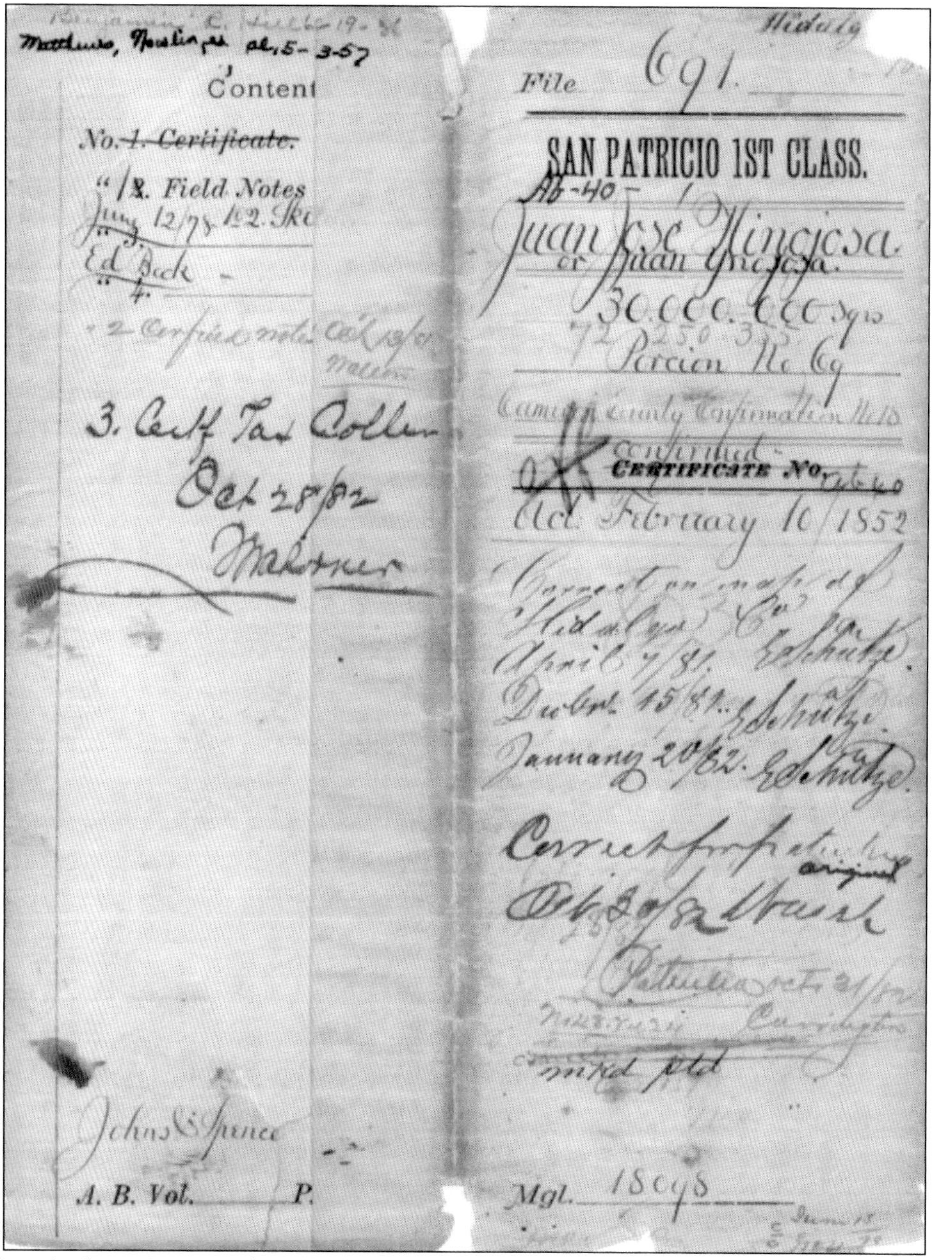

Matthews, Pauline pl. 5-3-57

Content

No. 1. Certificate.

" 1. Field Notes

3. Certif Tax Collec

Oct 28/82

File 691.

SAN PATRICIO 1ST CLASS.

Juan José Hinojosa

or Juan Ynojosa.

CERTIFICATE No.

Act February 10/1852

A. B. Vol. P.

Mgl. 18698

When the lower Rio Grande Valley became part of the United States in 1848, the Spanish and Mexican land grant holders were forced to defend their land claim in state courts. Many landholders were land-rich but cash-poor and were forced to pay their American lawyers' fees in acreage. The document above was Juan José Hinojosa's (sometimes spelled Ynojosa) Llano Grande Land Grant title, finally approved and certified by the Texas State Legislature in 1852 for his heirs. Large land grants such as this one were awarded only to favorites of the king or other crown officials. Called *mercedes reales*, or "royal grants," or *mercedes de tierra*, "land grants," these larger grants were intended to support hacienda-type ranching ventures. Before the 20th century in Hidalgo County alone, there were 43 porciones granted through the Reynosa jurisdiction, 12 intermediate grants, and 14 large land grants such as Hinojosa's. (Hidalgo County Historical Commission.)

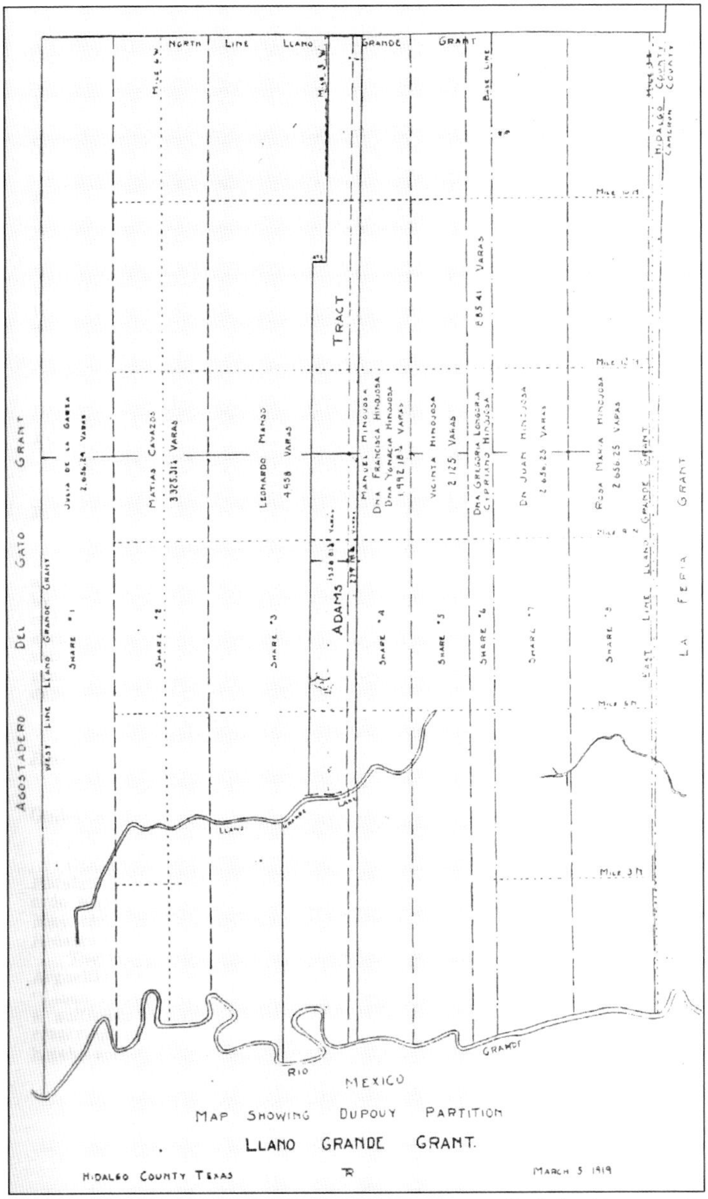

The map shown here of Hinojosa's Llano Grande grant is called the Dupouy Partition. It was originally prepared in 1848 by Alfredo Dupouy, the court surveyor in Matamoros, Tamaulipas, Mexico. By 1919, Hinojosa's children had already sold land to others as noted here. This map was used as part of the abstract of title obtained by the American Rio Grande Land and Irrigation Company on March 5, 1919, to show clean title to its purchase of lands in the Rio Grande Valley. Share one belonged to Julia de la Garza; share two belonged to Matías Cavazos; share three belonged to Leonardo Manso; share four belonged to Manuel Hinojosa, Francisca Hinojosa, and Ygnacia Hinojosa; share five belonged to Vicenta Hinojosa, share six belonged to Gregoria Longoria and Cipriano Hinojosa; share seven belonged to Juan Hinojosa, and share eight belonged to Rosa Maria Hinojosa. There was also a separately sectioned area called the Adams Tract, owned by William T. Adams and his wife, Virginia Adams. Mercedes is located in portions of shares five, six, and seven. (Hidalgo County Historical Commission.)

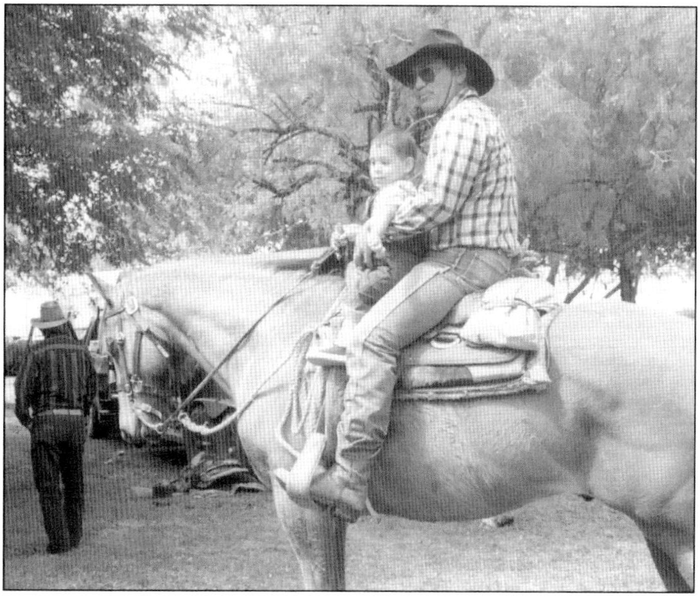

Although in the 1900s large-scale ranching in the Valley was gradually replaced by commercialized farming with the arrival of northern land developers, the love of the ranching era still survives today in many Mercedes residents. Pictured in 1975, seated on his Lineback Dun horse, is Rosendo Gonzales and his grandson Paul. Gonzales belongs to the Mid-Valley Horseman's Association. (Rosendo Gonzales.)

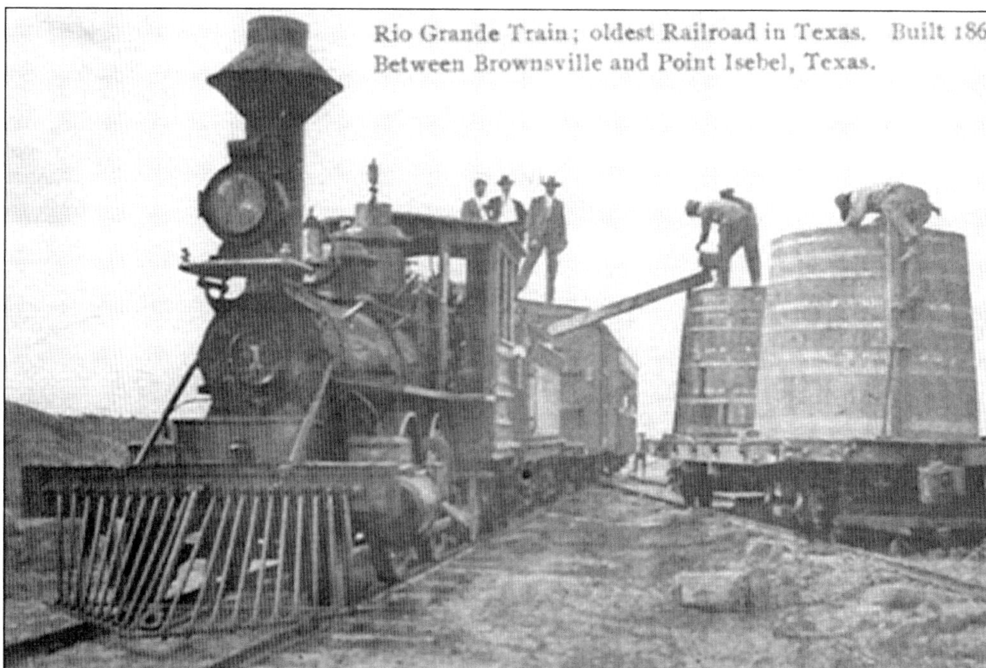

By 1868, as shown in this early postcard, the railroad had reached Brownsville. On July 8, 1904, the Sam Fordyce Branch of the St. Louis, Brownsville and Mexico Railway reached Section 14, the stop that would later become Mercedes, nicknamed "Sweetheart of the Branch." The coming of the railroad would be the first step in the development of the Rio Grande Valley into a highly profitable agricultural region. (Vito Buenrostro.)

Two

Founding a Town

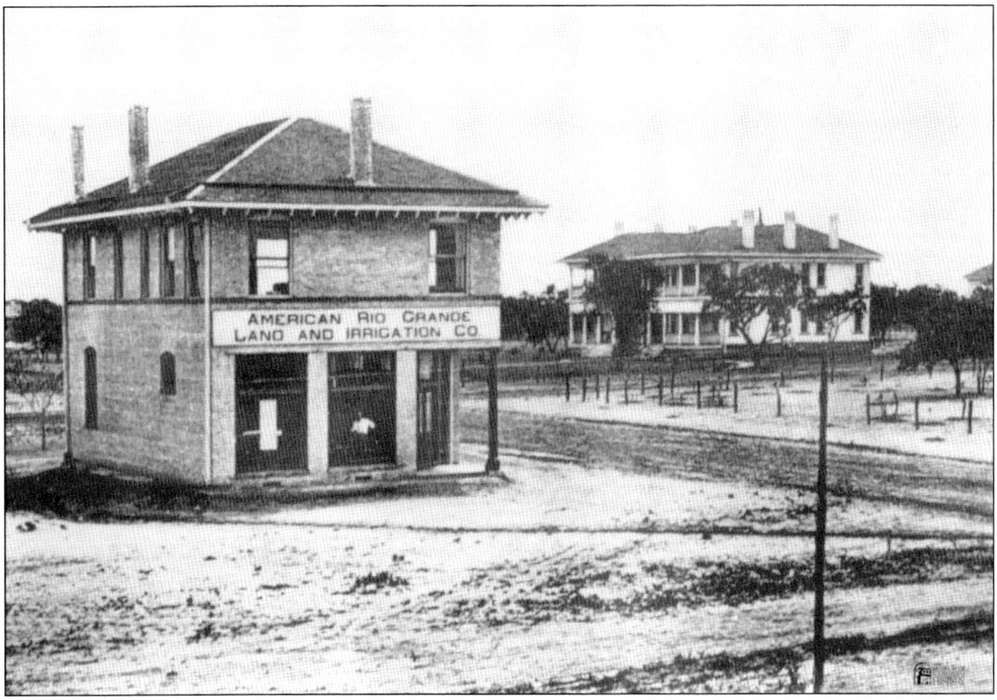

Mercedes was founded in 1907 to serve as the headquarters of the American Rio Grande Land and Irrigation Company. The company was formed expressly for the purpose of constructing an irrigation system pumping water from the Rio Grande to irrigate about 250,000 acres of land in Hidalgo and Cameron Counties. The first ARGL&I building seen here was located facing Texas Avenue near the corner with Second Street. (MSTH.)

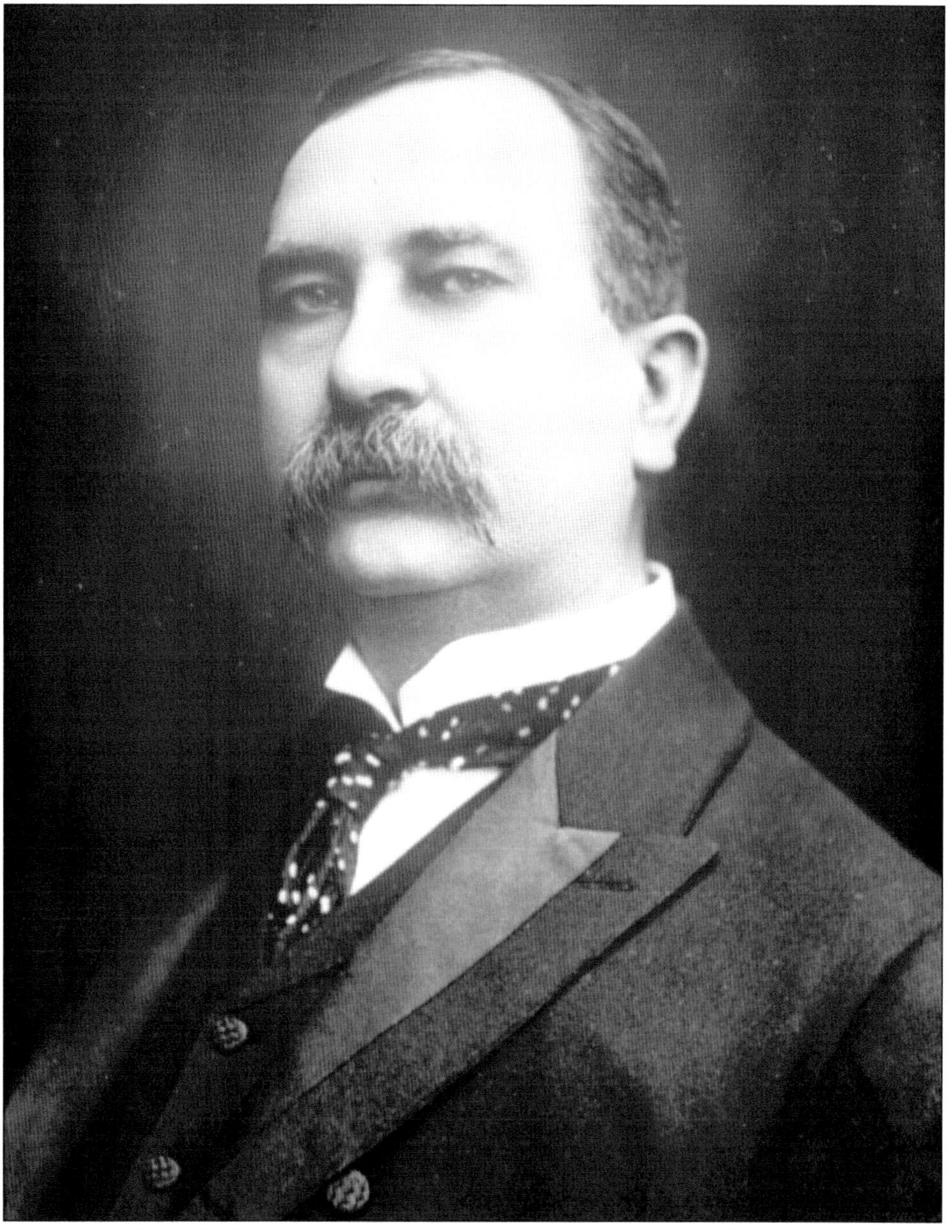

Benjamin Franklin Yoakum was born in Tehuacana, Texas, in 1859. He worked all his life in the railroad industry and knew every facet from surveying to engineering, construction, traffic, operating, and finance. Yoakum visited the Rio Grande Valley on various occasions and knew that by extending the railroad into the valley, commercialized agriculture was possible. With the help of Col. Sam Fordyce, he convinced a group of St. Louis investors to develop the American Rio Grande Land and Irrigation Company with a capital stock of $1,250,000. Early stockholders included Benjamin F. Yoakum, Sam Fordyce, Thomas W. Carter, Thomas H. West, Edward Whittaker, Edmund E. Elliot, Silas P. Silver, and DuVal West. The company was granted incorporation by the State of Texas on September 30, 1905. Although Yoakum never lived in Mercedes, he and his New York socialite daughter Bessie Yoakum frequently visited the town to see friends. (MSTH.)

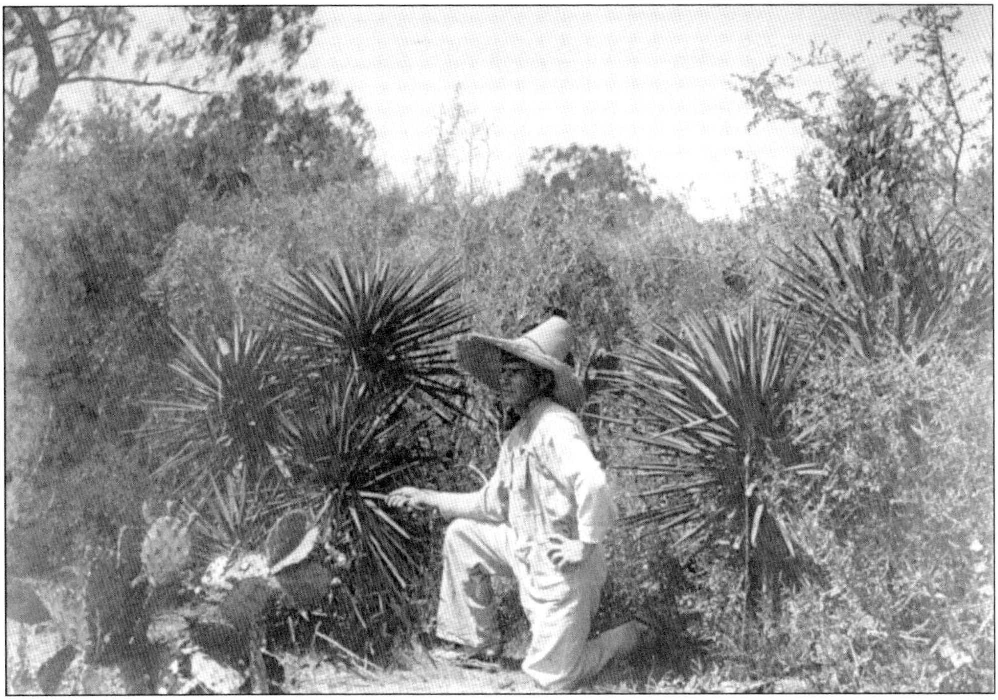

Yoakum knew that three things would be needed to make commercialized agriculture succeed in the Rio Grande Valley: an extensive irrigation system to water the farmlands, a railroad system to take the produce to northern markets, and a cheap labor force to clear the land, dig the canals, and work the fields once they were planted. Clearing the land, called "grubbing," was achieved by a large Mexican labor force that worked for pennies a day. (MSTH.)

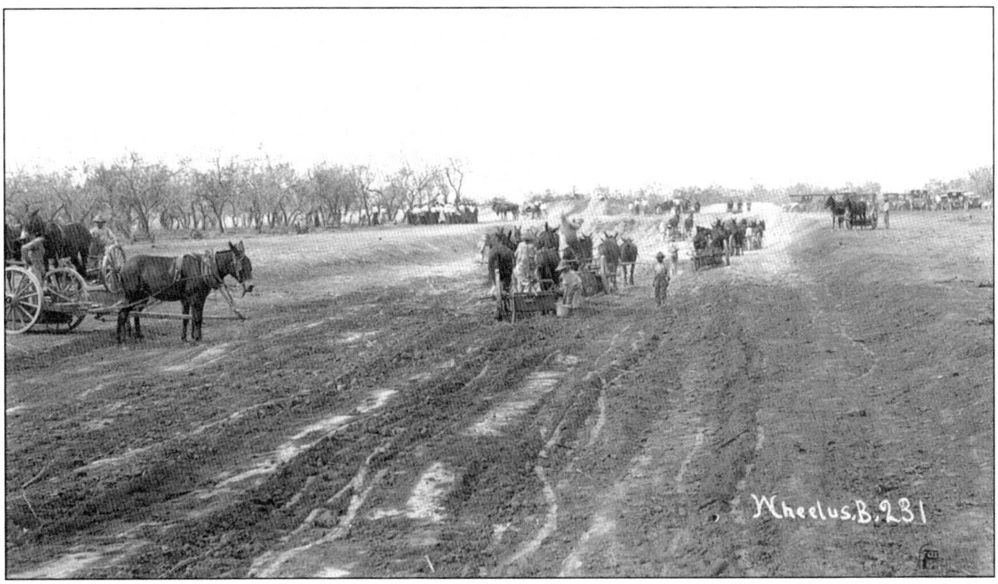

Col. Sam Robertson was the contractor for the earthwork on the Main North Canal built by the American Rio Grande Land and Irrigation Company. As seen in this photograph, he used 300 mule teams to dig a strip of land seven miles long from the river to the railroad in Mercedes to lay the Main Canal in 1906. (MSTH.)

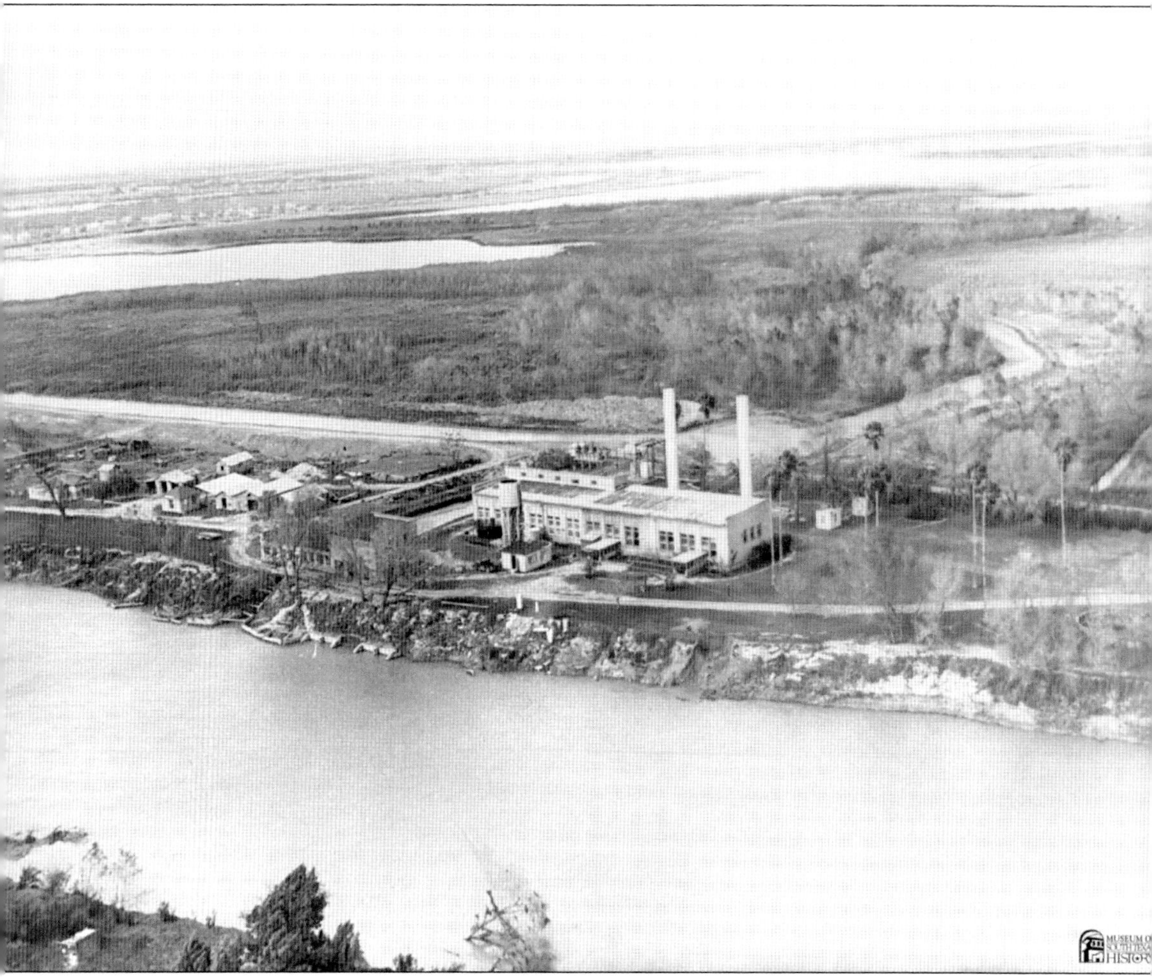

The first order of business in developing Mercedes and the surrounding mid-Valley area was to build a pumping plant on the Rio Grande. This was achieved in 1906 when the pumping plant was completed about eight miles south of Mercedes. A settling basin was also built west of the plant, with the Main Canal to carry water north by means of gravity; that is, utilizing the natural slope of the land to propel the water along the canals. The water must first be lifted out of the Rio Grande by the pumping plant. The pumping plant had a capacity of 300,000 gallons of water per minute, or 432,000,000 gallons every 24 hours. By 1923, the canal system totaled over 300 miles of canals, not including the smaller laterals serving individual farm tracts. (MSTH.)

William Francis Shaw served as chief engineer and vice president of the American Rio Grande Land and Irrigation Company in 1908. He also served the company as general manager from 1912 to 1930. He was the contact man for the American Company in setting up the canal system in the Mercedes area, and he assisted in laying out the town site of Mercedes and in organizing the electricity and water systems. (*Mercedes Enterprise.*)

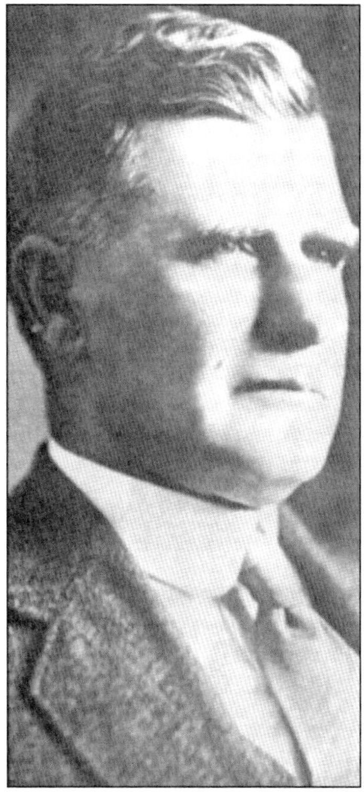

The river pumping plant had four pumps, two of which were 36 inches in size and were the largest pumps in the world at that time. Electrical power to run the pumps was run down from the electrical plant built in Mercedes. This 1915 photograph with unidentified persons shows some of the intricate machinery required to do the job. (MSTH.)

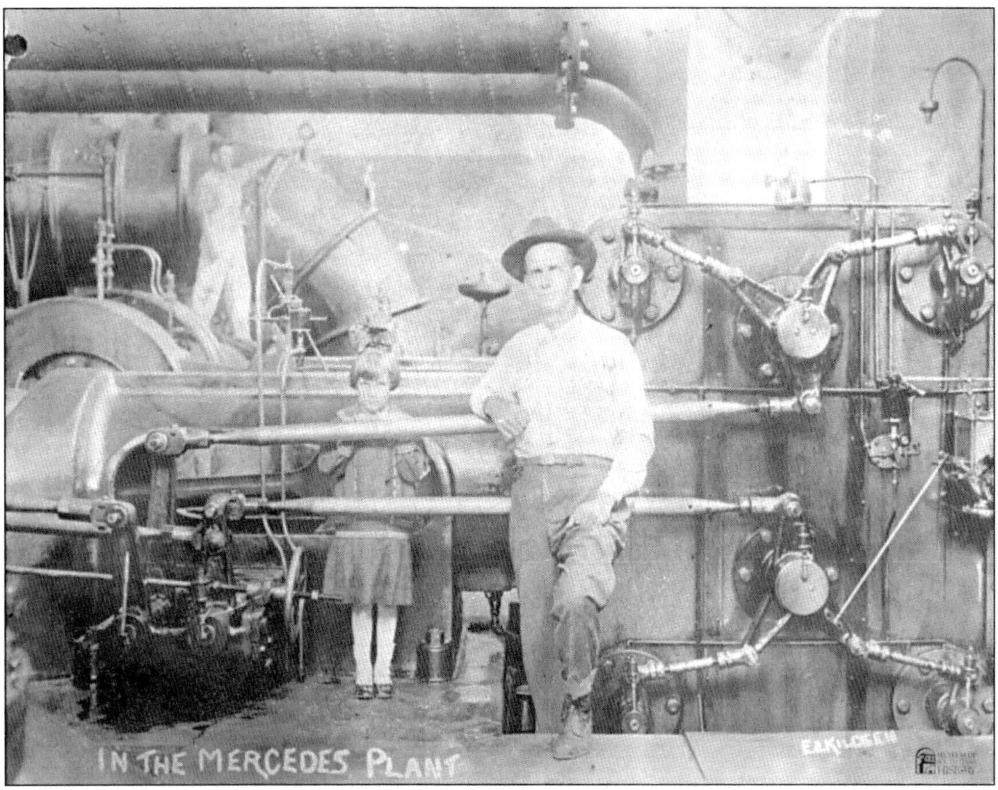

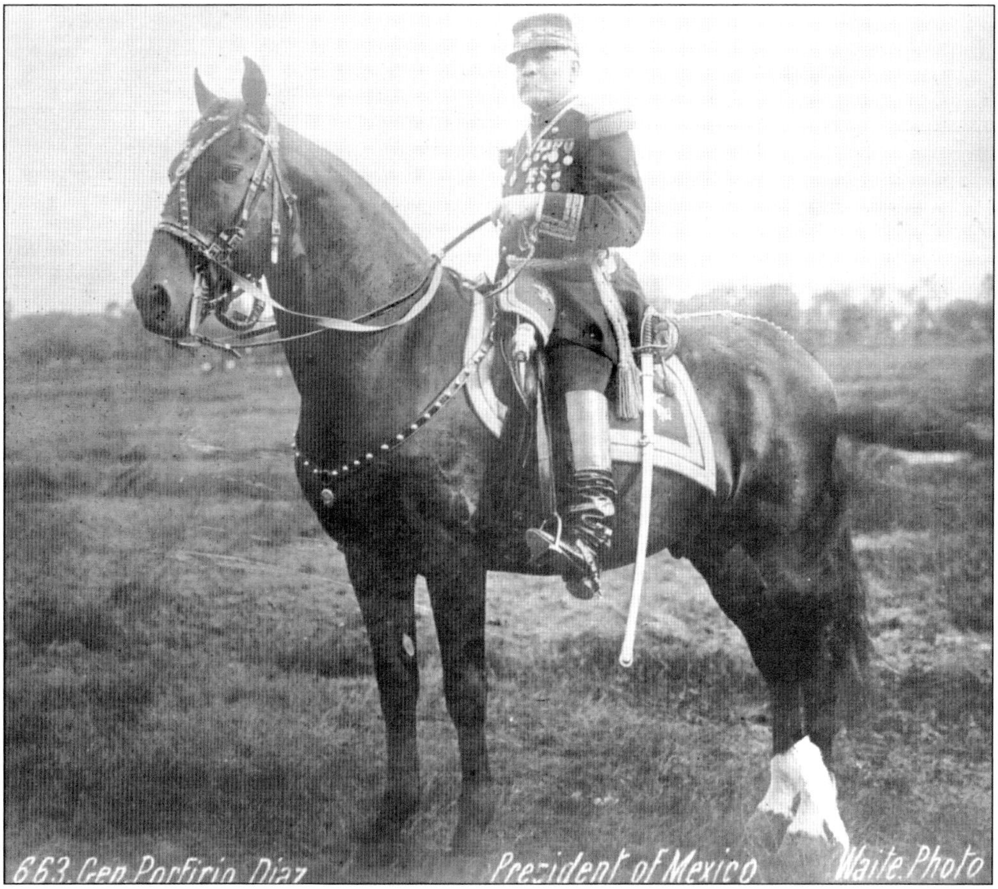

The American Company decided to name their headquarters "Díaz" in honor of Mexican president Porfirio Díaz, seen here, who was friendly toward American investors. Fearing the development of a revolt in Mexico and the inadvisability of that name, "Mercedes" was then chosen, supposedly to honor Díaz's wife; but Díaz was married first to Delfina Ortega and later to Carmen Romero. The origin of the name remains a mystery today. (National Archives.)

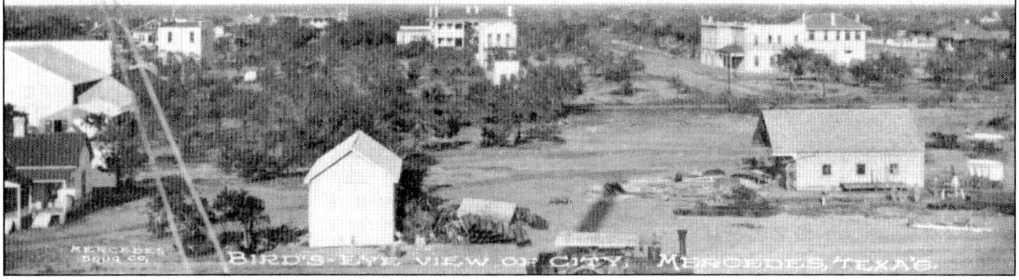

In this c. 1912 postcard, the photograph was taken facing west from the top of the Mercedes power plant next to the Main Canal. The Mercedes Hotel can partially be seen in the middle background. To the right of the hotel across Second Street can be seen the American Rio Grande Land and Irrigation headquarters, the Mercedes Drug Store, and the Hotel Annex. (Vito Buenrostro.)

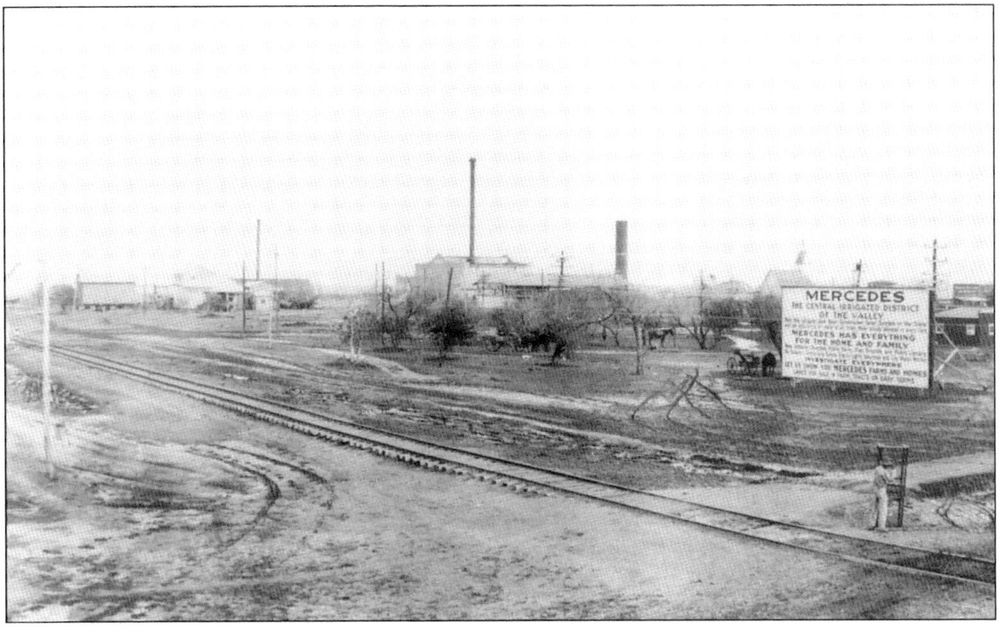

In December 1907, the original townsite of Mercedes was platted by American Company chief engineer Chester B. Davis. Streets were named and the map recorded in the Hidalgo County Courthouse. The large sign in this photograph encourages visitors to purchase land and homes in this growing community. (MSTH.)

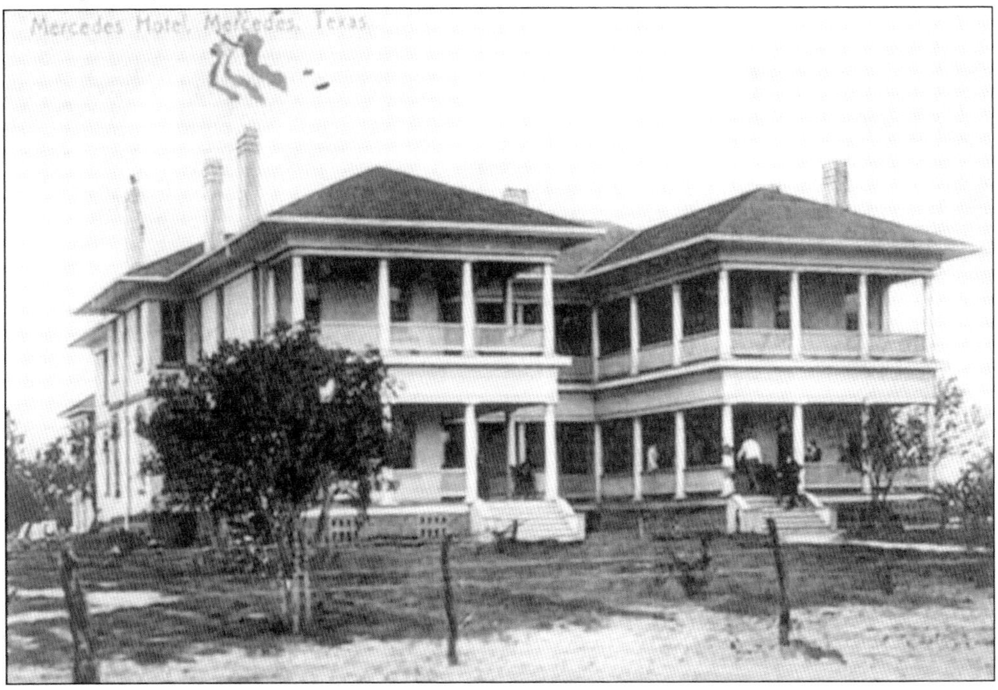

One of the first buildings in the new town was the Mercedes Hotel. When the engineers, railroad men, and other professionals came to Mercedes to work, there were no homes available yet. Many lived in boxcars on sidings when they first arrived, and they were greatly relieved when the hotel was completed. The hotel served very well until suitable homes could be built. (Vito Buenrostro.)

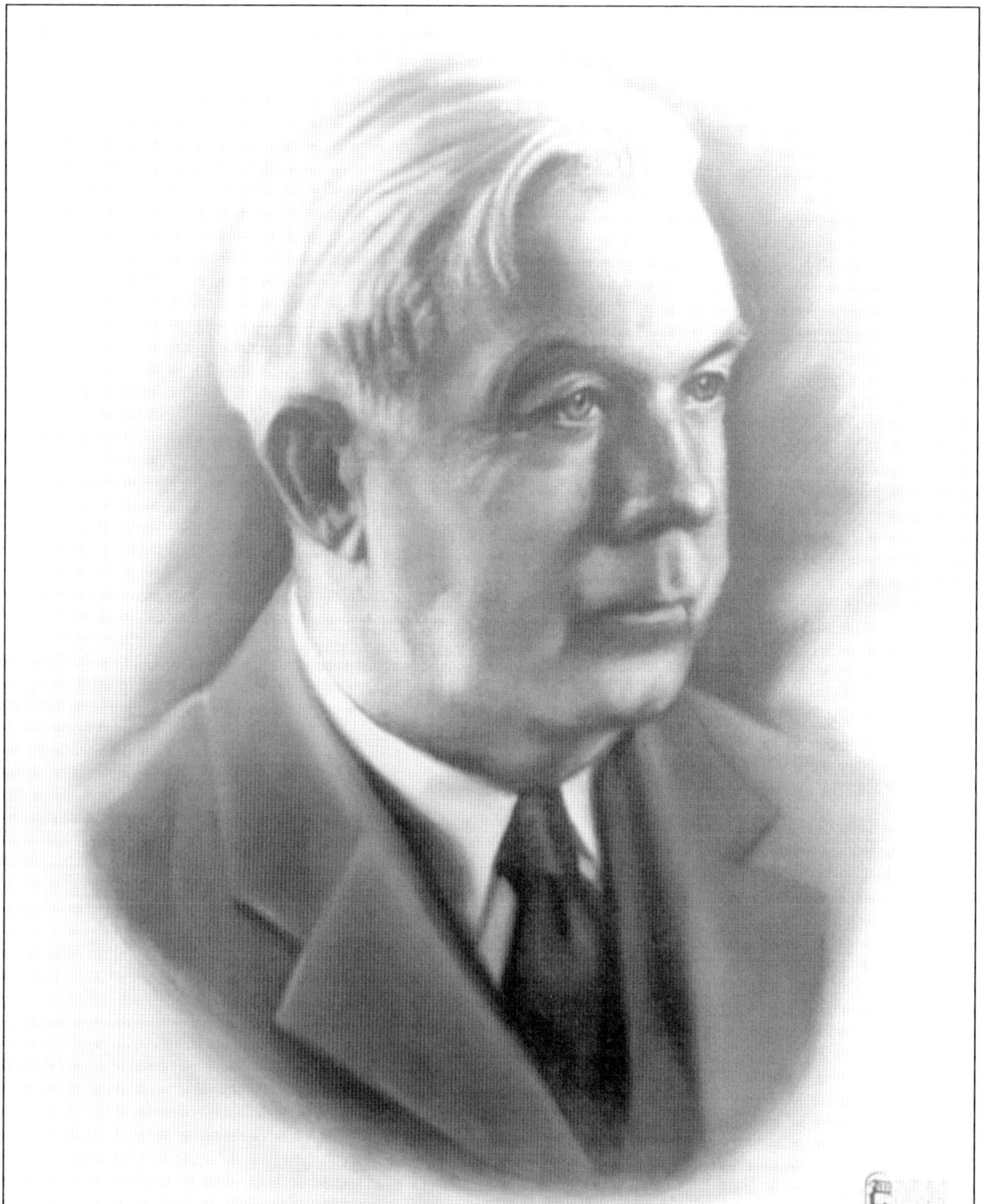

Silas Percy Silver served as the general manager of the American Rio Grande Land and Irrigation Company in 1905 and was instrumental in completing the irrigation system. He also ensured that land was sold, businesses were started, and city and school services were properly provided in Mercedes' early days. Under his direction, the American Company also donated land to churches and for cemeteries. Silver was born on November 3, 1866, in Mobile, Alabama. He was a graduate of Washington University with a degree in architecture. Examples of Silver's architectural talent are still evident in many of the buildings in Mercedes. Silver was the Hidalgo County judge when county residents voted to move the county seat from Hidalgo to Chapin (now Edinburg) in 1908. He served one term, from 1908 to 1909. Silas Percy Silver died on December 20, 1938, in Shreveport, Louisiana. (MSTH.)

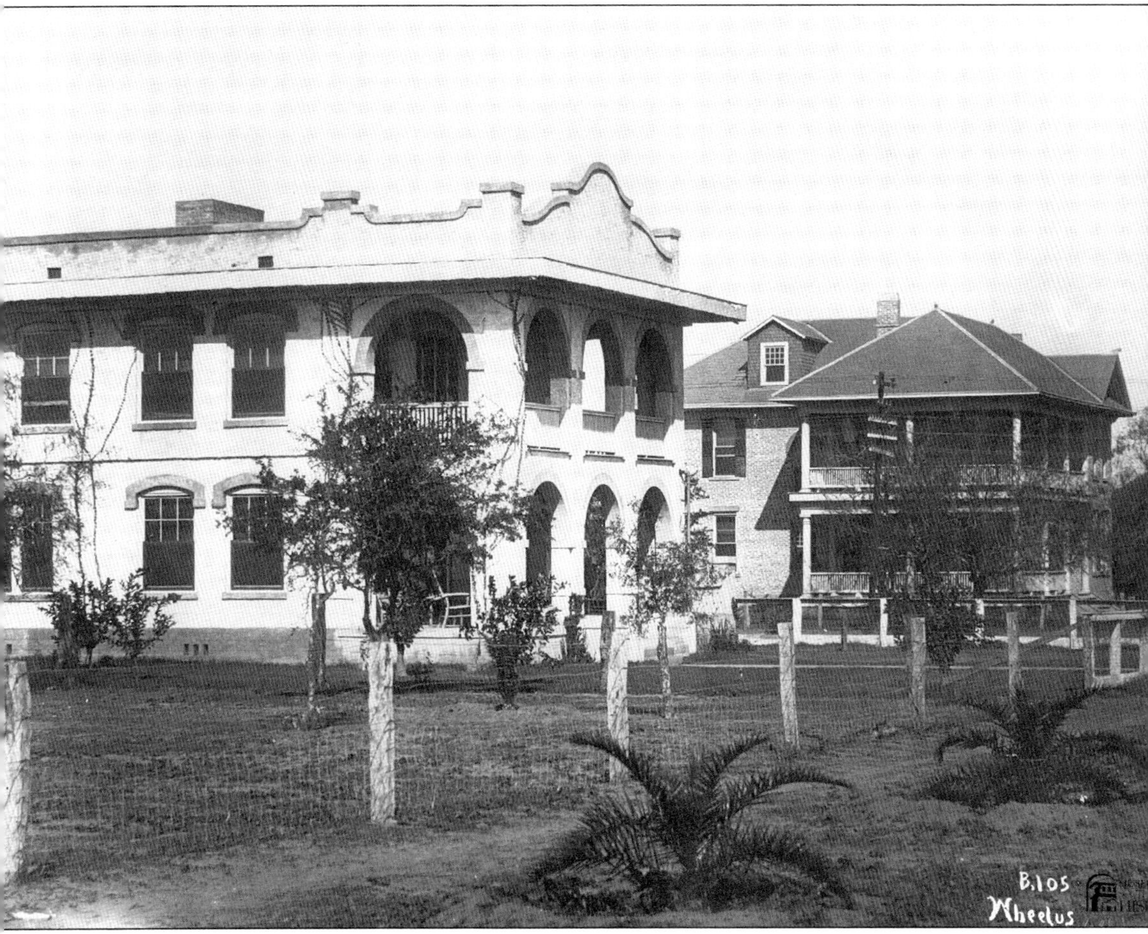

When Silas P. Silver, his wife, and young daughter arrived in the fledgling town of Mercedes in 1905, they were forced to live in a boxcar on a railroad siding because there were no homes built yet. Within a year, the American Company, as it was frequently called, had built the Silver family a company home, which is the house pictured on the right of the photograph. By 1908, Silver built his own home, the house on the left. The Silver house is still standing, located on South Missouri Avenue on the corner of Third Street. These homes both adhered to the restrictions placed by the city on new residences. The city ordinance required homes to be built of brick or stucco and not cost less than $2,000, which was a considerable amount in those days. Business buildings must be of brick or stucco and not cost less than $3,000. The early founders hoped to make the Mercedes downtown area a showplace that would attract new homeowners, farmers, and businessmen. (MSTH.)

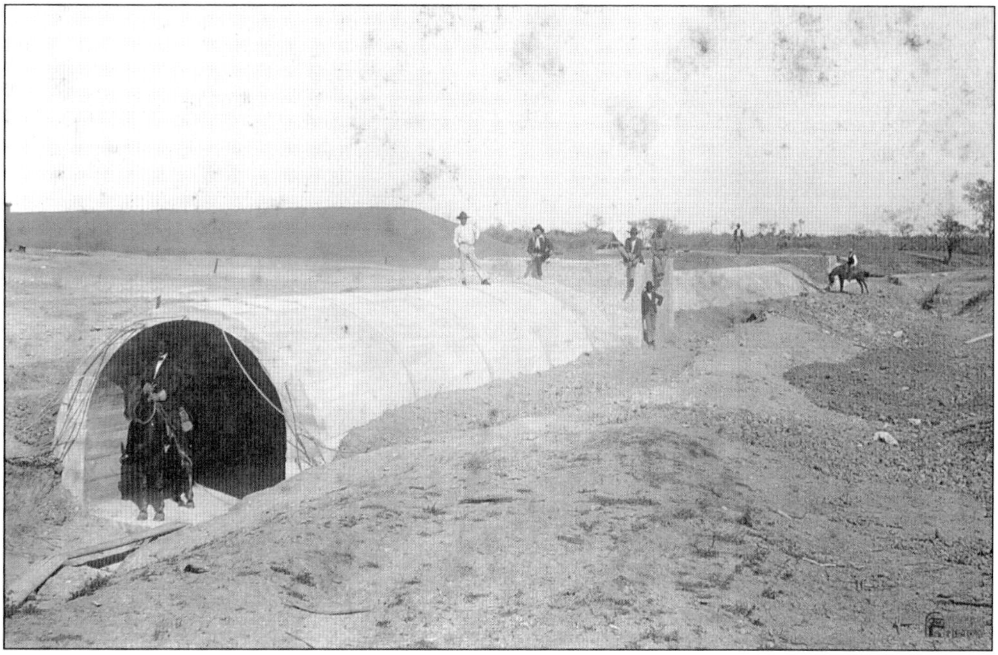

In this photograph, Silas Percy Silver rides his horse into a flume built as part of the canal system. One of the engineering advancements of this time was the use of reinforced concrete in the construction of the head gates, siphons, and flumes. The introduction in 1906 of this man-made "rock" by the American Company was new to Texas. (MSTH.)

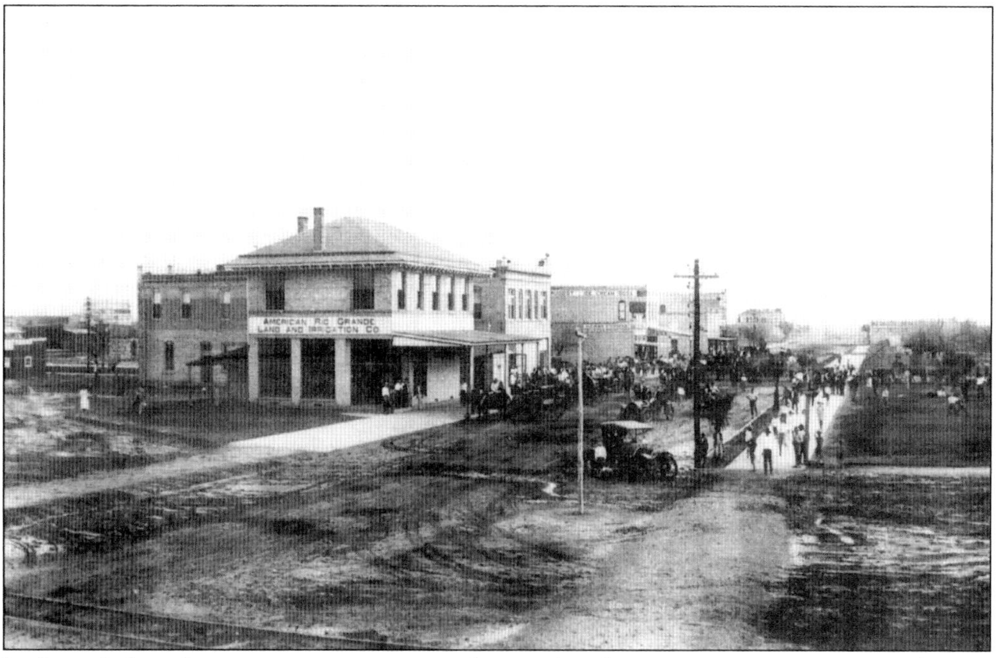

In the early days, there were no city services such as trash pickup or street repair, so a city ordinance was passed that required all male persons between 21 and 45 to work on, repair, and clean the public roads and streets. Ministers and firemen were exempt; however, just $2.50 would exempt any citizen for a year. (MSTH.)

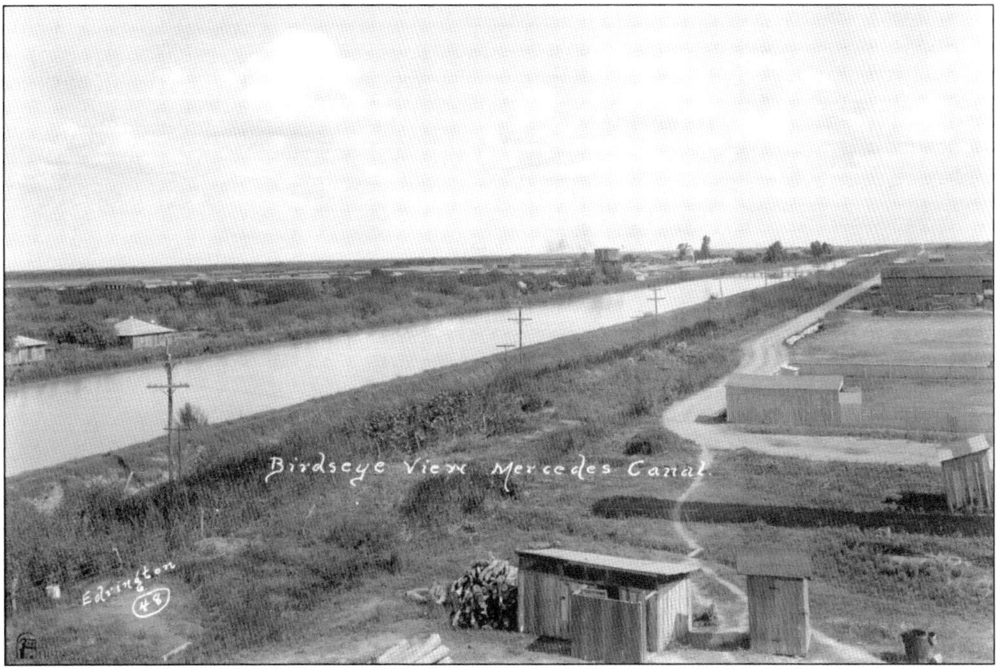

Some of the irrigation system construction was contracted out to Col. Sam Robertson until the crews of the American Company took over, extending the canals to Mile 12 North and Mile 2 1/2 West by 1912. This photograph shows the Main Canal, which runs just east of Mercedes. It was from 90 to 120 feet wide in places and from 15 to 20 feet deep. (MSTH.)

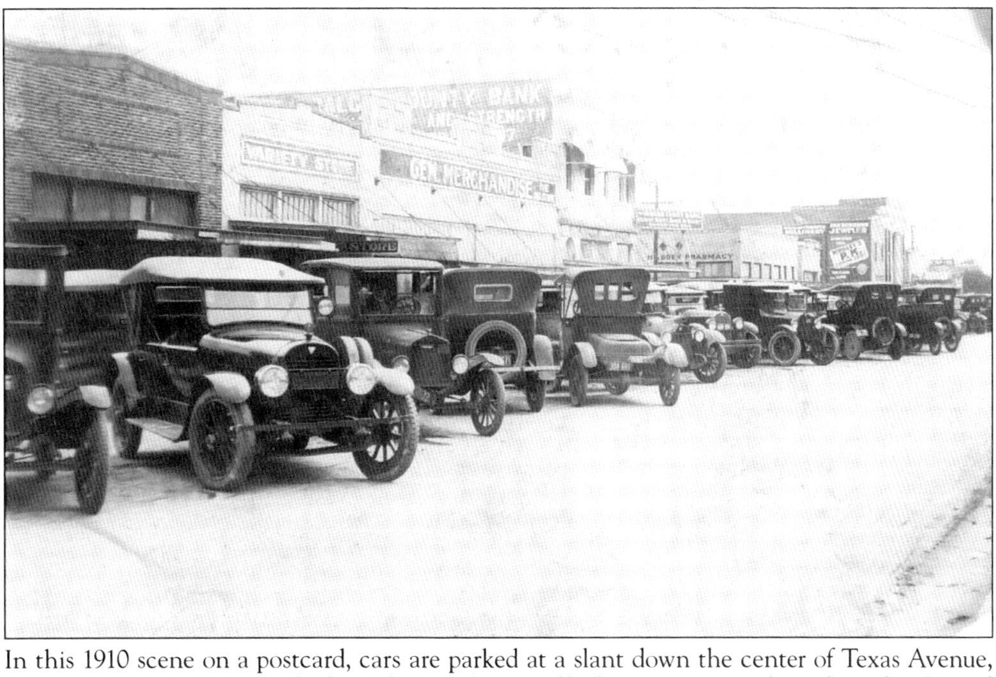

In this 1910 scene on a postcard, cars are parked at a slant down the center of Texas Avenue, the main street. City records show that uniform traffic laws were not adopted until 1930 and officers did not start handing out traffic tickets until 1939. Parking meters were installed in 1946, undoubtedly much to the dismay of downtown shoppers. (Vito Buenrostro.)

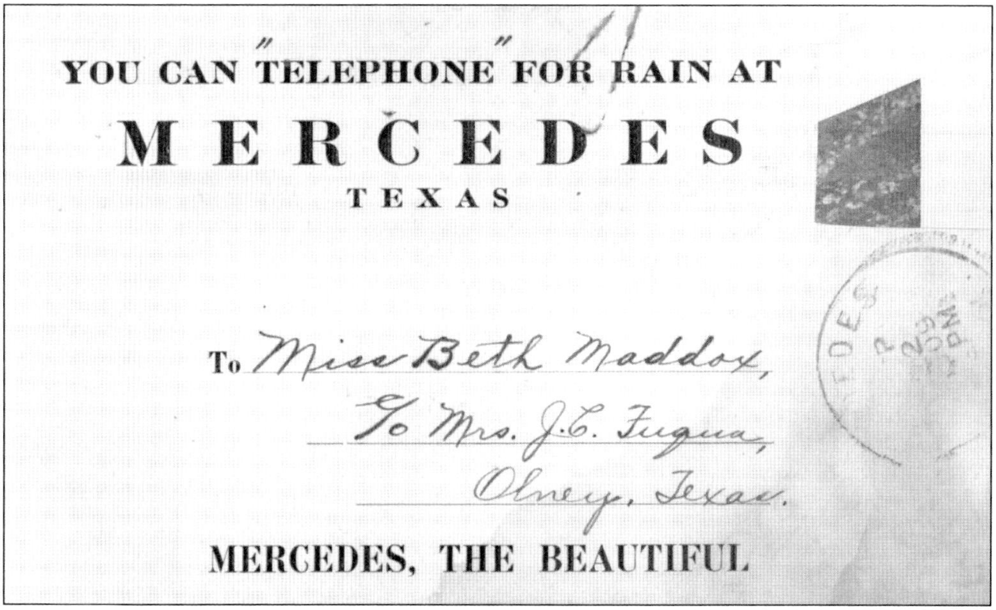

Postcards were very popular as a means of communicating with friends and family during the early 20th century. This is the cover of a used postcard that unfolded accordion-style to show many scenes of Mercedes around 1909. The stamp was cut off, but the postmark can still be partially seen. (Vito Buenrostro.)

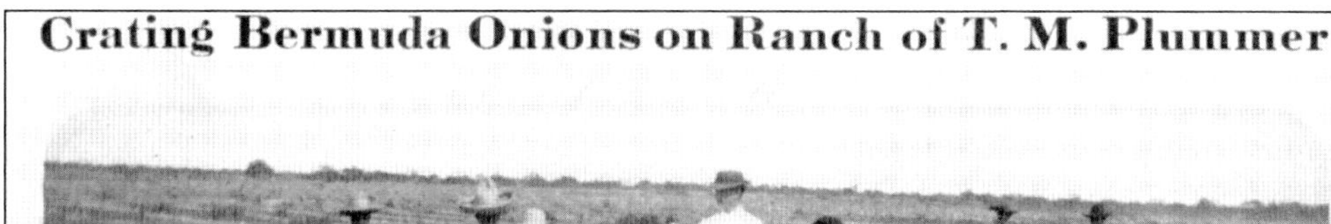

Within a few years of its founding, Mercedes was already producing large quantities of vegetables and fruits for shipping to northern and international markets. The Bermuda onion had already been introduced to south Texas in 1898 near Cotulla. With irrigation, onion farms like Theodore M. Plummer's (seen here) were highly successful, yielding about 3,000 crates per acre during a growing season. (Vito Buenrostro.)

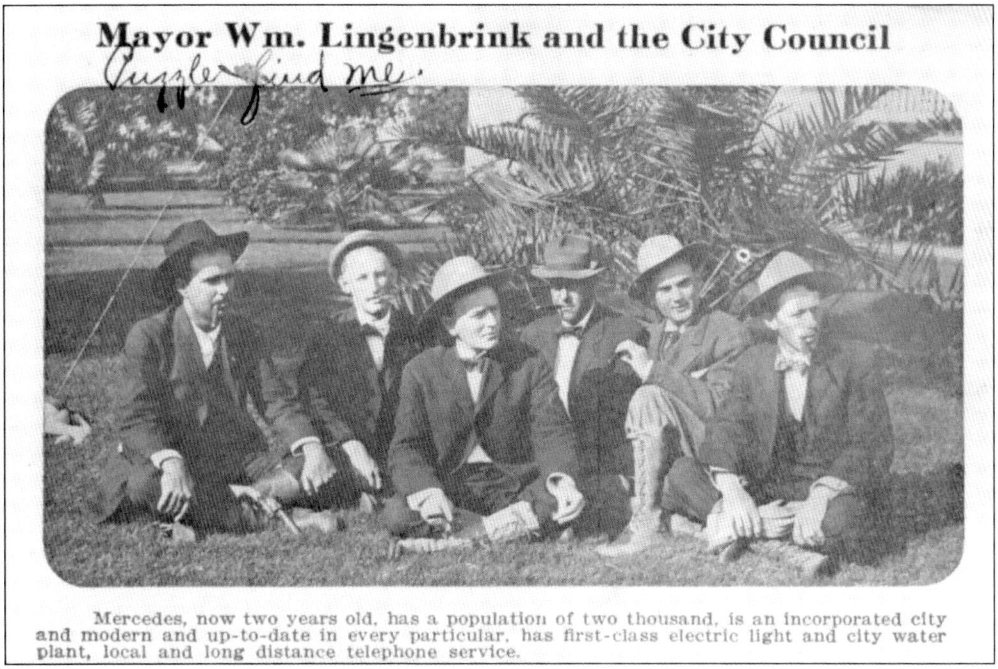

The gentlemen in this photograph are Mercedes's first mayor and city council after incorporation in 1909. From left to right are John Puckett, Gouverneur K. Wattson, Mayor William Lingenbrink, Dr. Edward C. Schoonmaker, Fred Cutting, and Lytle Harrison. They are sitting at the City Park, a popular gathering area because of its lush grass and palm trees. (Vito Buenrostro.)

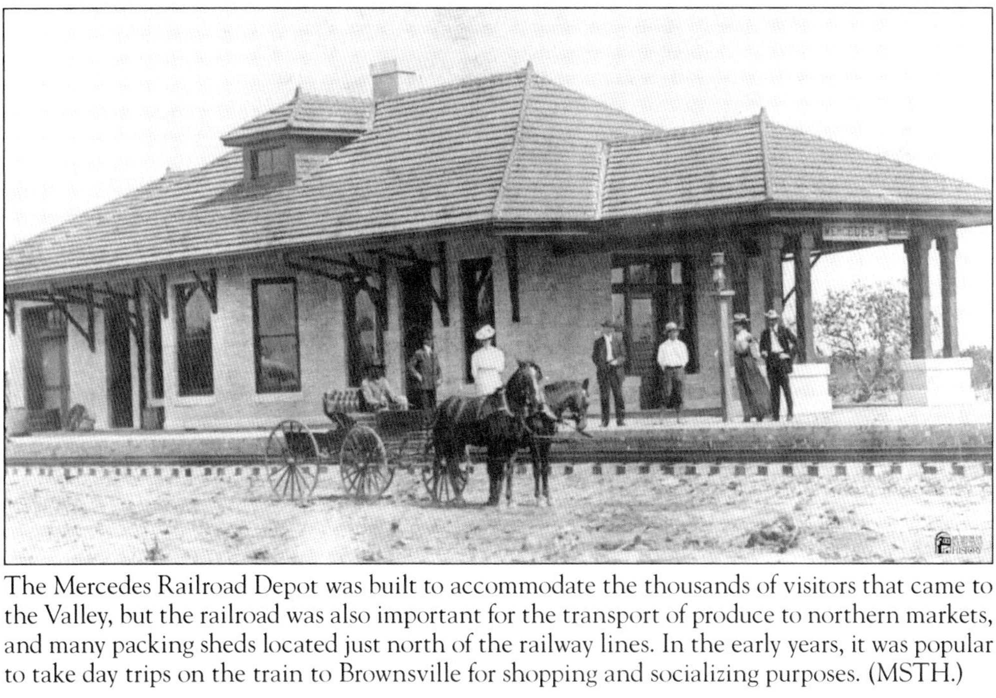

The Mercedes Railroad Depot was built to accommodate the thousands of visitors that came to the Valley, but the railroad was also important for the transport of produce to northern markets, and many packing sheds located just north of the railway lines. In the early years, it was popular to take day trips on the train to Brownsville for shopping and socializing purposes. (MSTH.)

FACTS

Mercedes Has—

The most complete irrigation canal in the United States.
Two Livery Stables.
Three Implement Houses.
Beautiful Tropical Park.
Three Physicians and Two Dentists.
Many Wholesale Houses.
$15,000 now being expended in additions this year.
A fine class of citizens from all parts of the country.

The richest soil in the United States.
Electric Lights, City Water.
Two Good Hotels.
Automobile Garage and Salesroom.

Public Library.	Bank.
One Lawyer.	Newspaper.
Cotton Gin.	Fine Residences.
Brick Yard.	Good Churches.
Two Lumber Yards.	Good Schools.
Ideal Climate.	Cheap Labor.

Local and long distance telephone, and nearly every class of business represented, and all within two years.

For Further information address the Secretary of the Mercedes Commercial Club.

OFFICERS AND DIRECTORS OF THE MERCEDES COMMERCIAL CLUB.

OFFICERS:

F. J. Cutting, President — **S. P. Silver, 1st Vice-Pres.** — **W. A. Fitch, 2d Vice-Pres.**
Alex Wheless, Secretary — **Theo. M. Plummer, Treasurer**

DIRECTORS:

J. M. Johnston, Jr., — **W. S. Chaplin** — **G. K. Watson** — **Dr. E. C. Schoonmaker**
Lytle Harrison — **Alex Champion** — **J. Winthrop Campbell**
Geo. S. Freeman — **W. Lingenbrink** — **Robert Brogleman**

In this panel of an accordion postcard, the Mercedes Commercial Club, forerunner of the Mercedes Chamber of Commerce, listed all of the amenities to be had in the new city. Mercedes had grown very quickly by 1909 with more than 1,000 inhabitants, but the American Company still had many farm tracts to sell and hoped to attract buyers from the northern and Midwestern states. The use of postcards was one of the marketing strategies, since the new citizens of Mercedes were sure to send them to friends and family where they would be seen by potential investors. The scene below shows the train depot in the background with the "beautiful tropical park," as described above, shown in the foreground of the photograph. (Vito Buenrostro.)

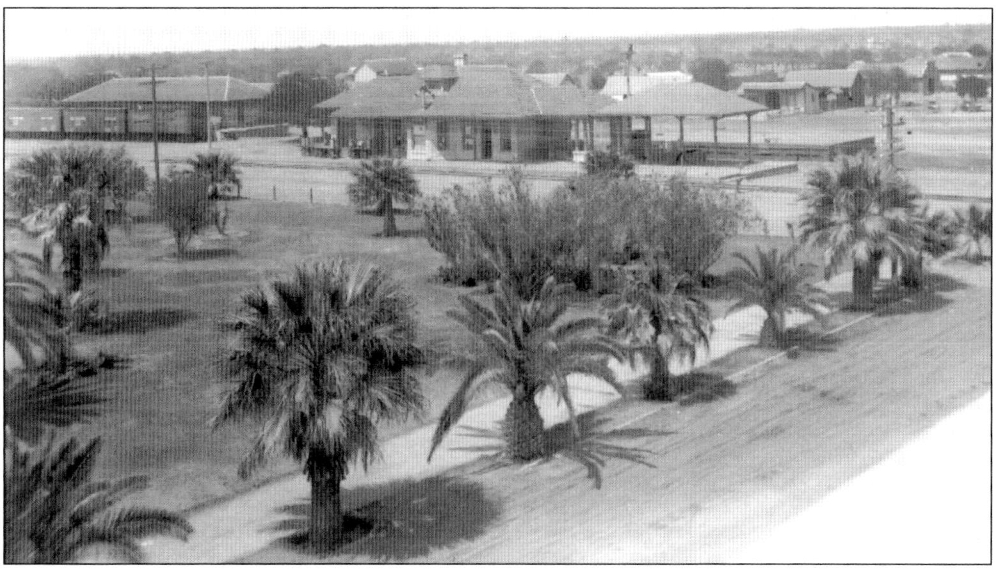

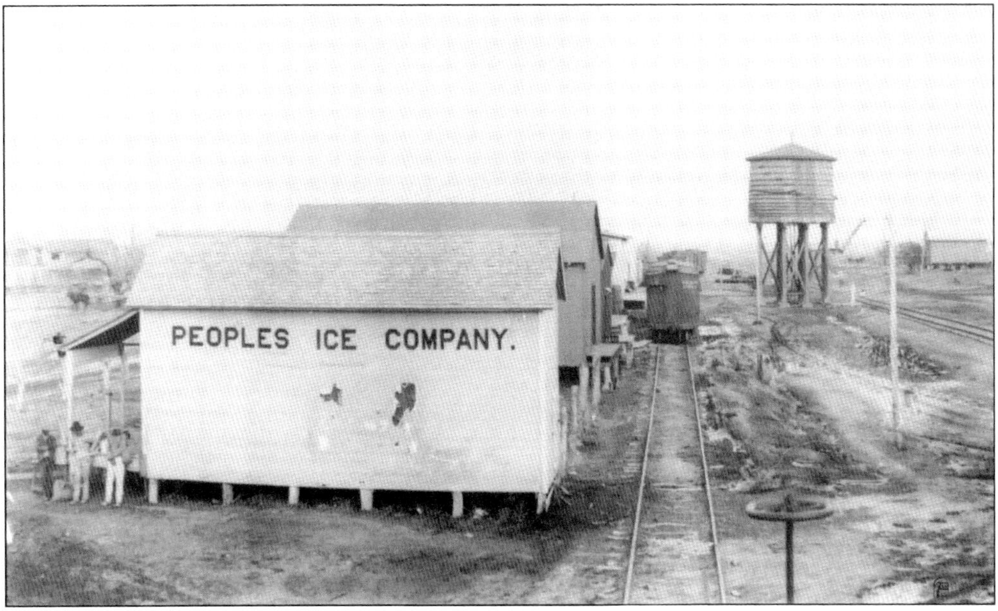

Most of the vegetables and fruits produced in the Valley faced a long train trip to northern and sometimes international markets. This required the produce to be iced down for shipping. Icehouses such as this one were common sights near the packing sheds and railroad tracks. With the advent of mechanically refrigerated boxcars in the late 1940s, icehouses became largely obsolete. (MSTH.)

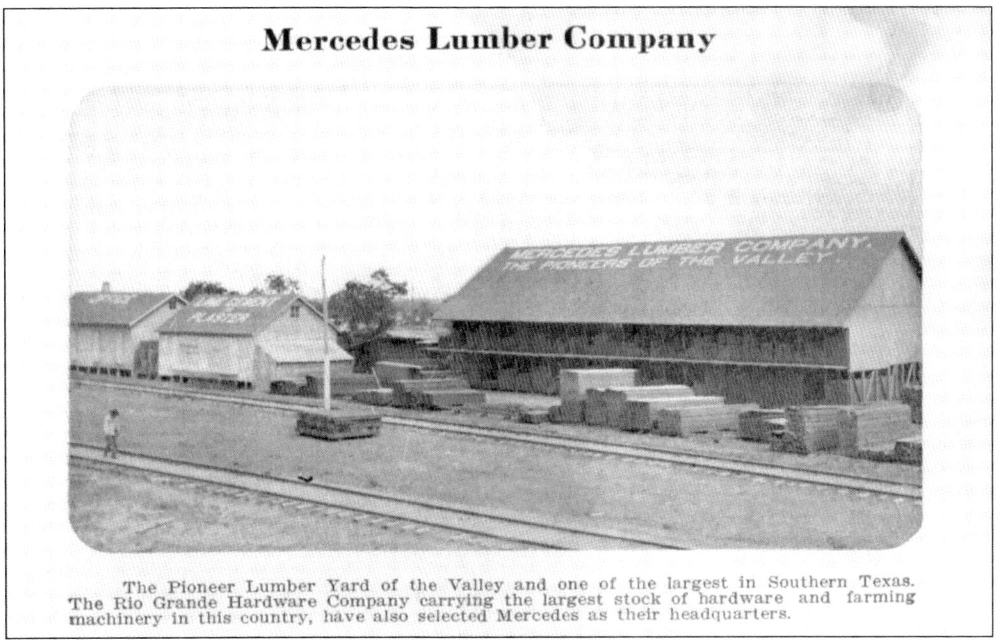

The first business owners in the new town of Mercedes were John D. White, general foreman of all laborers and construction work; Fred Cutting and Charles Campbell, who built the first lumber yard, the Mercedes Lumber Company as seen here; and Alex Champion, who built the first general merchandise store. The first blacksmiths were Ben Brooks Jr. and Pablo López. (Vito Buenrostro.)

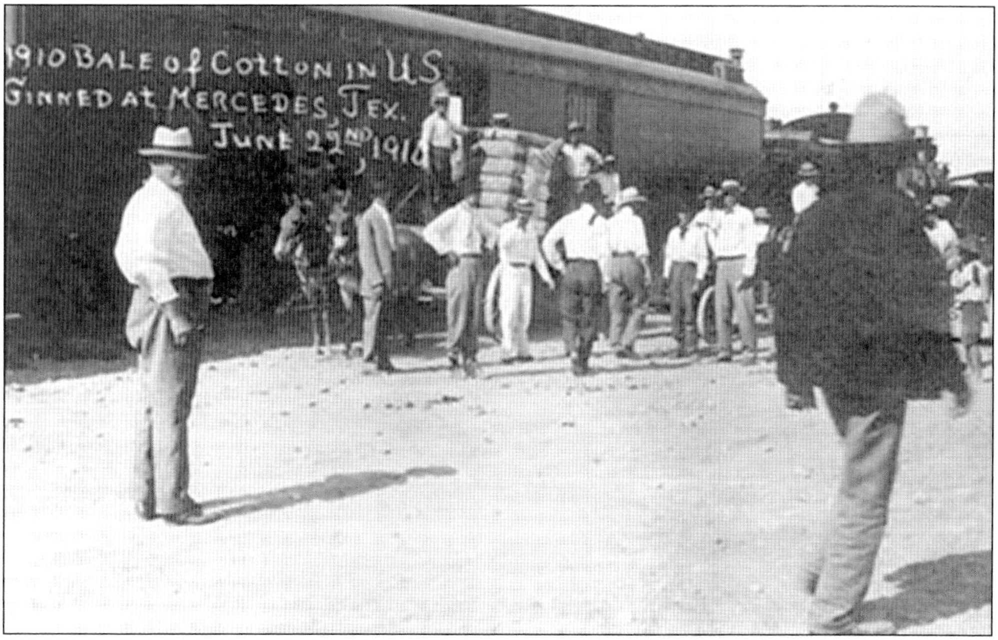

As shown in this postcard, on June 22, 1910, the first bale of cotton in the United States for the season was ginned in Mercedes. Cotton was sometimes planted between rows of cabbage or corn that was harvested first while the cotton grew to maturity. This gave the cotton a head start at being ginned first in the nation. (Vito Buenrostro.)

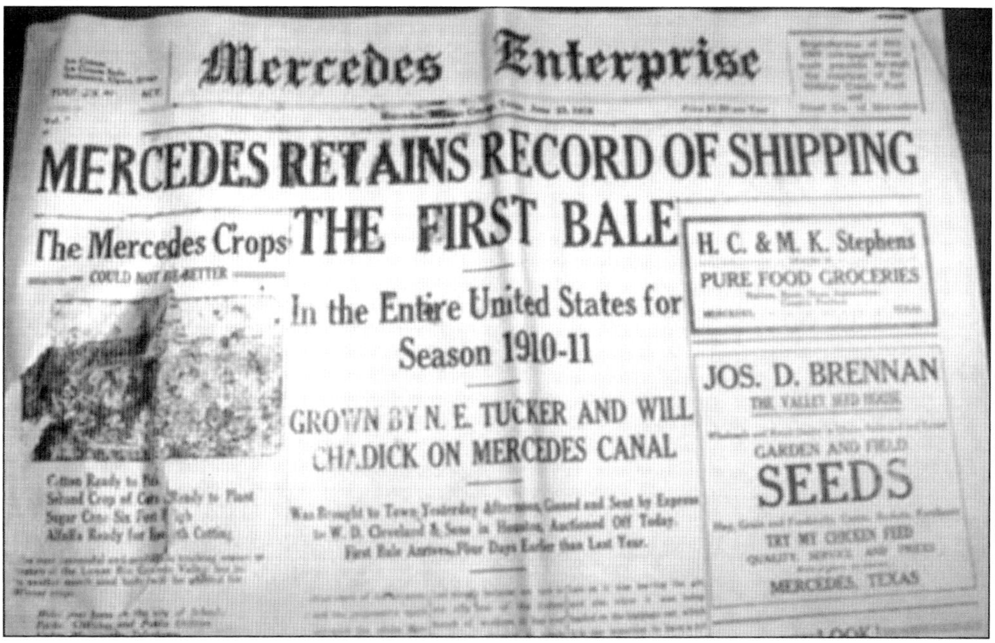

Mercedes Enterprise

MERCEDES RETAINS RECORD OF SHIPPING

THE FIRST BALE

In the Entire United States for Season 1910-11

GROWN BY N. E. TUCKER AND WILL CHADICK ON MERCEDES CANAL

The Mercedes Crops

COULD NOT BE BETTER

H. C. & M. K. Stephens

PURE FOOD GROCERIES

JOS. D. BRENNAN

THE VALLEY SEED HOUSE

GARDEN AND FIELD

SEEDS

TRY MY CHICKEN FEED

MERCEDES, TEXAS

The *Mercedes Enterprise* is the local newspaper whose origins go back to 1908 when Isadore Moritz, previously of the *Brownsville Herald*, decided to start up a periodical in the fledgling town. The *Enterprise* is still being published today with its original name. In this issue, the big story was the ginning of the nation's first bale of cotton for the 1910 season in Mercedes. (*Mercedes Enterprise*.)

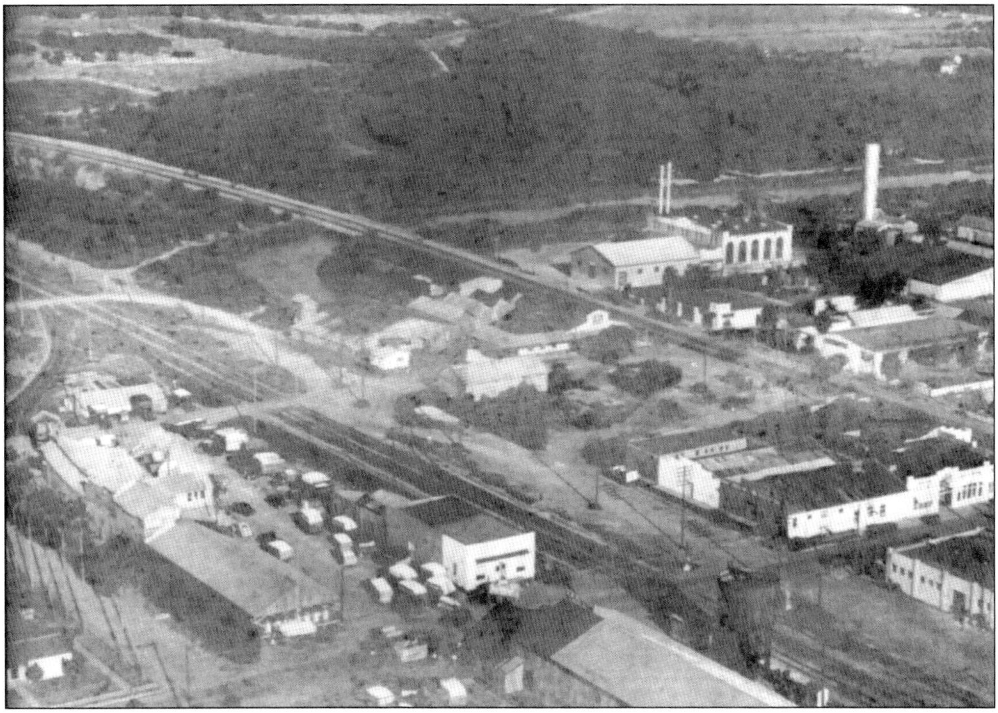

In this aerial view of Mercedes looking southeastward, packing sheds are seen in the bottom left area, located alongside the railroad tracks. The Main Canal can be seen running behind the power plant, the building with the arches in front. The main roadway going from top left to bottom right is Second Street after it was designated US Highway 83. This photograph was taken around 1935. (Weslaco Museum.)

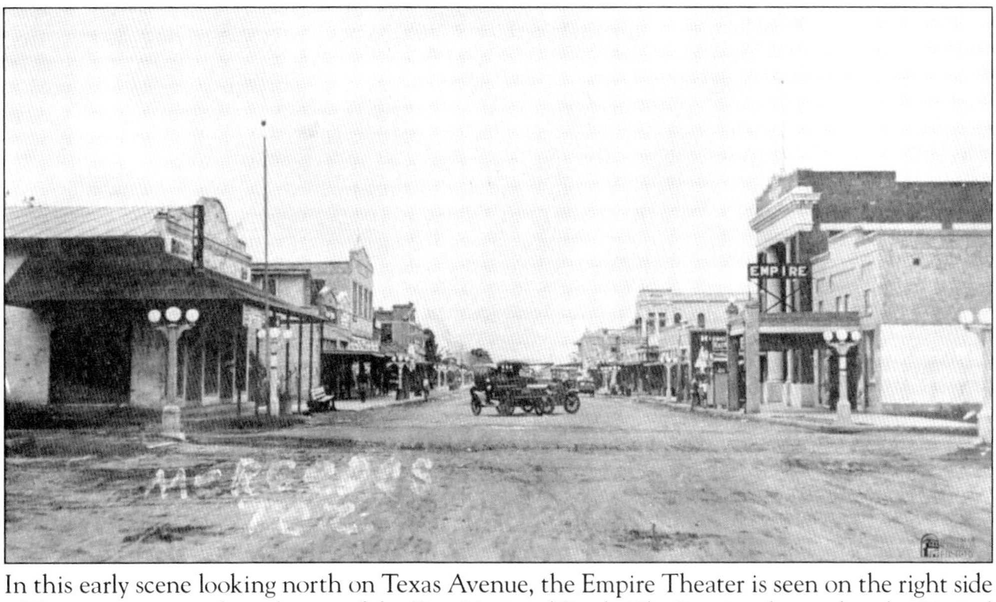

In this early scene looking north on Texas Avenue, the Empire Theater is seen on the right side of the street next to the columns of the First National Bank. The Empire changed to the Capitol after the hurricane of 1933, and later to the State Theater. Across the street on the corner is the mercantile store opened by Amador Fernández of the Toluca Ranch. (MSTH.)

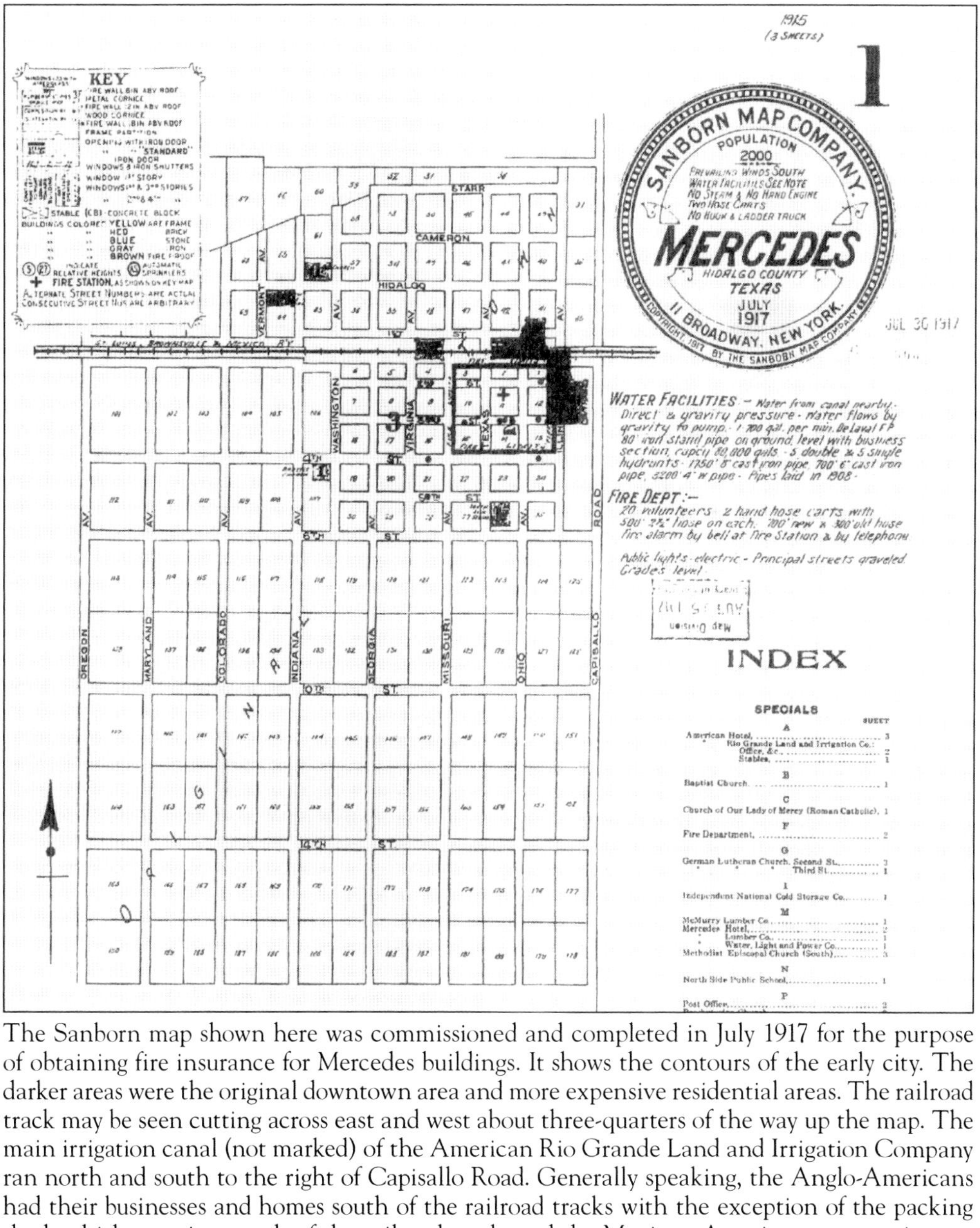

The Sanborn map shown here was commissioned and completed in July 1917 for the purpose of obtaining fire insurance for Mercedes buildings. It shows the contours of the early city. The darker areas were the original downtown area and more expensive residential areas. The railroad track may be seen cutting across east and west about three-quarters of the way up the map. The main irrigation canal (not marked) of the American Rio Grande Land and Irrigation Company ran north and south to the right of Capisallo Road. Generally speaking, the Anglo-Americans had their businesses and homes south of the railroad tracks with the exception of the packing sheds which were just north of the railroad track; and the Mexican American community was located north of the railroad tracks. This type of separation occurred in every town of the lower Rio Grande Valley of this era, with exceptions sometimes made when the Mexican American family or business owner was well-to-do. (City of Mercedes.)

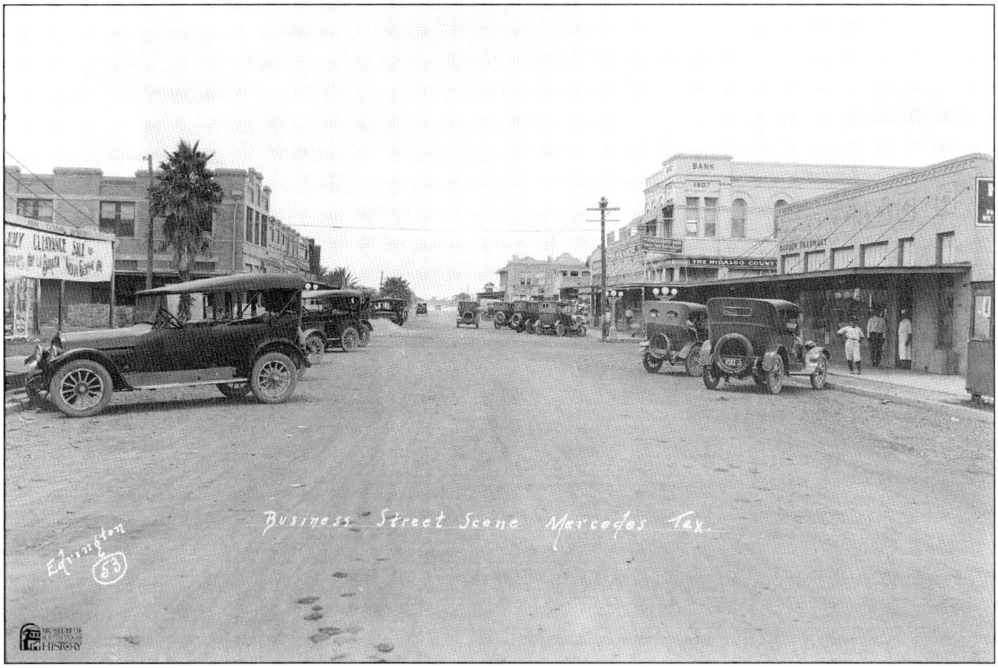

In the above 1922 photograph of the Mercedes downtown area, the cars are parked at a slant and next to the sidewalks rather than in the middle of the street. This is Texas Avenue looking north. The two-story building on the right with light-colored brick is the second building used by the Hidalgo County Bank and Trust. It was located on the northeast corner of Texas Avenue and Third Street. In 1928, the bank built a new brick three-story building across the street on the southwest corner of Texas and Third Streets as seen in the photograph below. This edifice still exists today although it has been remodeled to face a new parking lot south of the building. (Above, MSTH; below, *Mercedes Enterprise*.)

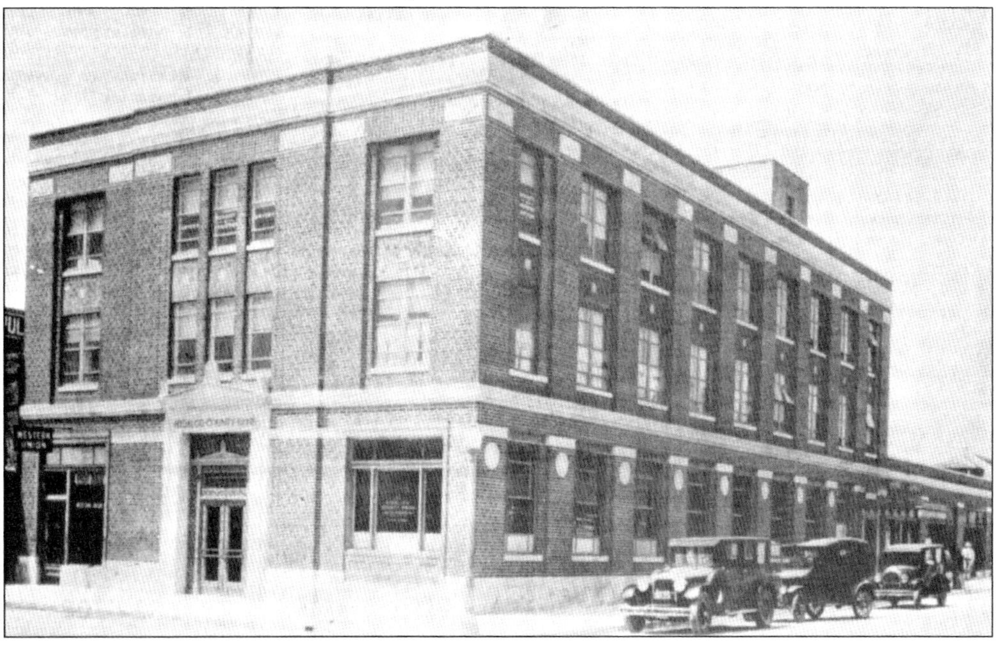

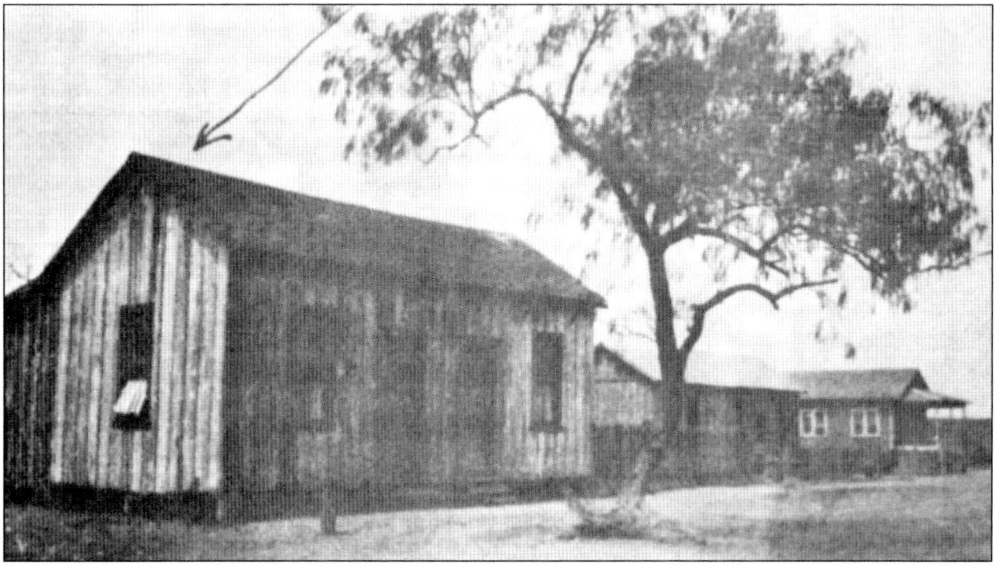

This small frame building, which faced Third Street downtown, was first used by the Hidalgo County Bank and Trust Company in 1907. When the new brick building on South Texas Avenue was built later that same year, the frame building was used as a primary classroom with Miss Boyd as teacher. (*Mercedes Enterprise.*)

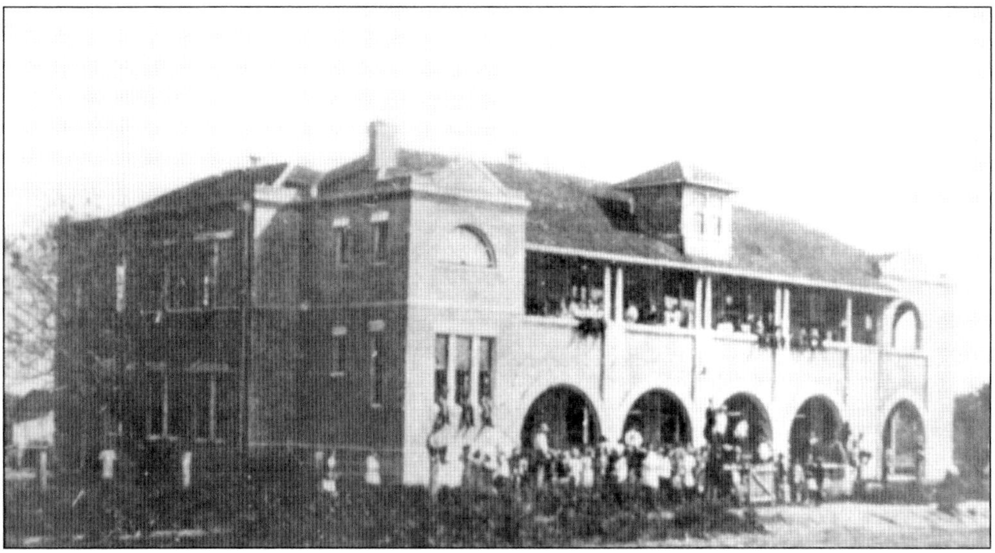

After holding classes in several buildings in town, a more permanent structure was finally completed facing Texas Avenue. This school, built in 1912, housed students from primary grades to high school grades. It was named for Harriet Claycomb Buck who was the mother of Nannie Mer Buck, the Mercedes superintendent of schools from 1915 to 1923. The building was demolished after irreparable damage in the hurricane of 1933. (Mercedes ISD.)

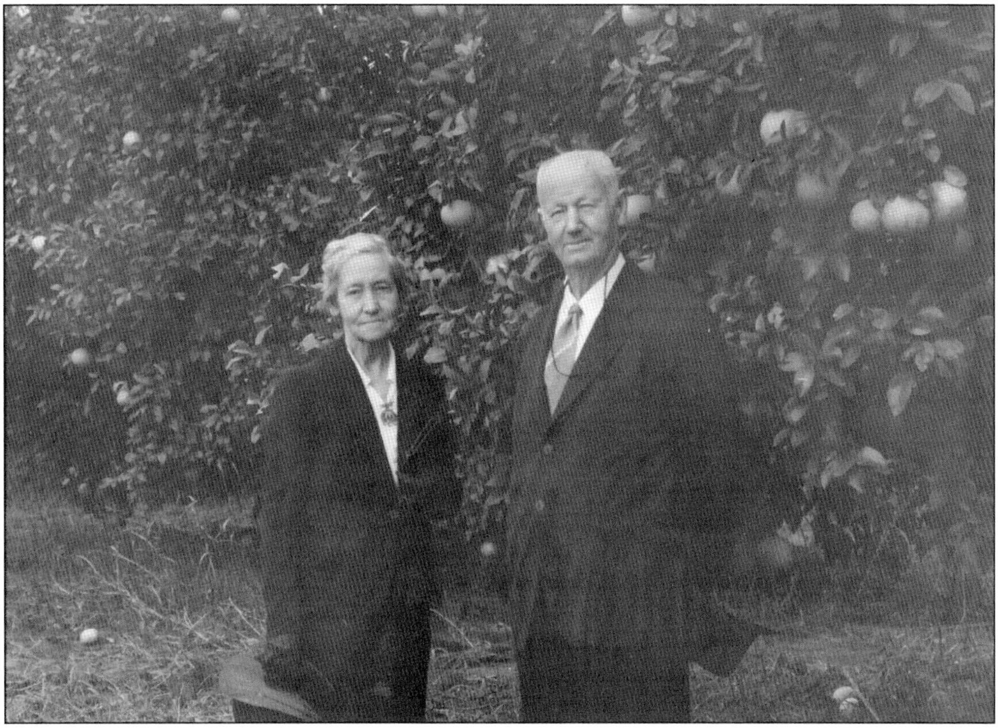

Elizabeth Riess (left), Gustavus K. Riess, and their two children Marion and Malcolm relocated to Mercedes from the northeast in 1910. Both "Gus" and "Lizzie" were active in their community, serving on the school board and city council from 1912 to 1914. Gus was a railroad station agent, and Lizzie is reputed to have developed the first pink grapefruit in the Rio Grande Valley. (Riess family.)

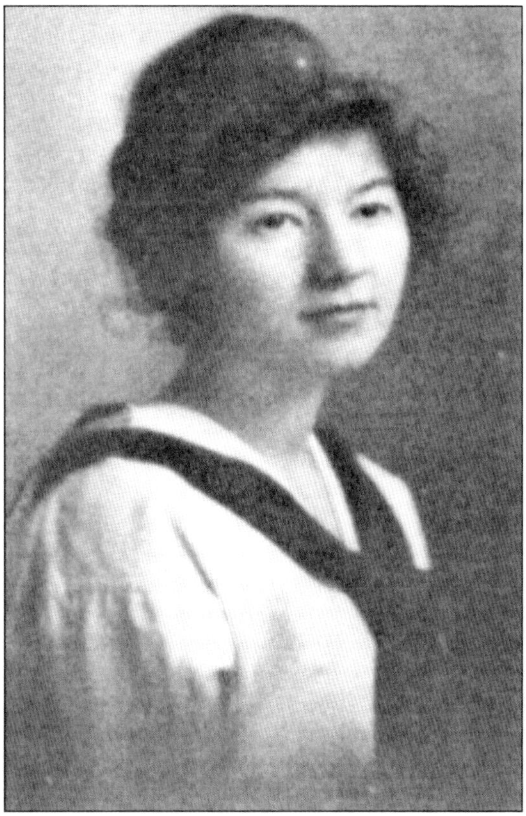

Although schoolchildren in Mercedes had been attending school in makeshift classrooms beginning in 1907, the first student to complete her studies and graduate from the Mercedes school district in 1914 was Marion Riess, daughter of Gus and Lizzie Riess. She later became a teacher and principal in Mercedes. She married Rev. Herbert Haslam of Philadelphia, had five children, and helped with her husband's ministry while also continuing to teach. (Mercedes ISD.)

GRADUATING EXERCISES

Mercedes High School

FRIDAY, MAY 21ST, 1915

EIGHT O'CLOCK P. M.

MOVING PICTURE THEATRE

Programme

"Welcome, Sweet Springtime" .... High School
Address to Graduates .... Judge L. T. Hoyt
"Hungarian Rapsodie Mignonne," Carl Koelling ....Beatrice Diehl
Address for Class .... Martha Wright
"Rhapsody," March, Franz Liszt ...... Beatrice Diehl and Gertrude Carter
Farewell to Graduates .... Mildred McCall
"Scarf Dance," C. Chaminade .... Mary Ellen Silver
Presentation of Diplomas .... Wm. Dietel
"Questions" .... High School

"MISS BLUE BONNET"

Comedy in Two Acts, by Brooke W. Leman

SYNOPSIS OF PLAY

Jas. Dudley, a crabbed millionaire, is father of an attractive daughter, by name Jane. She, against his will, runs away to meet her fiance, Walden. To prevent their meeting and subsequent marriage, Dudley engages Pace, a young attorney. Action starts where Pace attempts to prevent the meeting of the runaway girl and her sweetheart at the mountain station of Dodge.

He is guided merely by the description of a "very attractive young lady, wearing a blue traveling suit and a blue hat." A young lady of this description arrives and is taken by Pace for Miss Dudley. Her supposed fiance does not appear on time, and the attorney while watching for him, becomes deeply interested. His interest increases, and finally he grows to love her. Still supposing she is Miss Dudley, and realizing the hopelessness of his suit in this event, he decides to give up the task. This he does, only to learn that the couple he was to have pursued have gone the other way, and that the young lady of the blue bonnet is his for the asking.

And he asks.

CAST OF CHARACTERS

Hon. Jas. Dudley, a millionaire .... Aloysius Regan
Rodman Pace, attorney .... Albert Rothrock
Smith, station agent .... Wm. Ragland
Winters, who is suspected .... Aloysius Regan
Jane, the woman involved .... Pearl Hearing
Agnese, very charming .... Nellie Linemann

Place—Dodge, a mountain station.

Time—A Saturday night and December morning in December.

In 1914, only one person graduated from high school—Marion Riess. The next year, Mercedes High School graduated four students—Pearl Hearing, Nellie Linemann, Martha Wright, and Albert Rothrock. The program shown here describes the graduation ceremonies held on May 21, 1915, at the Moving Picture Theater. The program included poetry recitations, songs, several speeches, piano pieces, presentation of the diplomas, and a short play with the graduates participating. This play was the forerunner of the "Senior Play" tradition at Mercedes High School, although the play is no longer presented during the graduation ceremonies because of time constraints. On May 18, 1915, the junior class had honored the senior class with a banquet given at the Mercedes Hotel. On the menu were fruit cocktail, fried chicken, cream gravy, hot biscuits, currant jelly, mashed potatoes, string beans, pears, olives, and the new sensation from New York City: Waldorf salad. (Mercedes ISD.)

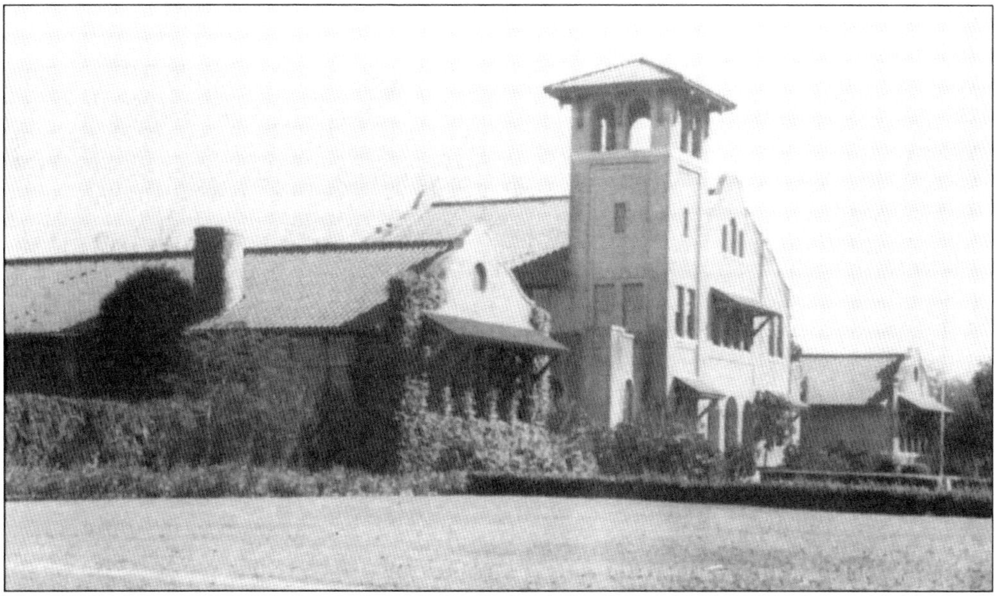

South School, later renamed for Leon R. Graham, the superintendent of schools from 1941 to 1951, was built in 1921 facing Ohio Avenue between Ninth and Tenth Streets. Since its construction and through various remodeling projects and additions, Graham School served as a primary school, a junior high, a high school, and a migrant school. (Mercedes ISD.)

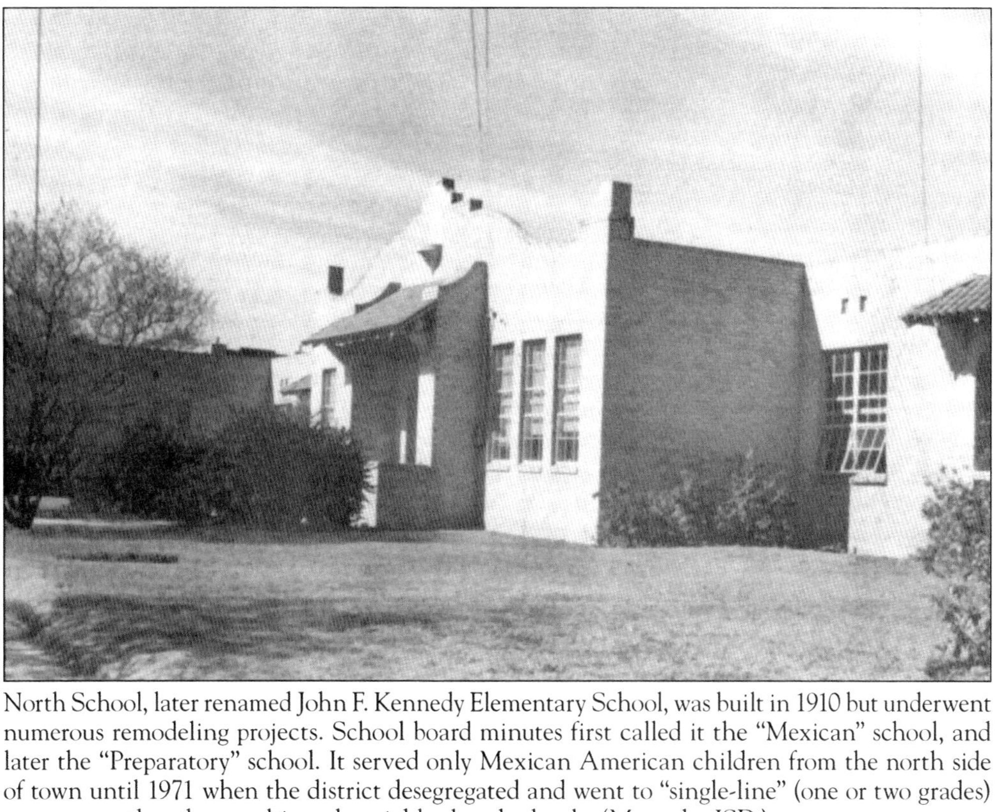

North School, later renamed John F. Kennedy Elementary School, was built in 1910 but underwent numerous remodeling projects. School board minutes first called it the "Mexican" school, and later the "Preparatory" school. It served only Mexican American children from the north side of town until 1971 when the district desegregated and went to "single-line" (one or two grades) campuses rather than multi-grade neighborhood schools. (Mercedes ISD.)

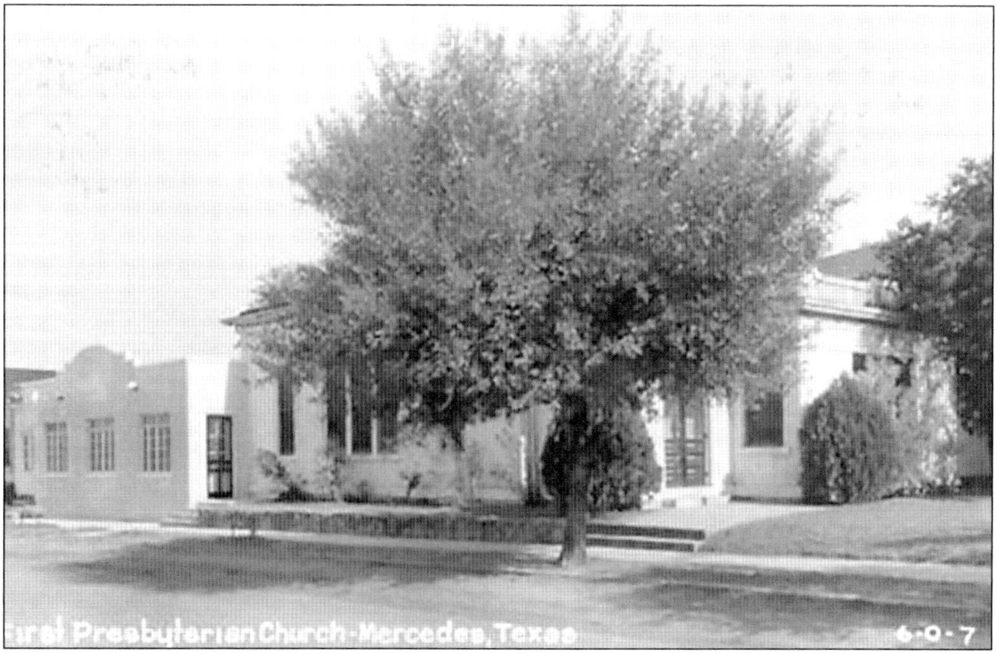

In 1909, the first Presbyterian congregation of 19 members was organized by Rev. William W. Doggett. The church seen in this photograph was built in 1912, located on the corner of Fourth Street and Missouri Avenue with the Rev. Samuel M. Glasgow as the first resident pastor. (Vito Buenrostro.)

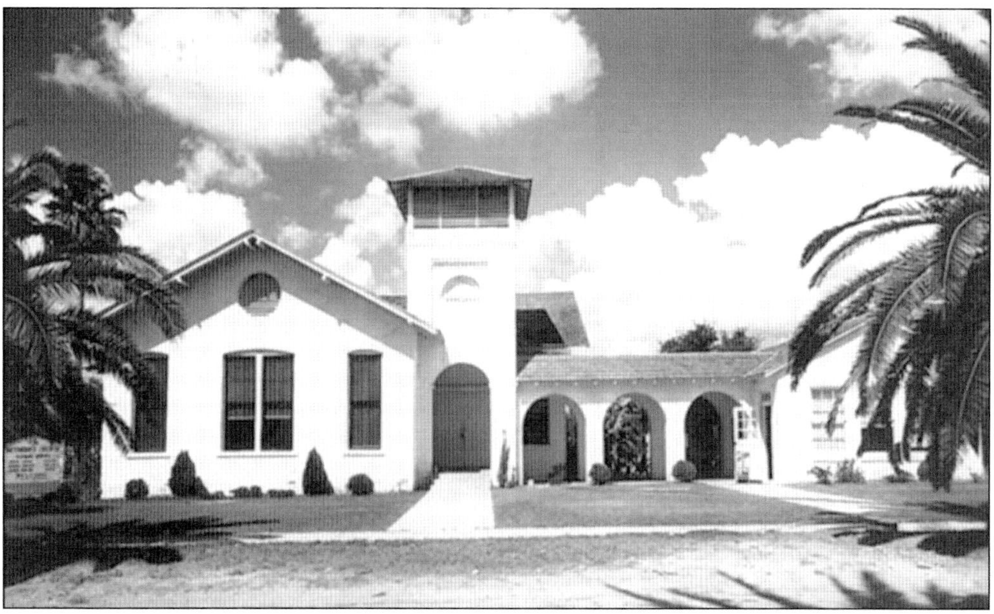

This photograph shows the first building of the First United Methodist Church built in 1936. It was later used for the Spanish-speaking congregation with the name El Buen Pastor Iglesia Metodista, or the Good Shepherd Methodist Church. A new structure was built on Sixteenth Street in the 1960s. (Vito Buenrostro.)

Raquel Gonzales Palacios stands in the center front during an Easter Pageant with other unidentified girls in the spring of 1932. They are holding palm leaves and flowers as is traditional for this religious holiday. According to family members, the steps where the girls posed are most likely those of the rectory at Our Lady of Mercy Catholic Church. (Irma Palacios.)

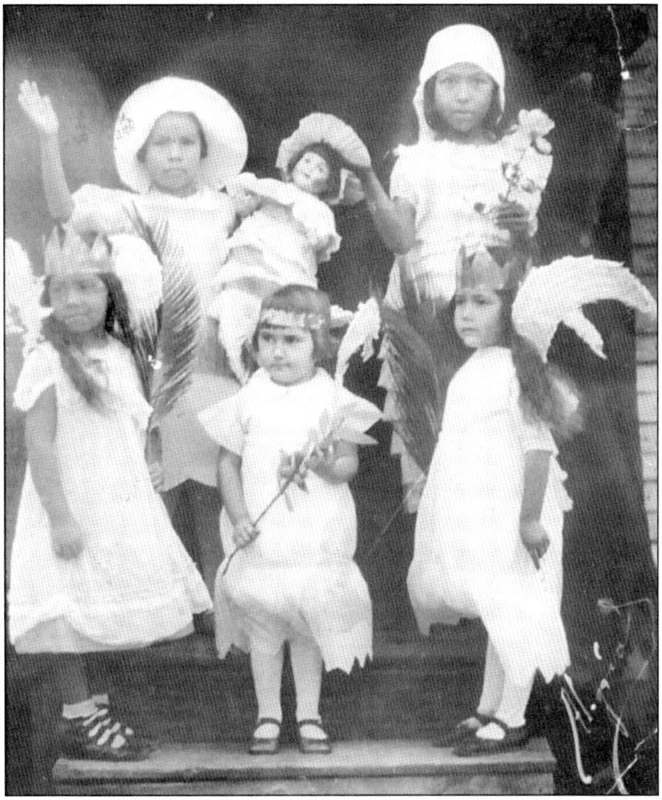

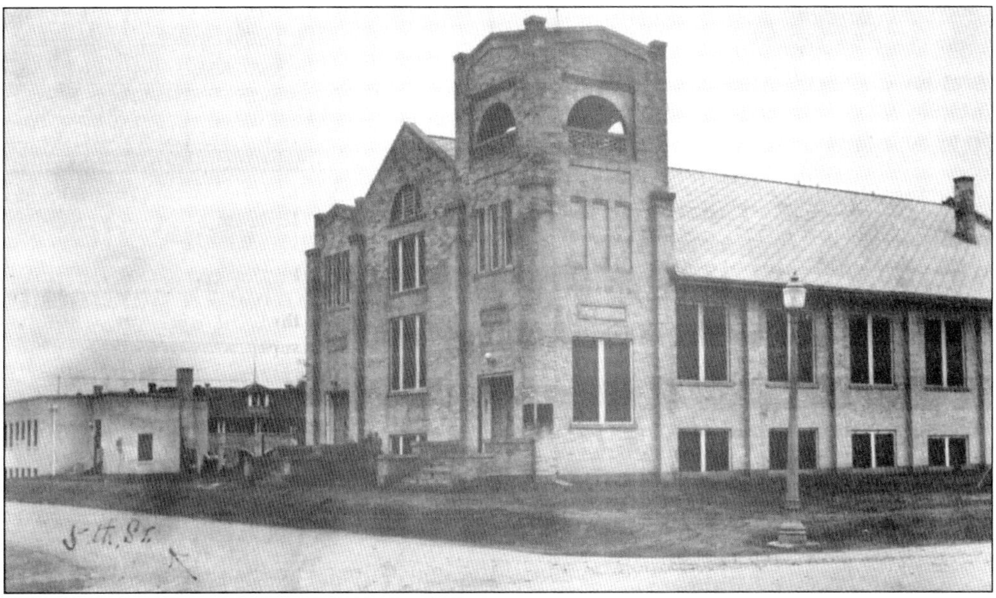

The First Baptist Church of Mercedes was organized in 1907 with four charter members: Mrs. Fred Cutting, Mrs. Jimmy Johnson, and Mr. and Mrs. Lewis Boothe. They were served by missionaries until the building of the present church seen in the photograph. The new complex includes an auditorium, Sunday school classrooms, kitchen, and fellowship hall; it was erected in 1920 during the pastorate of the Rev. John C. Boyd. (*Mercedes Enterprise*.)

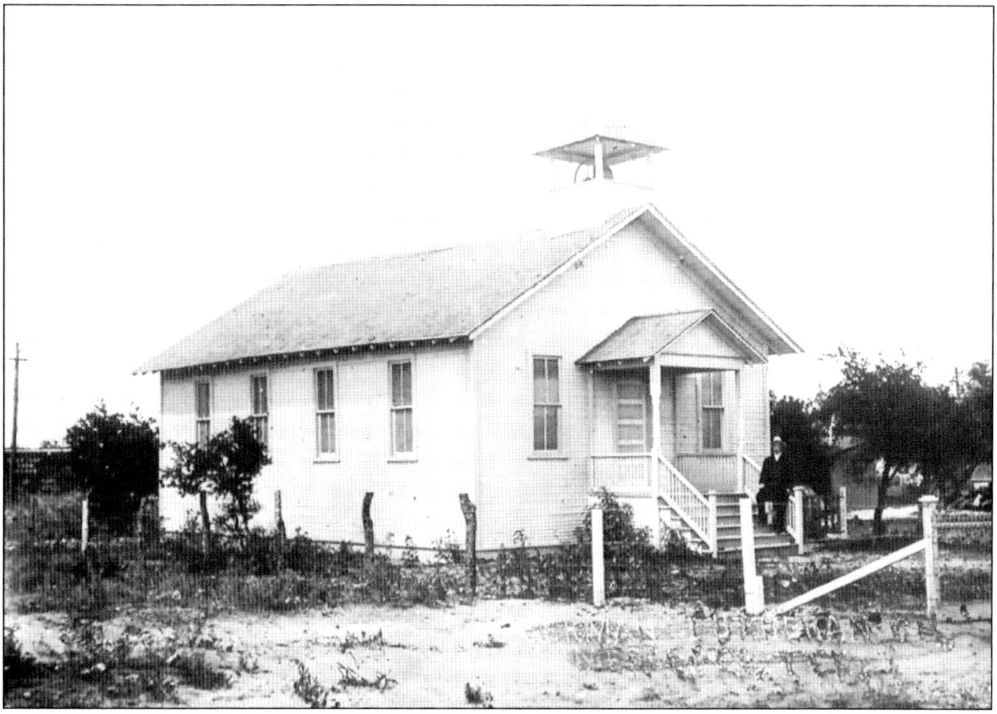

The Immanuel Lutheran Church, first called the German Lutheran Church, was the first Lutheran church established in the Rio Grande Valley in 1910. The first pastor, Rev. Ernest J. Moebus stands on the steps in this early photograph. Using the Mercedes church as his headquarters, Rev. Moebus founded many preaching stations in the Valley. Most of the town's population of German heritage attended this church in the early days. (Library of Congress.)

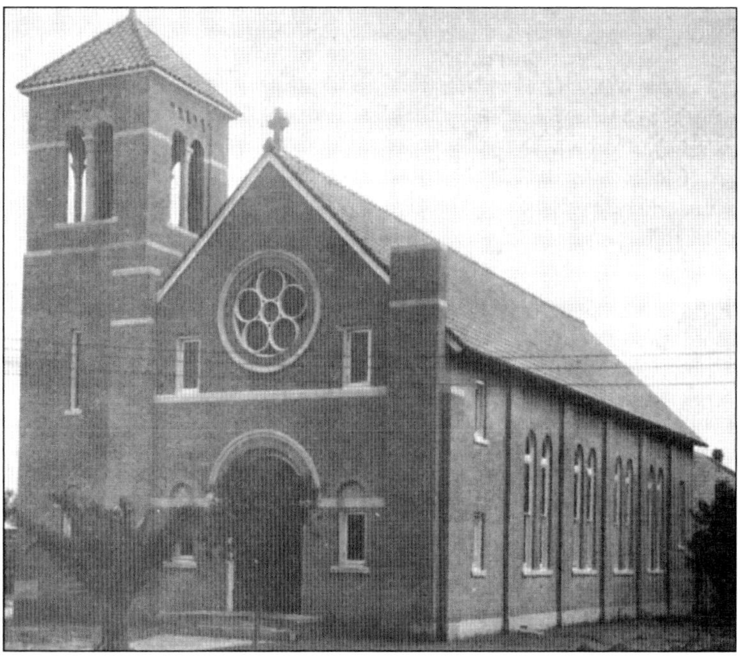

The Immanuel Lutheran Church was moved to its present location at South Washington Avenue and Third Street where this brick structure was completed in 1929. Later additions included a parochial school, meeting rooms and a kitchen. Well known in the community is the excellent school that, although it has had to close on past occasions, is fully operating again. (*Mercedes Enterprise*.)

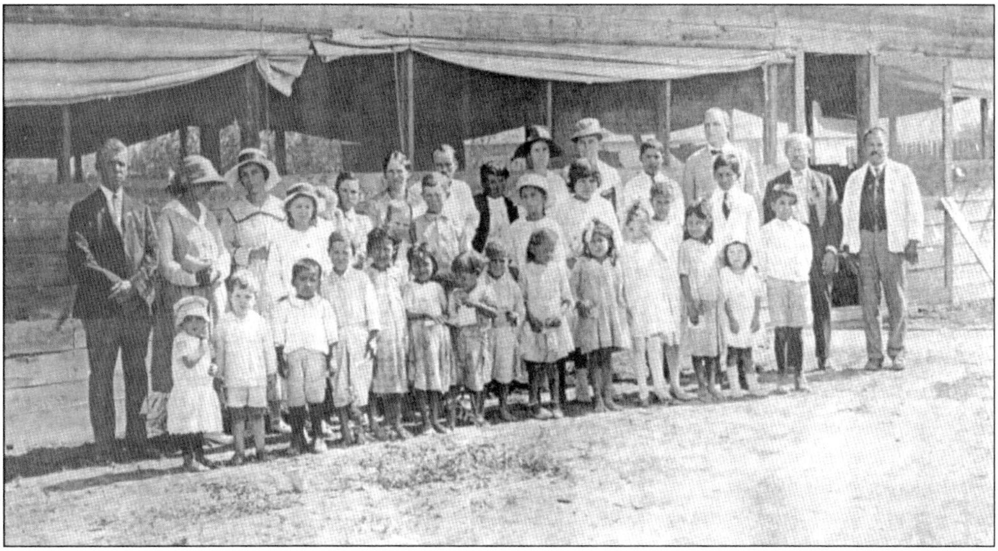

Pictured here is a Baptist mission group in 1916 in a temporary building on North Missouri Avenue with Howell and Zepeda family members among others. This group would meet in the Mercedes Community Building at first but later built the Primera Iglesia Bautista Mexicana, or First Mexican Baptist Church. (Eddie Howell Sr.)

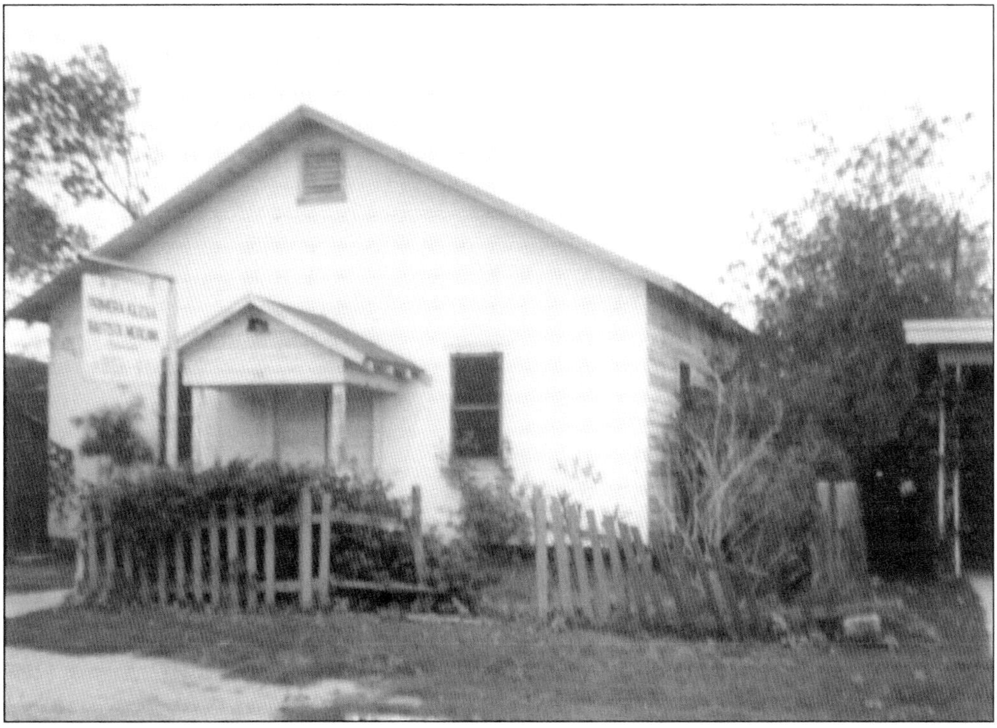

The Primera Iglesia Bautista Mexicana shown here was built around 1918, with Joseph Henry Howell as the first missionary preacher. Howell's father, William Albert Howell, had been a Union soldier captured by the Confederacy who escaped to Mexico and later wound up in Port Isabel. He opened a dry goods store there and raised a family, with Joseph Henry eventually relocating to Mercedes. (Carolyn C. López.)

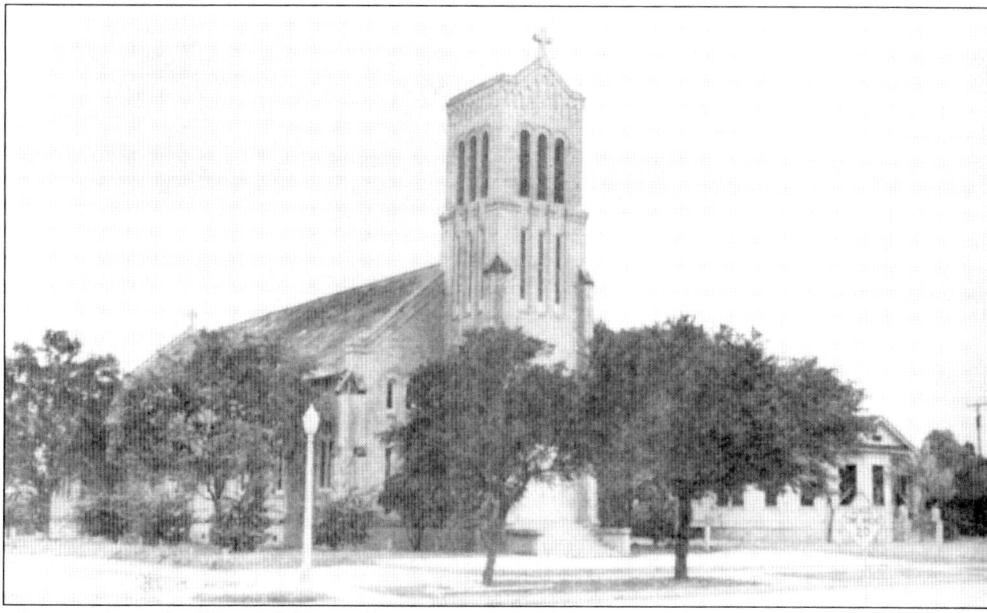

The first frame building of Our Lady of Mercy Catholic Church was erected on the north side of Hidalgo Street in 1909 on land donated by the American Rio Grande Land and Irrigation Company. The new church was built in its present location on Vermont Avenue and Third Street as seen here, and it was formally dedicated on October 22, 1922. (Our Lady of Mercy Church.)

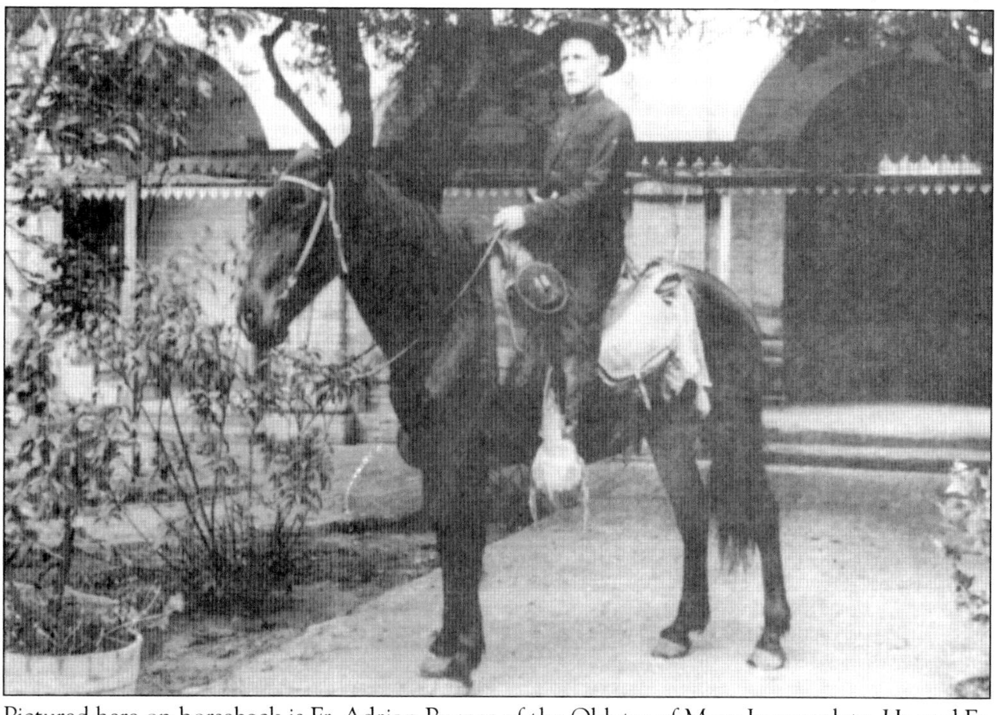

Pictured here on horseback is Fr. Adrian Bornes of the Oblates of Mary Immaculate. He and Fr. Paul Hally were the first resident priests assigned permanently to Our Lady of Mercy Church at Mercedes in 1909. They served not only Mercedes but the surrounding missions as well, traveling to them on horseback. (Our Lady of Mercy Church.)

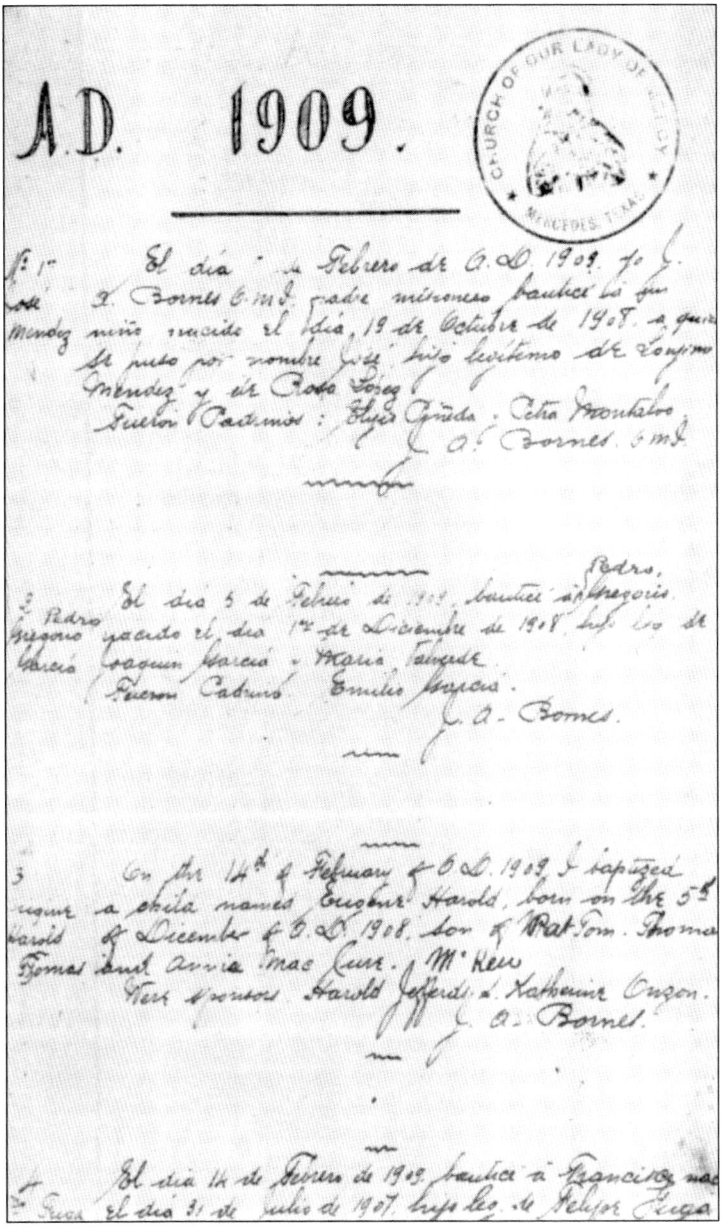

The first baptisms were performed and recorded in this registry at Our Lady of Mercy Catholic Church in February 1909. The children baptized were José Méndez, Pedro Gregorio García, and Eugene Harold Thomas. All three were born in late 1908 but had to wait for the priest to arrive early the next year in order to be baptized. The first two entries are written in Spanish and the third is written in English, undoubtedly to conform to the identities and ethnicities of the parents. The entries contain the date of baptism, the date of birth for the child, the condition of legitimacy, the parents' names, the "padrinos" or sponsors' names, and the priest's signature, Fr. Adrian Bornes, OMI. Baptismal records such as these are very important resources not only for genealogists or those who wish to trace their ancestry but also for historians. In many baptismal registries, if the family was an important one, the grandparents' names would also be included. (Our Lady of Mercy Church.)

Mercedes Telephone Co.

DIRECTORY

List of Subscribers Revised and Printed November 1st, 1909

44 American Hotel
40 Anglin E.
A. R. G. L. & I. Co.
- 21 W. S. Chaplin, President
- 37 General Office
- 41 Corral
- 50 Store Room

48 Appel H. A., store
49 Appel H. A., residence

2 Brennan Joseph D.
23 Buck Chas. B., M. D., res.

12 Caldwell T. J., M. D., res.
28 Champion, Alex & Bro.
43 Champion, L. & Bro.
34 Chaplin W. S., res.
18 Chapman A. E.
14 Cutting F. J.

27 Harrison Lytle, res.
11 Hidalgo County Bank

8 Johnson J. M., res.

3 Kay D. E. res.

38 Mercedes Dray Co.
17 Mercedes Drug Company
15 Mercedes Dry Goods & Gro. Co.
30 Mercedes Grain Co.
46 Mercedes Hotel
19 Merceds Livery Co.
33 Mercedes Lumber Co.
47 Mercedes Plantation Co.
9 Mercedes Publishing Co.
20 Moritz Isadore, res.
22 Murray S. J., res.
32 McMurry Lumber Co.

4 Ogle J. E.

42 Plummer T. M.

26 Rio Grande Hdw. & Mch. Co.

6 Schoonmaker E. C., M. D., office
25 Scobey F. E., res.
13 Silver S. P. res.
31 Smith R. J., office
29 Stephens H. C. & M. K.
16 St. L. B. & M. Ry Depot

24 White J. D., store

36 Young's Pharmacy
45 Young D. J., res.

10 Zachry Mercantile Co.

Please call by number.
When through talking please RING OFF.
Subscribers will be held responsible for all long distance calls made over their telephones.

This was the first Mercedes Telephone Directory issued in November 1909. It was reprinted in the 25th anniversary issue of the *Mercedes News-Tribune* on September 16, 1932. After only two years of founding, Mercedes had more than 1,000 inhabitants and more than 30 businesses that included two hotels, several drugstores, dry goods and general merchandise stores, a newspaper office, hardware and lumber companies, pharmacies, churches, hospitals, and doctors. Notice in the listings that the town still accommodated those who used horses, buggies, and wagons with a livery stable. In 1909, the streets in Mercedes were not yet paved, but business was brisk and the downtown area was very active. At that time, Mercedes was considered the "Queen City" because it was the premier mid-Valley town and the fastest growing settlement in Hidalgo County. (*Mercedes Enterprise*.)

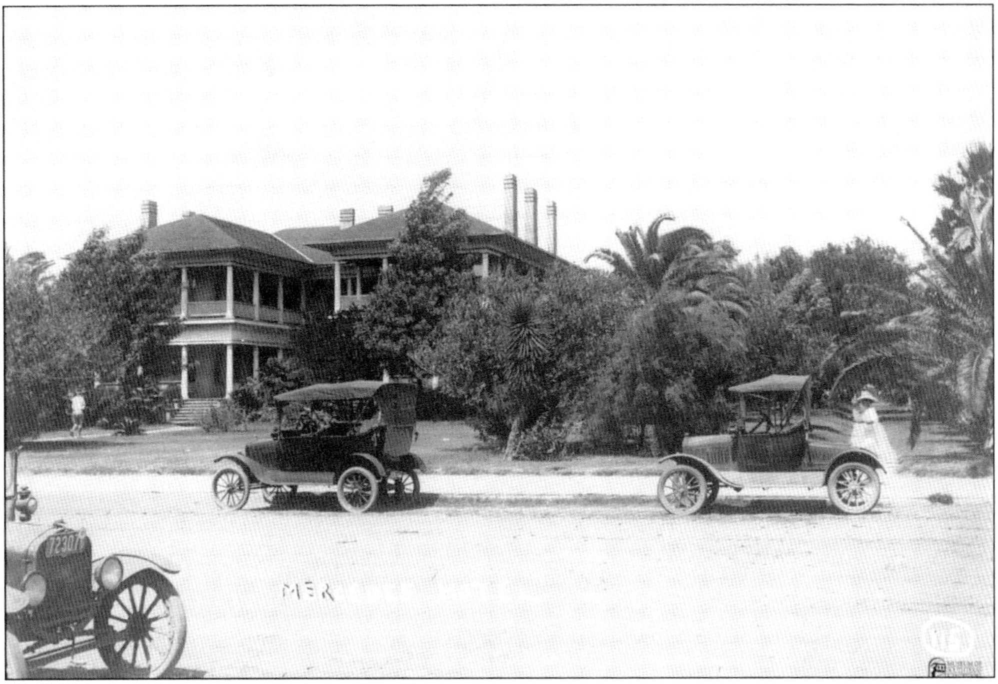

Mercedes had become very prosperous very quickly. The Mercedes Commercial Club had succeeded in attracting a large number of "newcomers" to the town through its aggressive marketing strategies. The town was well-tended and progressive, with important Valley-wide meetings sponsored by the American Rio Grande Land and Irrigation Company often held at the Mercedes Hotel pictured here. (MSTH.)

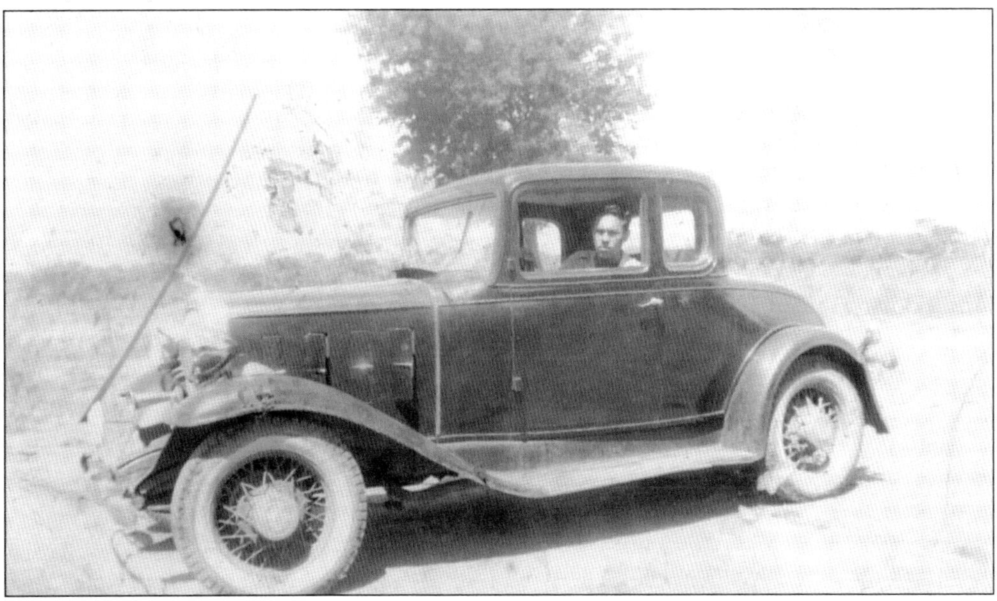

Cato Palacios goes for a ride in the 1932 Chevrolet two-door coupe owned by his father, Abraham Palacios. By 1915, Mercedes had streets paved with caliche (or gravel) and had added streetlights to the downtown area. In 1933, Second Street was widened to asphalt-paved two lanes with shoulders, and it became US Highway 83. (Irma Palacios.)

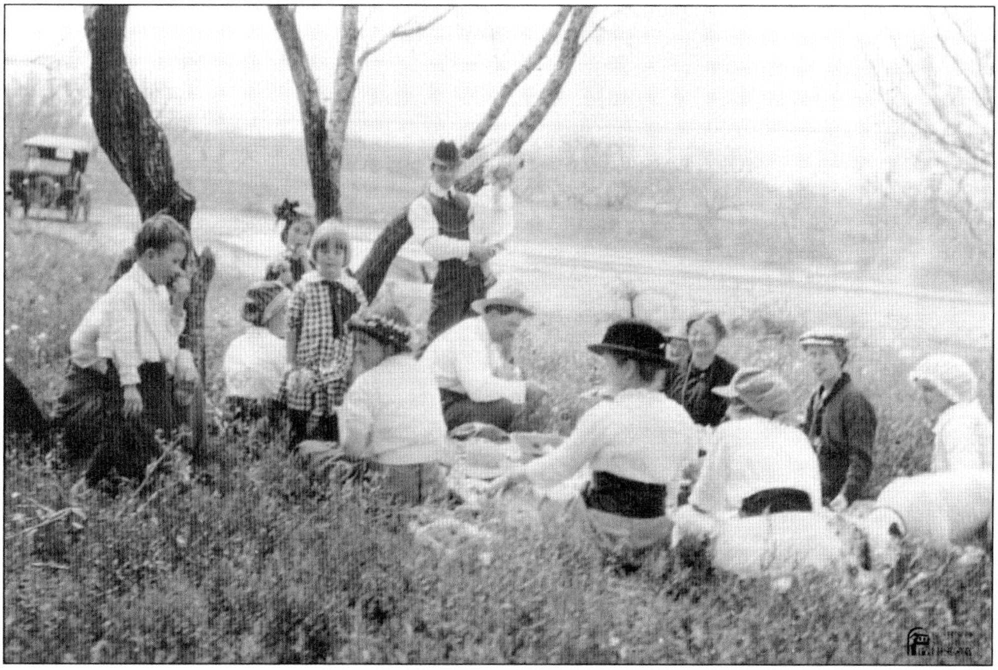

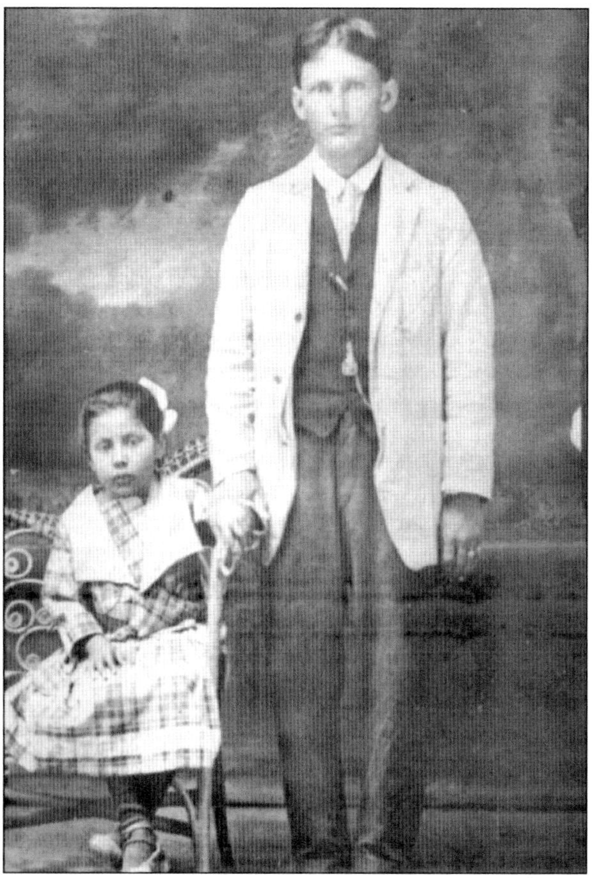

The Baker, Montgomery, and Closner families enjoy a picnic at Lake Campacuás c. 1915. The lake, also known as Tampacuás or Carter's Lake, is about two miles north of Mercedes. It is part of the delta system of *resacas* and arroyos that once were channels of the Rio Grande. It is about two miles long and is 700 feet wide at its broadest point. (MSTH.)

Pictured here in 1920 is Julián Villarreal (standing) with his daughter Adela. Julián and his bride, Dolores, arrived in Mercedes in 1912 and established a small grocery store at 117 North Texas Avenue. He also operated a bakery and often served as a foreman for agricultural work crews. Adela, now Mrs. Ramírez, says they took the picture while waiting for a train to Brownsville, where she was to see a doctor for an ear infection. (*Mercedes Enterprise*.)

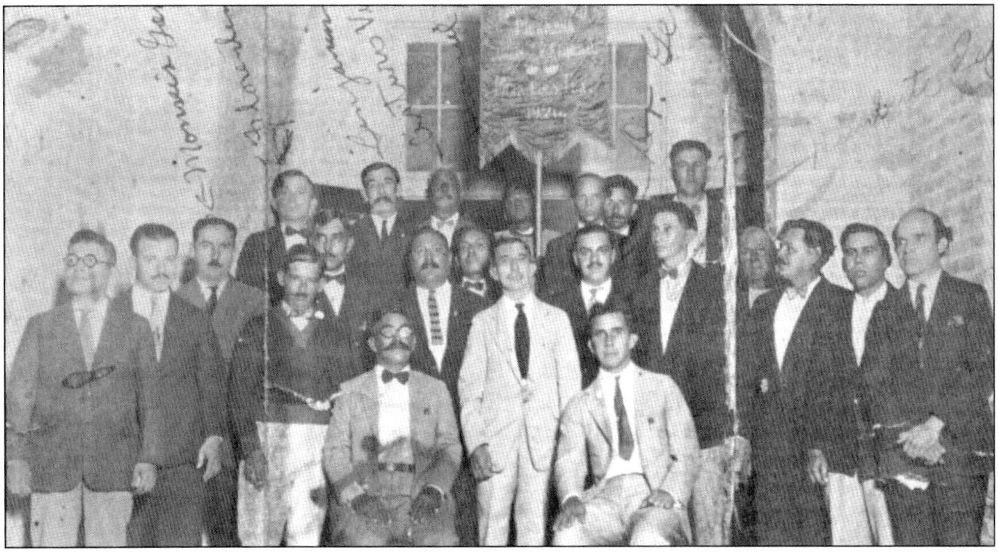

These gentlemen belonging to the Mercedes Mexican American Chamber of Commerce posed for a group picture in 1926. Mexican American businessmen in Mercedes organized early compared to other Valley cities in order to mutually support their business efforts. In the early years, most Mexican American businesses were located north of the railroad tracks because of residential segregation. (*Mercedes Enterprise.*)

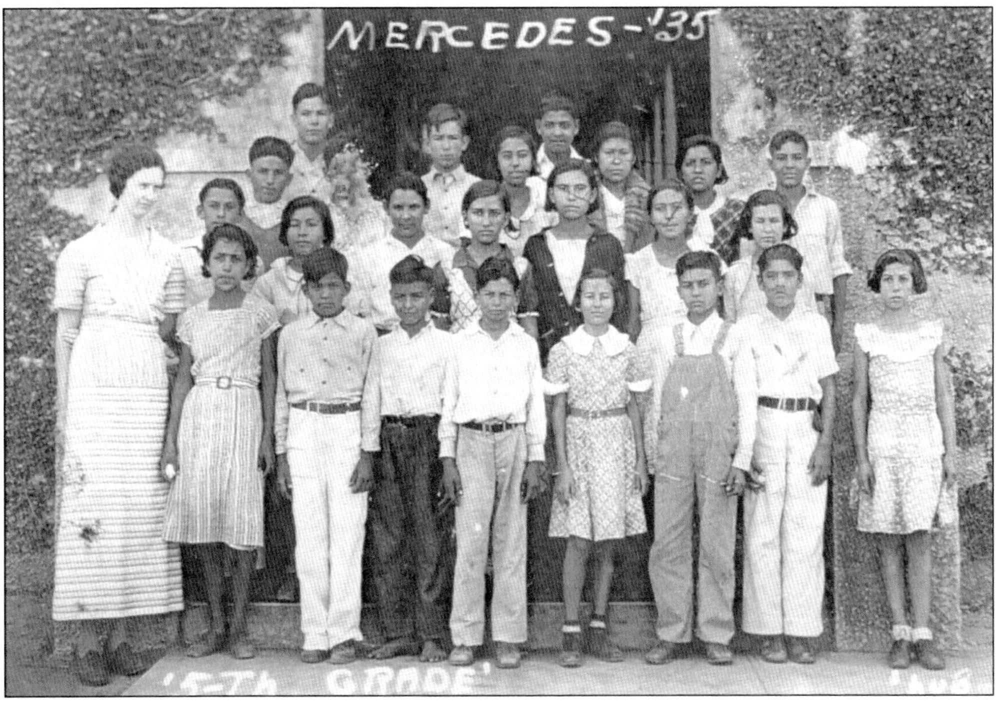

Pictured here is Alma Whatley's fifth-grade class at North Ward School in 1935. The front row includes, from left to right, Whatley, Andrea Barrera, Guadalupe Galván, Cuitláhuac García, Guadalupe Castañeda, unidentified, Juventino de León Jr., Juan Torres, and Adelita Marroquín. In the back rows are unidentified students. Whatley later taught English classes for many years at the Mercedes High School. (Delia de León.)

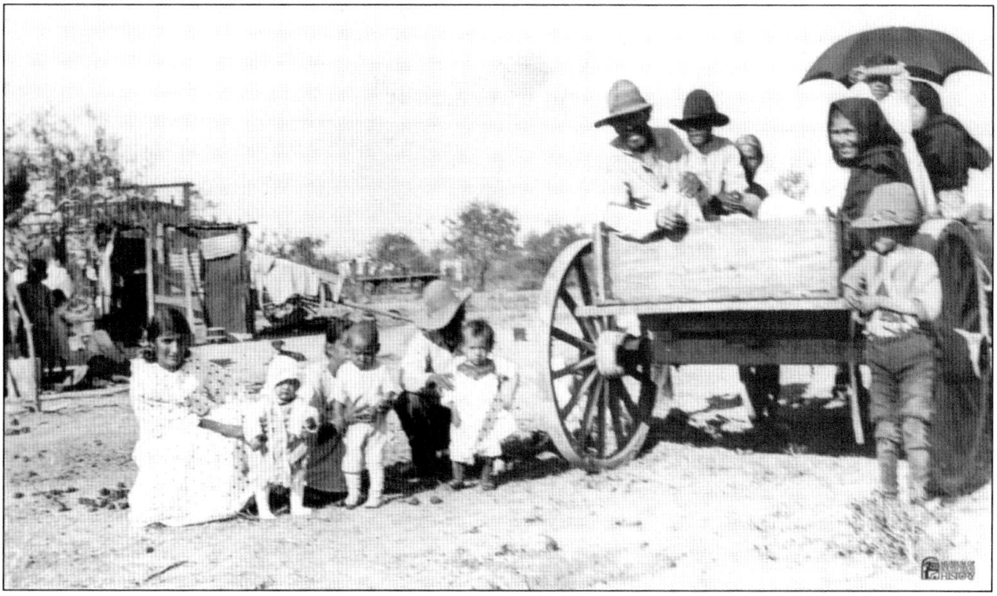

Word of the bonanza, or "abundance of work," in the newly formed town of Mercedes reached the ears of workers on existing ranches as well as Mexican nationals. Many came seeking work, and they were readily hired to clear the land, work on the new farms, construct businesses and residences, and do general labor. (MSTH.)

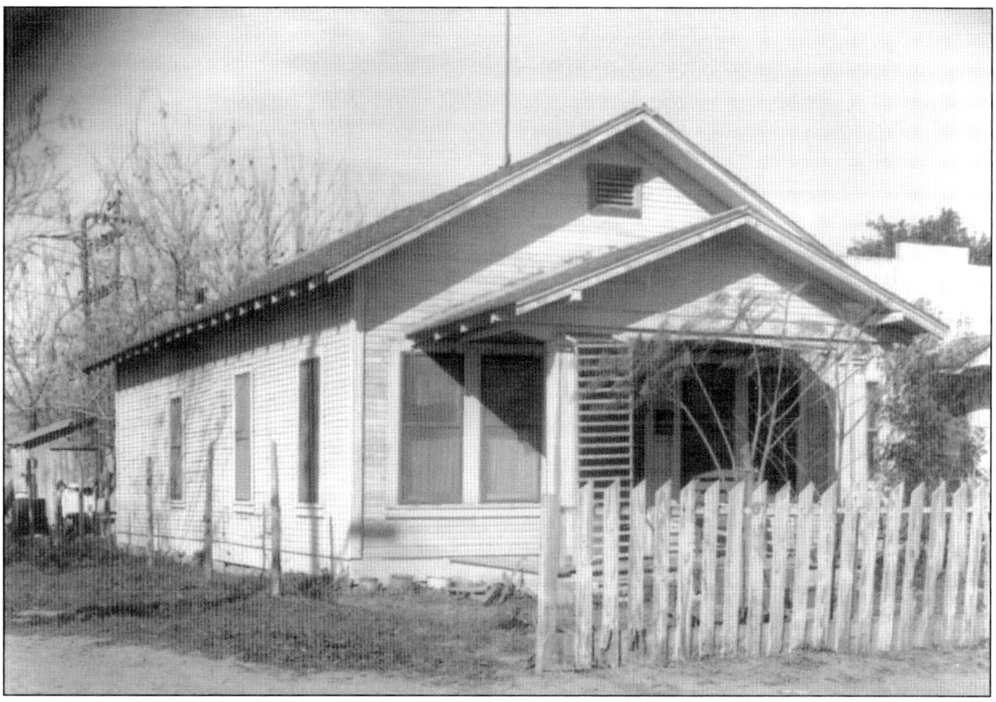

Some labor families were able to move into town where their housing was better. For those who lived in town, there was ample work at canning factories, produce sheds, and downtown stores and businesses. This home at 106 North Ohio Avenue, built around 1918, belonged to Calixta Ruelas Ortega, who willed it to her brother Severo Ruelas and family in 1936. (Carolyn C. López.)

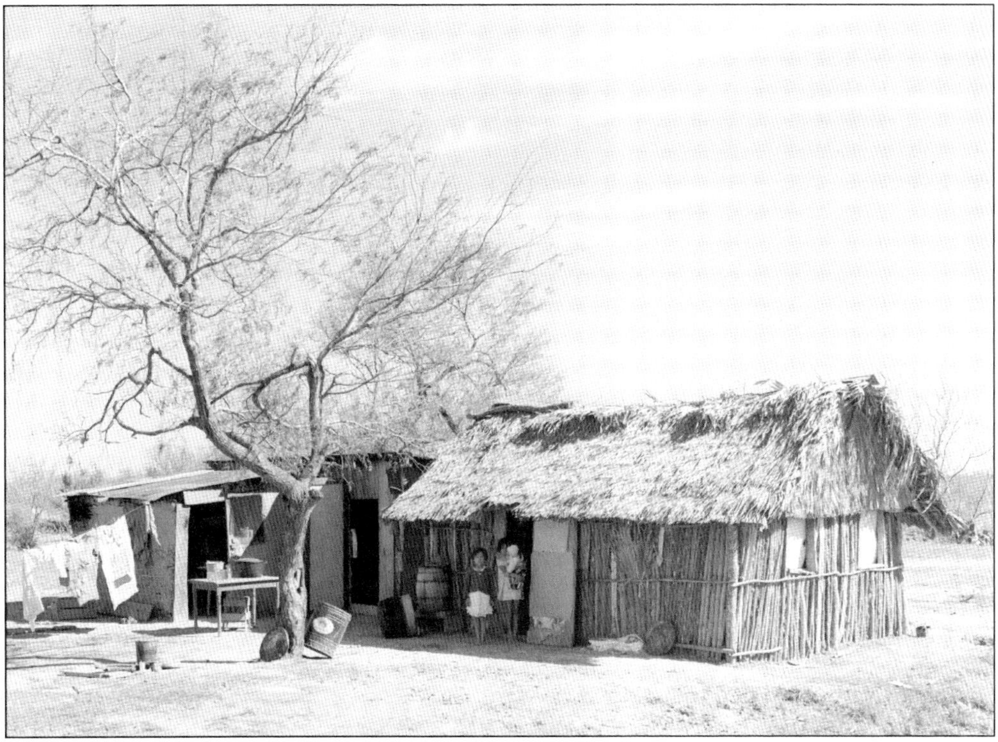

Many labor families lived in small huts, or *jacales*, made of available mesquite wood or old boards with thatched roofs. Water was available from wells or had to be purchased from water sellers. Winters were especially difficult because of the cold and wet. Many of these jacales did not survive the hurricane of 1933. (National Archives.)

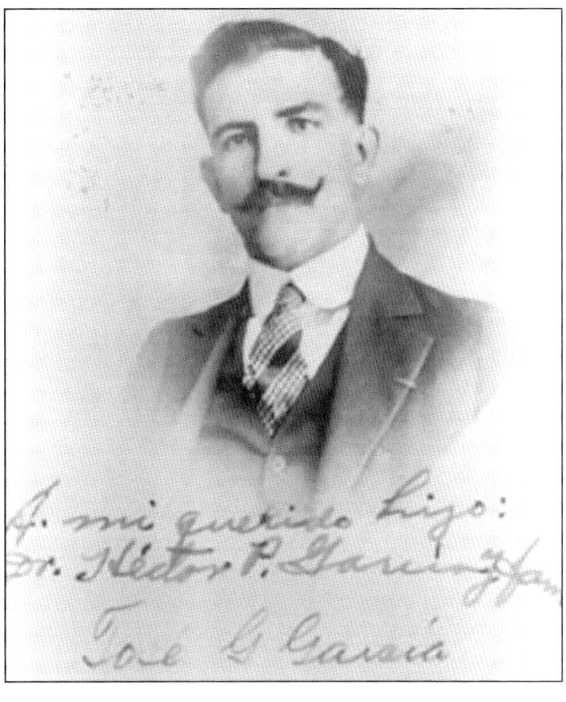

José García was a schoolteacher in Mexico who fled with his family in 1910 to the United States when the Mexican Revolution brought great disorder in Mexico. Together with several brothers, they opened multiple businesses in Mercedes including a drugstore, a clothing store, and many grocery stores. (García family.)

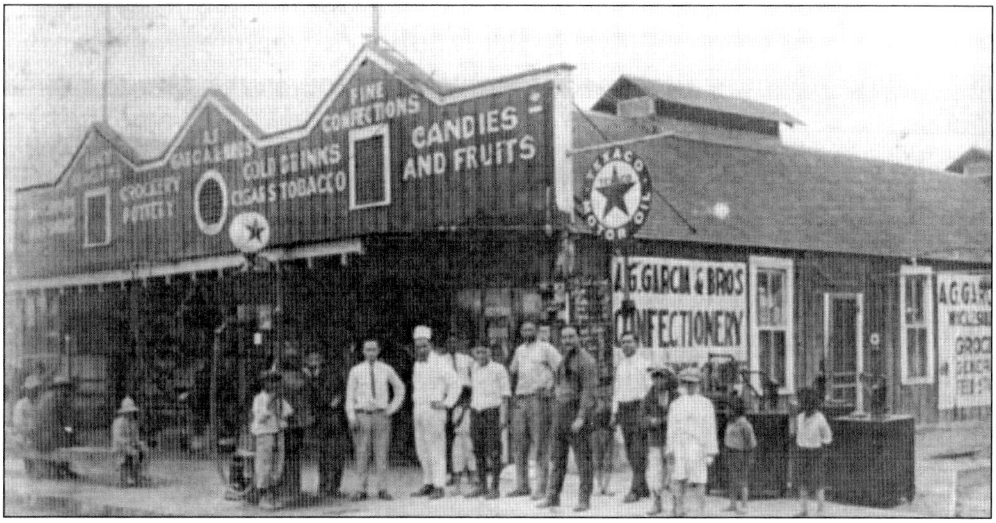

The García family opened this store, A.G. García and Brothers Confectionery, on the corner of Hidalgo Street and Texas Avenue in 1920. The original store was started in 1913 and had customers from as far away as Brownsville and Rio Grande City. This store later burned down and was not rebuilt. (García family.)

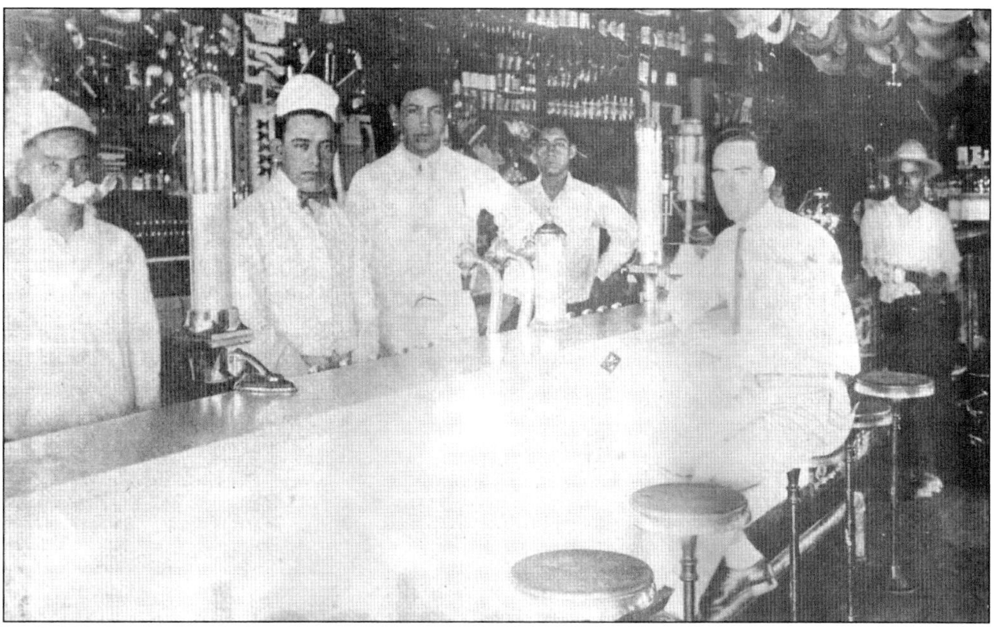

A drugstore and fountain was run in one corner of the García store. Pictured from left to right are José T. Leal, Octavio García, Leopoldo Solís, Elizandro Peña, Odón G. García (seated), and an unidentified patron standing to the back. (García family.)

When the American Rio Grande Land and Irrigation Company was scouting a location for its pumping plant in 1906, it wished to avoid the possibility of the river suddenly changing course. Without seeking permission, the company dug a channel at the Horcón Tract site to divert the river flow, illegally changing an international boundary. The company paid a fine and the channel stayed. (Hidalgo County Historical Commission.)

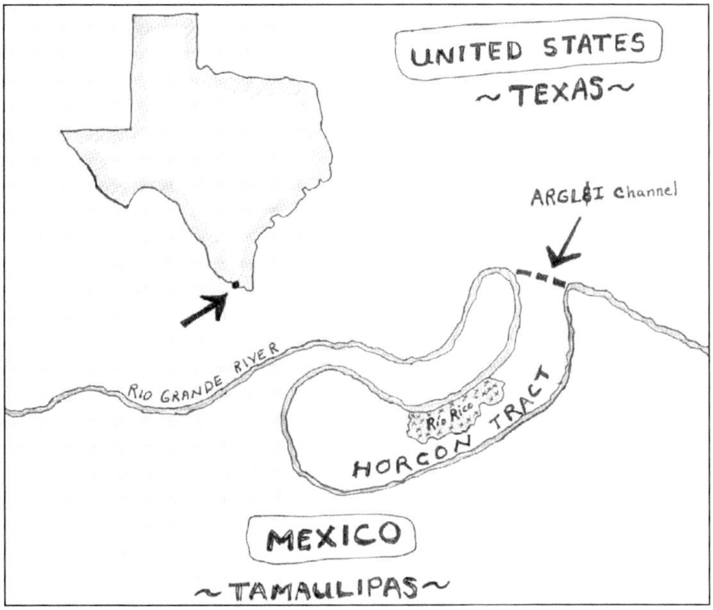

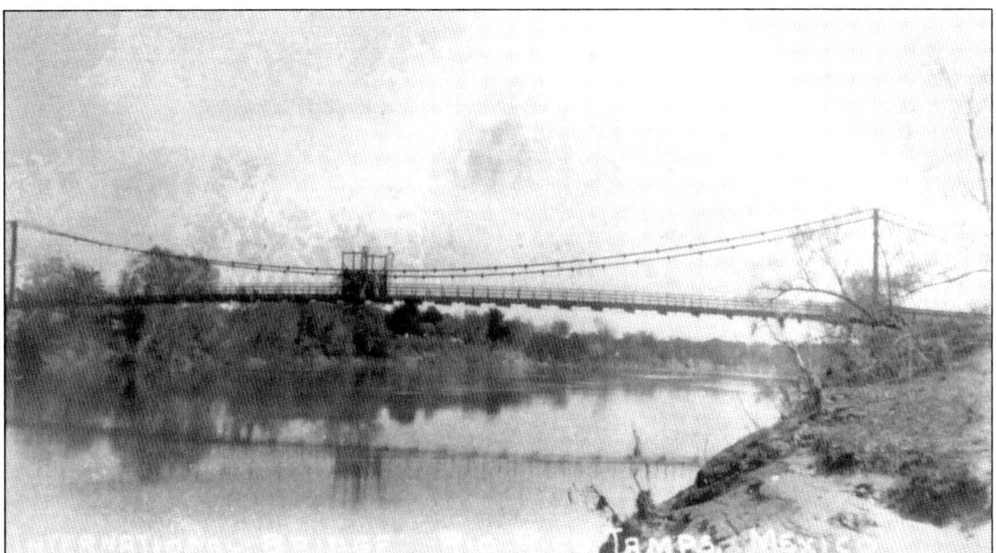

A bridge was built to connect the small town of Río Rico on the Mexican side in the Horcón Tract site to Thayer on the American side. Both sides of the river had custom houses, and the bridge allowed both Mexicans and Americans to buy products available only in the other's country. (Hidalgo County Historical Commission.)

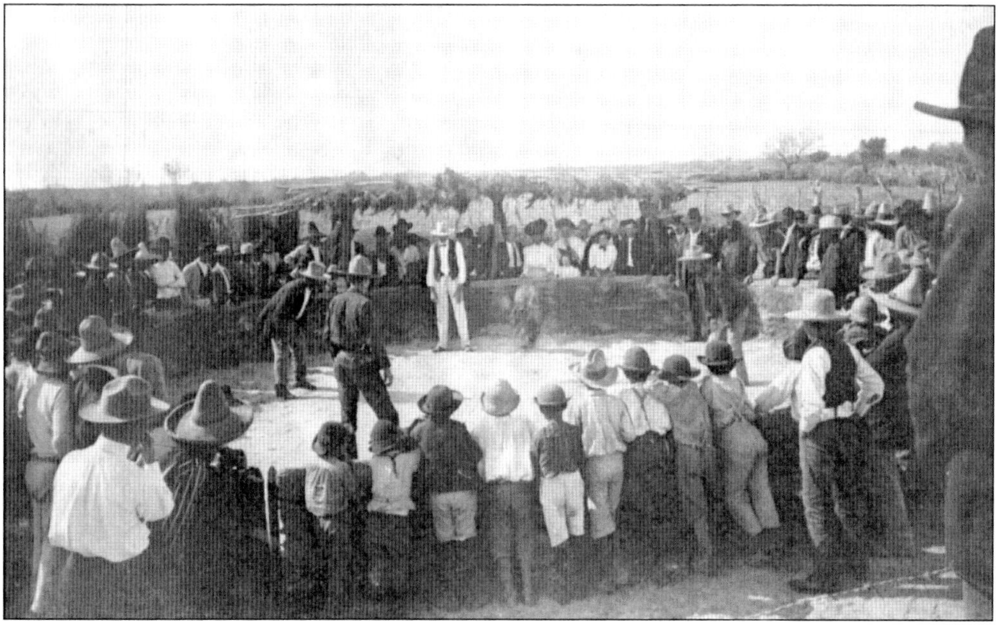

Many visiting land parties and excursion groups were taken to Rio Rico for entertainment. In this photograph, an excursion group is watching a cockfight, and undoubtedly laying wagers on the outcome. In addition to cockfights, northerners could attend dog races and bullfights and could dine and dance. During Prohibition, Río Rico was a popular destination for many Valley residents. (Hidalgo County Historical Commission.)

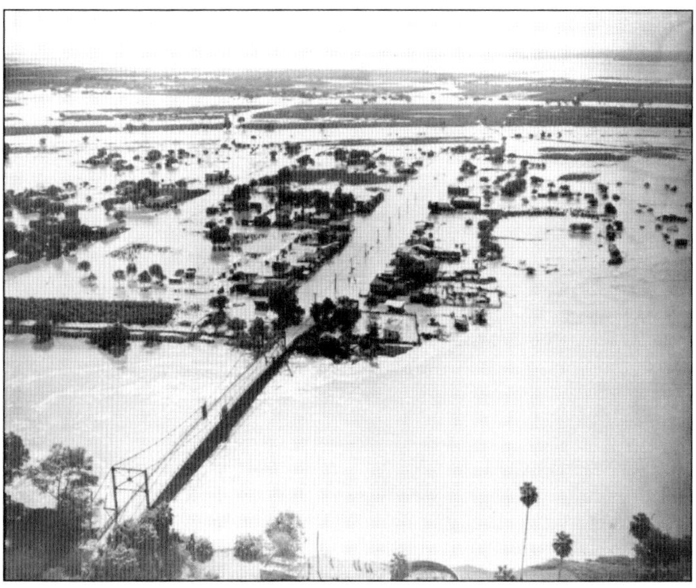

The Rio Grande flooded regularly before Falcon Dam was built upriver in 1954. This photograph shows the Thayer–Río Rico Bridge in 1941 when a severe flood caused great devastation in the area. Both American and Mexican businesses in Río Rico suffered great losses. (Hidalgo County Historical Commission.)

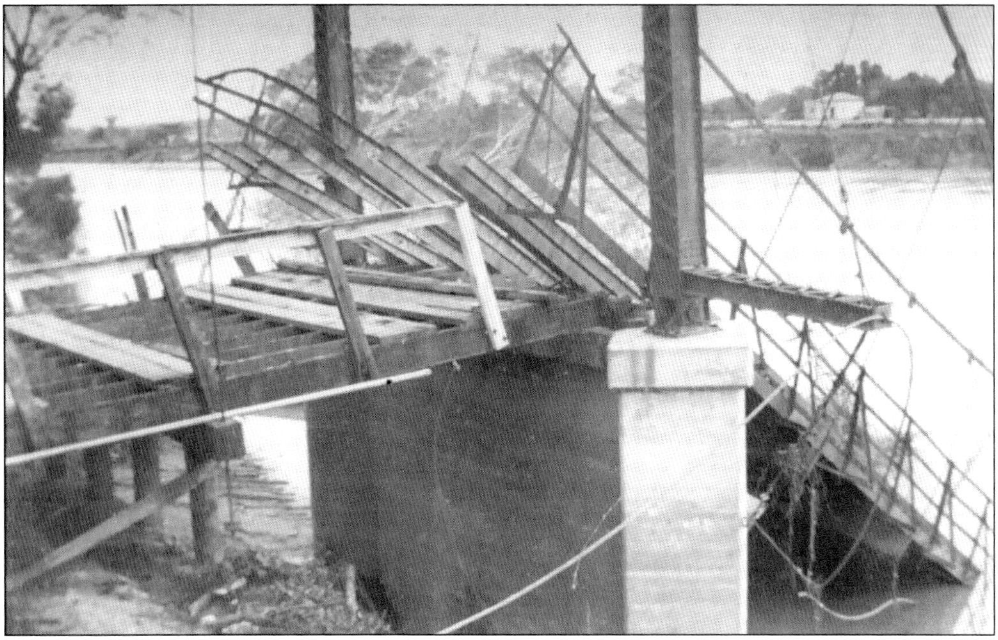

The 1941 flood caused the riverbanks to erode and the Río Rico Bridge to collapse completely. Previous floods had curtailed tourism in Río Rico, but the collapse of the bridge ended almost all river crossings. Only those willing to cross over on small boats provided any commerce to Río Rico businesses. (Hidalgo County Historical Commission.)

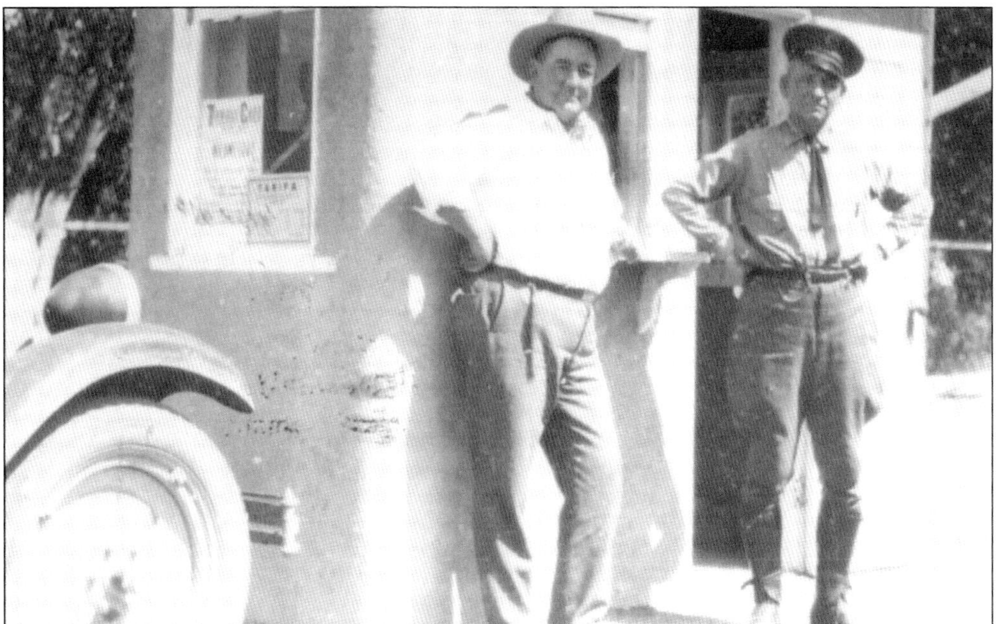

William "Andy" Tullis (left) and immigration officer White stand in front of the customs booth at the Río Rico Bridge in 1932. Tullis was manager of the B&P Bridge Company and oversaw operations there for many years. When the Río Rico Bridge collapsed in 1941, a new site was selected two miles upriver. The B&P completed the Nuevo Progreso Bridge in 1952. (Hidalgo County Historical Commission.)

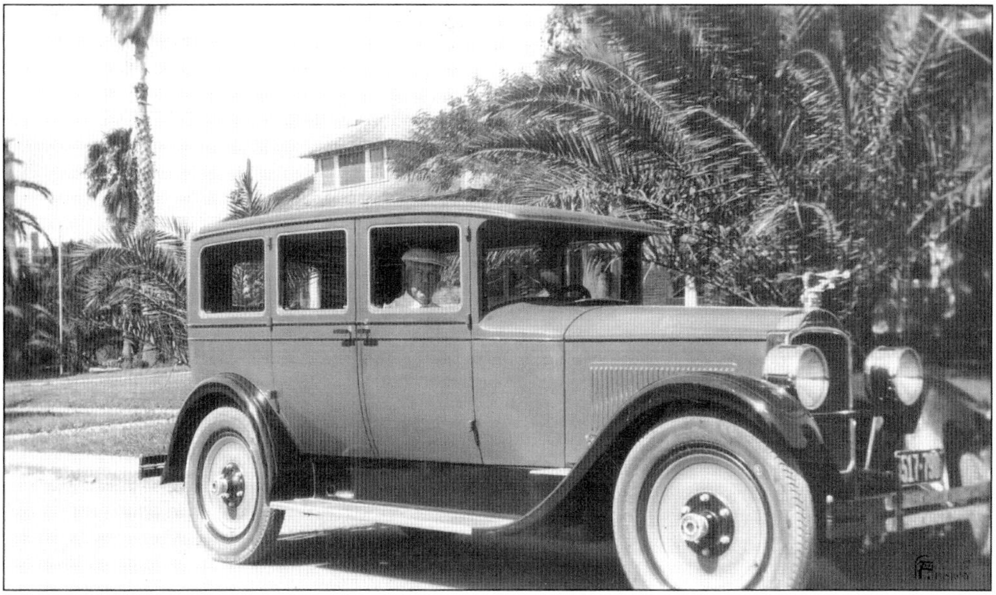

Judge Silas P. Silver, general manager of the American Rio Grande Land and Irrigation Company, rides as a passenger while driven by his chauffer in a Packard Touring car in this c. 1930 image. In his later years, Silver suffered a stroke and was partially disabled, but he remained active in city and county politics for many years. (MSTH.)

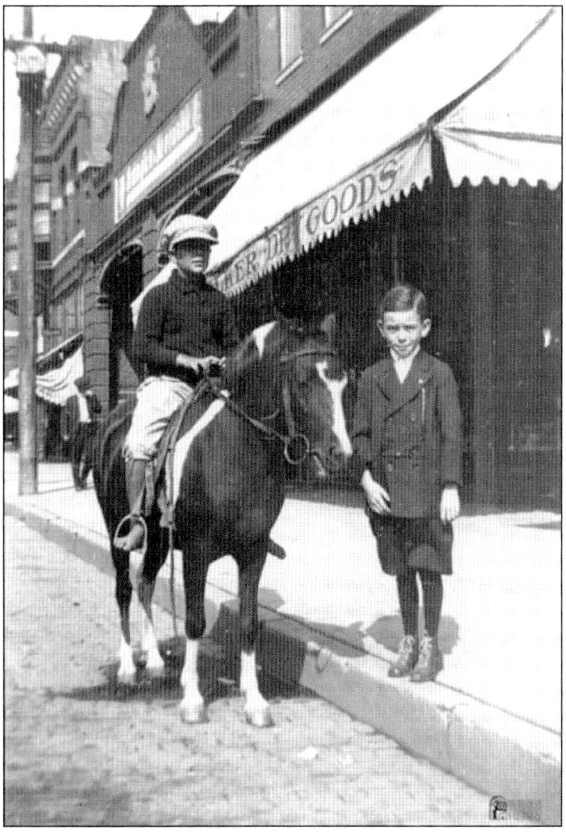

Silas P. Silver's grandson Albert Stephens, seen here wearing short pants, was the son of Silver's only daughter, Mary Ellen, who married Charles Stephens of Louisiana. Here, Albert is shown on a trip to Silver's hometown of St. Louis, Missouri, in the 1920s. The boy on the horse is unidentified. (MSTH.)

Three

Building the Community

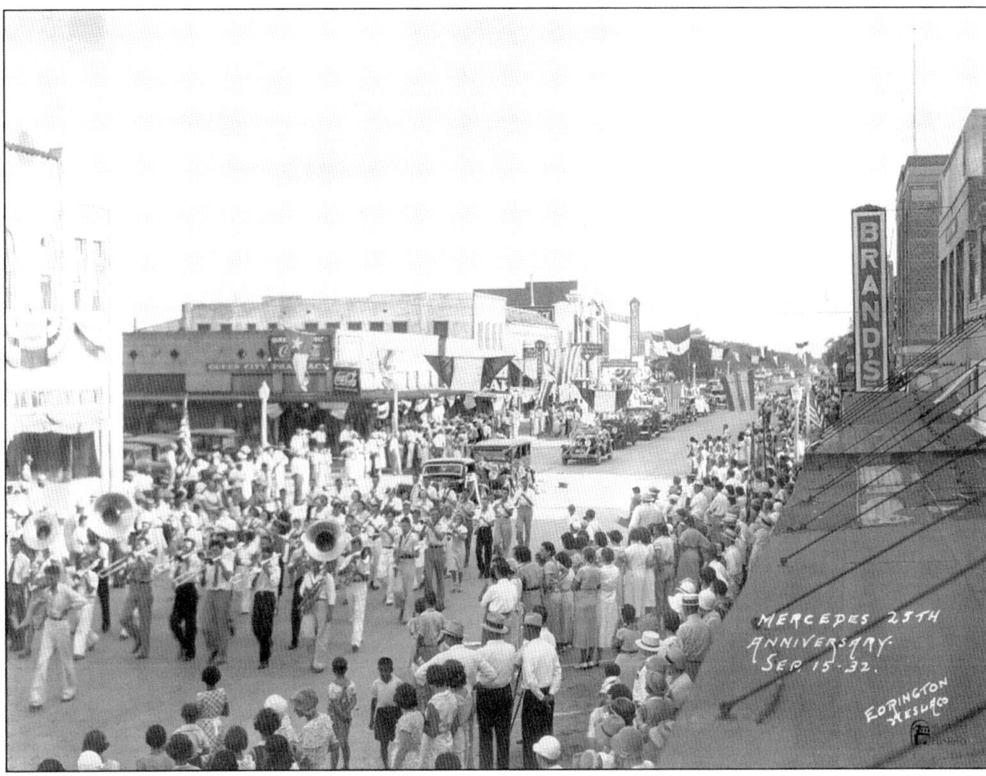

On September 15, 1932, Mercedes celebrated its 25th anniversary with a variety of events including the parade shown in this photograph. All the Valley towns were invited to the celebration. The highlight of the first day was the Cavalcade of the Lower Rio Grande Valley, an elaborate pageant with more than 400 characters depicting the history of the area from 1519 to 1932. (MSTH.)

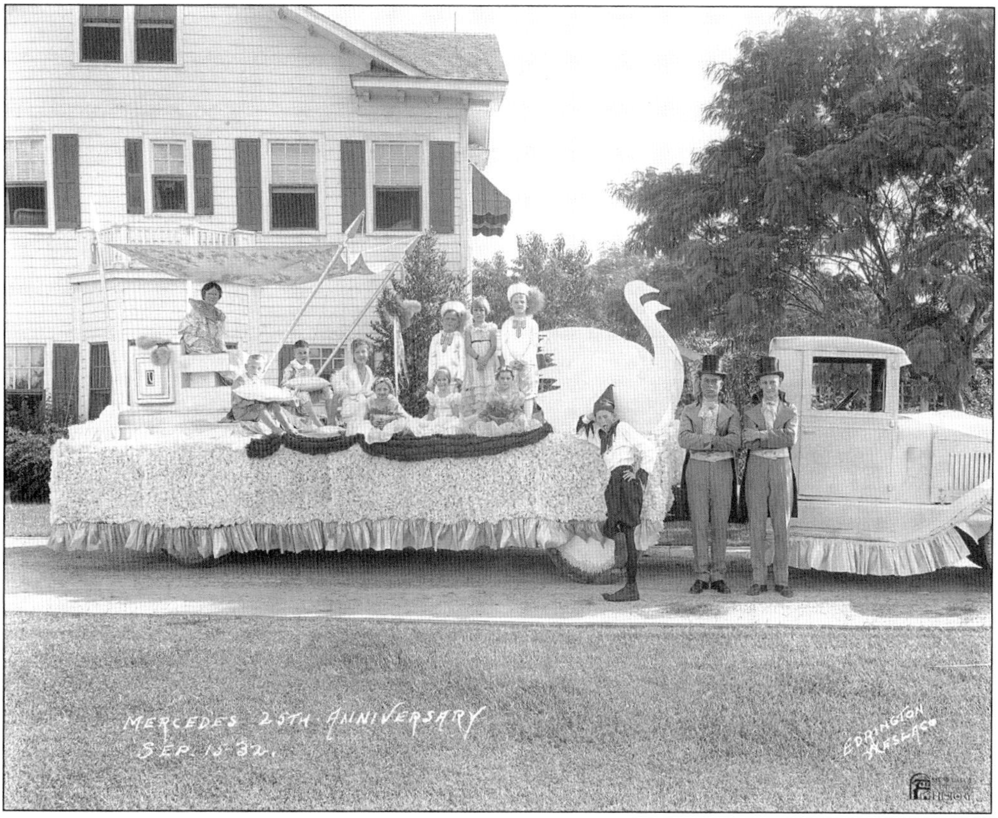

This 1932 photograph shows one of the more popular floats on which the Silver Queen of the 25th anniversary celebrations, Ida Greene Wattson, rides with her court. Elaborate costumes in white, gold, and silver were worn by all. Also included in the day's celebration were an art exhibit, a banquet, the Cavalcade performance, and a Founders' Day Ball at the Elks' new hall. (MSTH.)

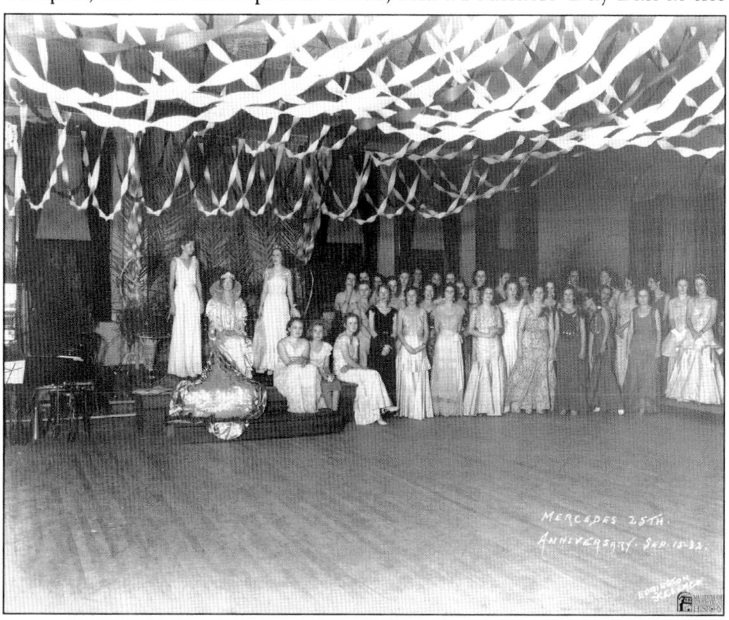

The Founders' Day Ball was held in the Elks Lodge the night of September 15, 1932. Many Valley towns were represented in the queen's court by the duchesses. Participating towns included Alamo, Brownsville, Edinburg, Harlingen, La Feria, McAllen, Mission, San Benito, San Juan, and Weslaco. The Elks Lodge building still exists today but is now known as the second Mercedes Hotel. (MSTH.)

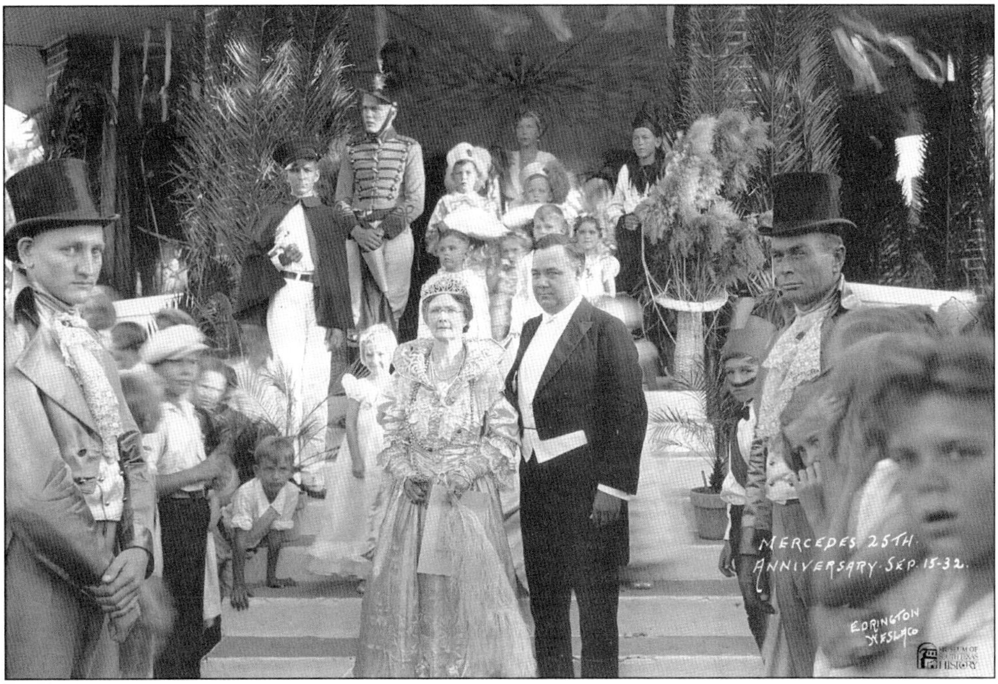

Ida Greene Wattson was crowned "Silver Queen" by Mercedes mayor William D. Chadick during the presentation ceremonies at the Founders' Day Ball. Chadick was the nephew of entrepreneur Col. Sam Fordyce and was involved in city and Hidalgo County politics. He was elected mayor of Mercedes in 1932. (MSTH.)

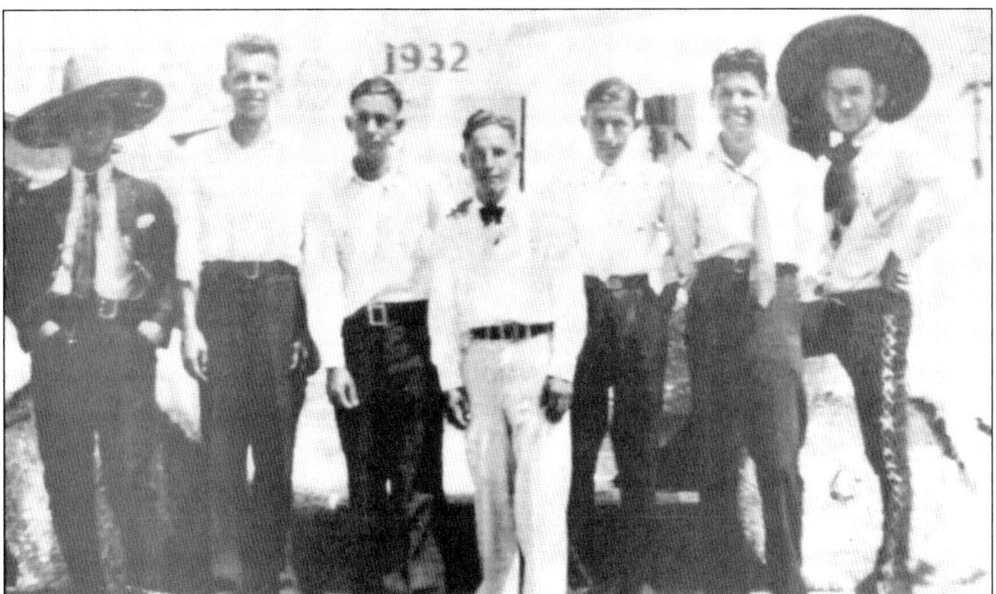

These gentlemen participated in the celebration of Mercedes's 25th Anniversary on September 16, 1932, with some dressed in their Mexican Independence Day costumes. Pictured from left to right are José T. Leal, Alfredo García, David Sáenz, Candelario Marín, Rafael Hinojosa, Rogelio Hinojosa, and Jesús García. (*Mercedes Enterprise*.)

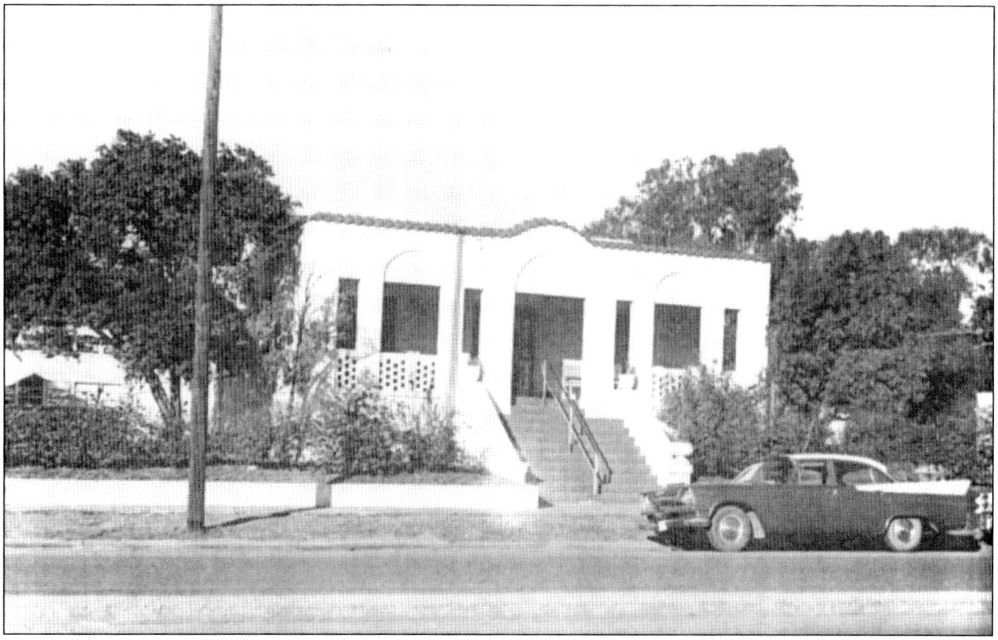

The Mercedes General Hospital seen here was organized in 1922. It was first located on Ohio Avenue and Sixth Street but was later moved to South Texas Avenue. It was originally set up by doctors Charles B. Buck, John G. Webb, and Daniel L. Heidrick, who bought the instruments and equipment from the Malone Brothers Hospital. (Carolyn C. López.)

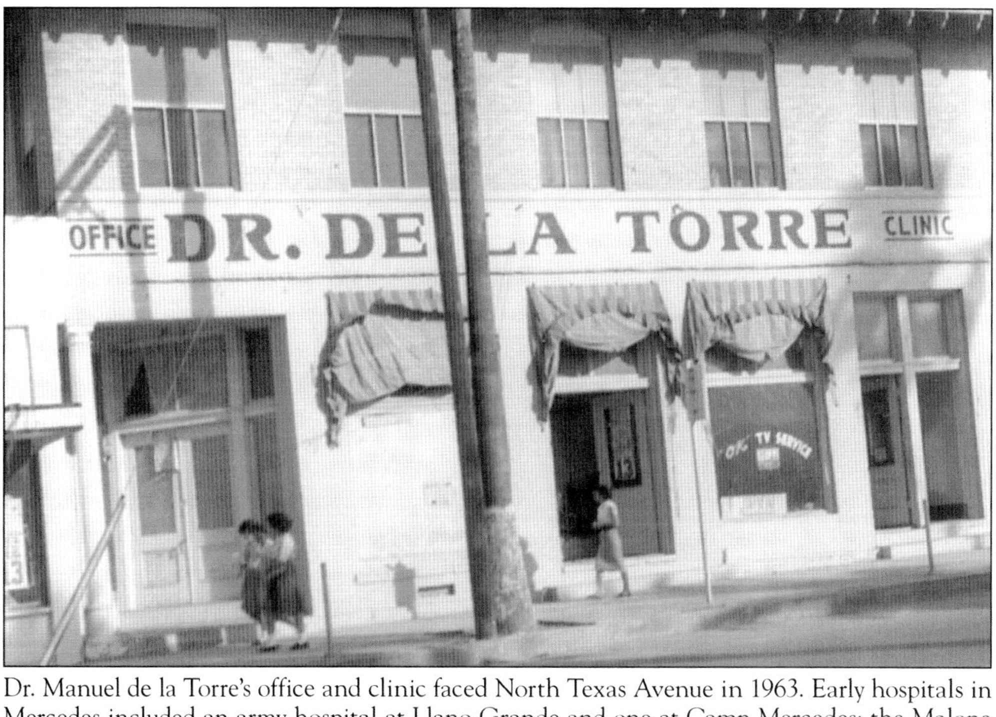

Dr. Manuel de la Torre's office and clinic faced North Texas Avenue in 1963. Early hospitals in Mercedes included an army hospital at Llano Grande and one at Camp Mercedes; the Malone Brothers Hospital, set up by the mid-1920s at 430 South Texas Avenue; the Mercedes General Hospital; the Lawler Clinic; and the Caballero Clinic. (Carolyn C. López.)

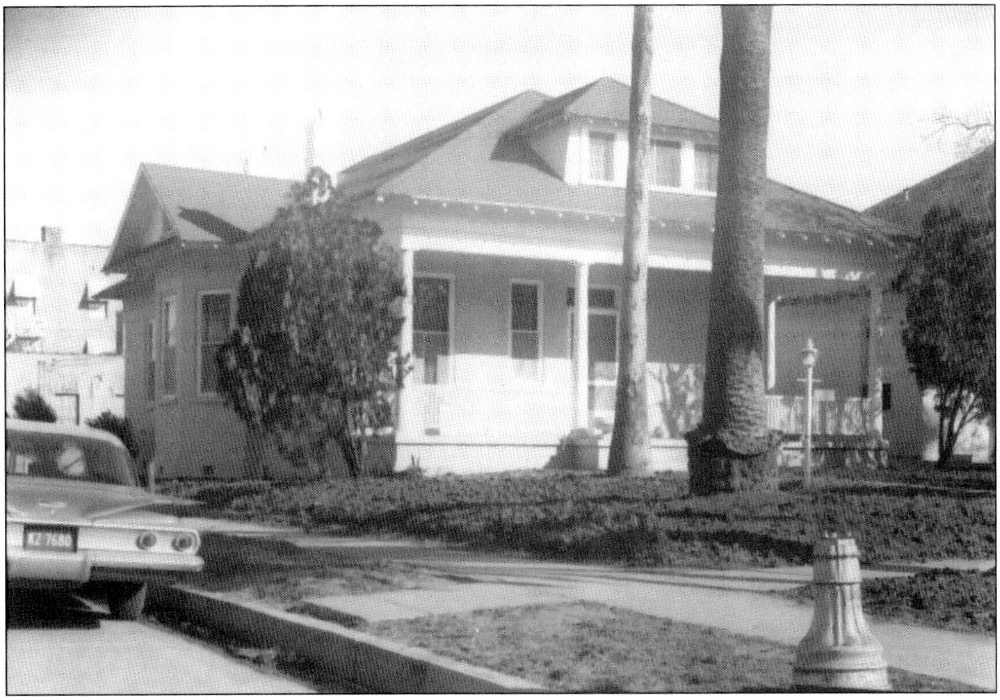

Dr. Gonzalo Caballero's home was on the corner of Third Street and Missouri Avenue, and his clinic was just across the street. The clinic used to be Dr. Robert Johnston's when he still practiced. Today, the Caballero Clinic is still run by Gonzalo's son Dr. Eduardo Caballero. (Carolyn C. López.)

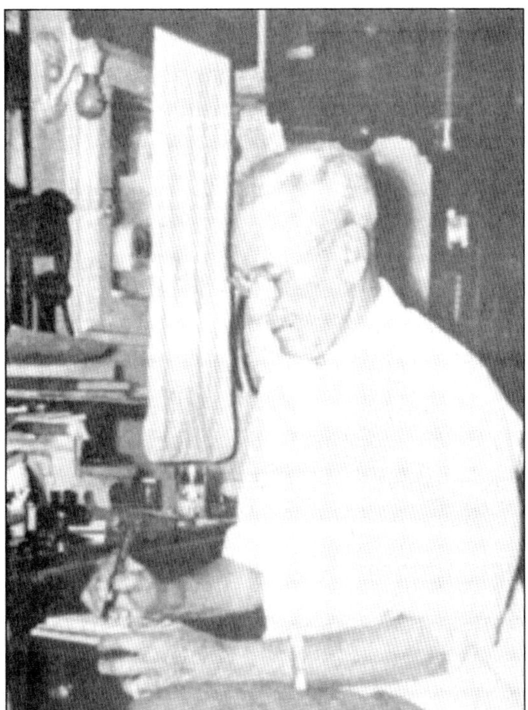

Dr. Daniel L. Heidrick came to Mercedes with the 16th Cavalry when he was the Army camp doctor. When he was discharged from military service he returned to Mercedes to practice. Many said he must have delivered at least half the babies in Mercedes, and he is remembered for never turning anybody away because they could not pay. His home and office were located at 446 South Texas Avenue. (*Mercedes Enterprise*.)

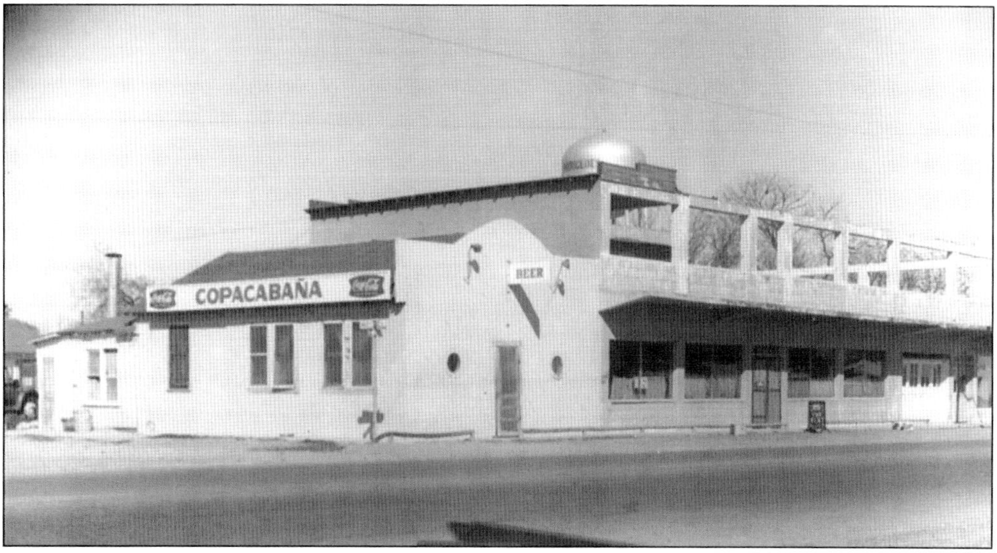

The Copacabaña was a popular night spot in Mercedes beginning right after World War II. It was established by the Sáenz brothers and their brother-in-law Ciro L. Uribe. It had a restaurant, a banquet room, and a terrace on the second floor for dances and parties. It was also later used for vocational training for returning GIs and later served as a migrant worker recruitment center. (Carolyn C. López.)

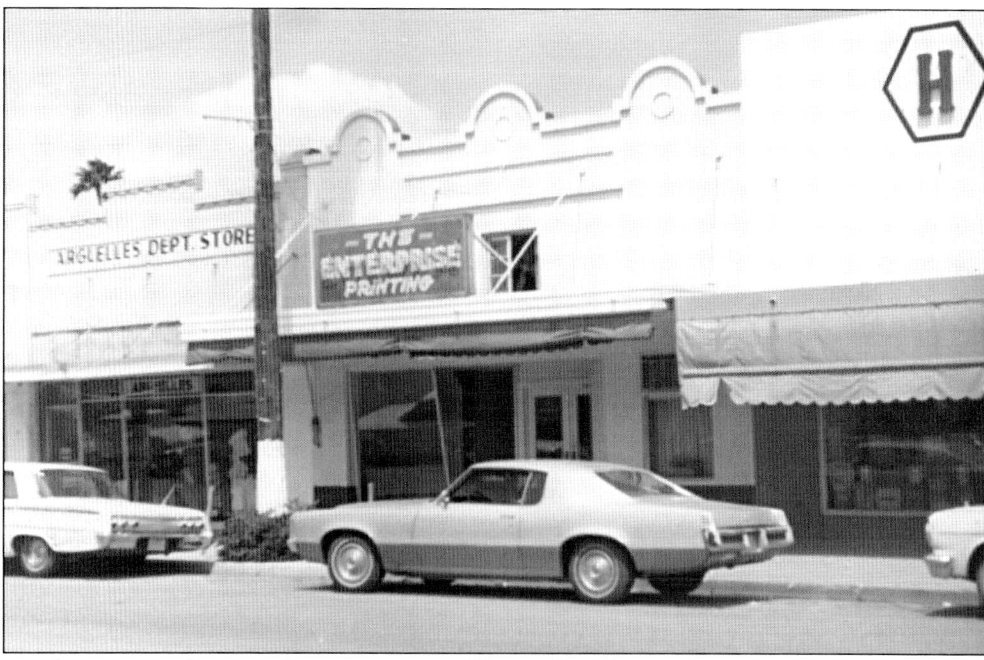

Local newspaper the *Mercedes Enterprise* is still located in the old Rex Theater building on Texas Avenue in downtown Mercedes. When first established, it also took care of other printing needs for the community such as billboards, posters, flyers, brochures, and pamphlets. It has previously also had the names *Mercedes Tribune*, *Mercedes News-Item*, *Mercedes News*, and *News-Tribune*. (Carolyn C. López.)

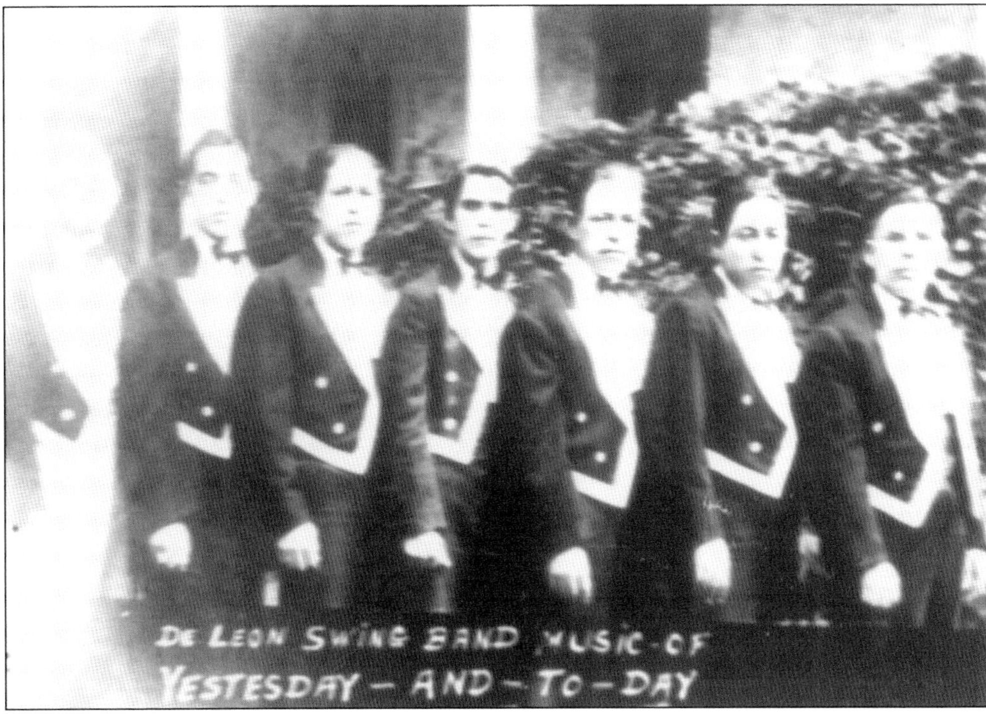

The De León Swing Band entertained many Mercedes residents in the 1930s and 1940s with popular American and Mexican dance music. Pictured from left to right are two unidentified musicians, Felipe "Pipe" Olivárez, José Serna, Octavio García, Concepción "Chon" García, and band leader Juventino "El Maestro" de León Sr. (Delia de León.)

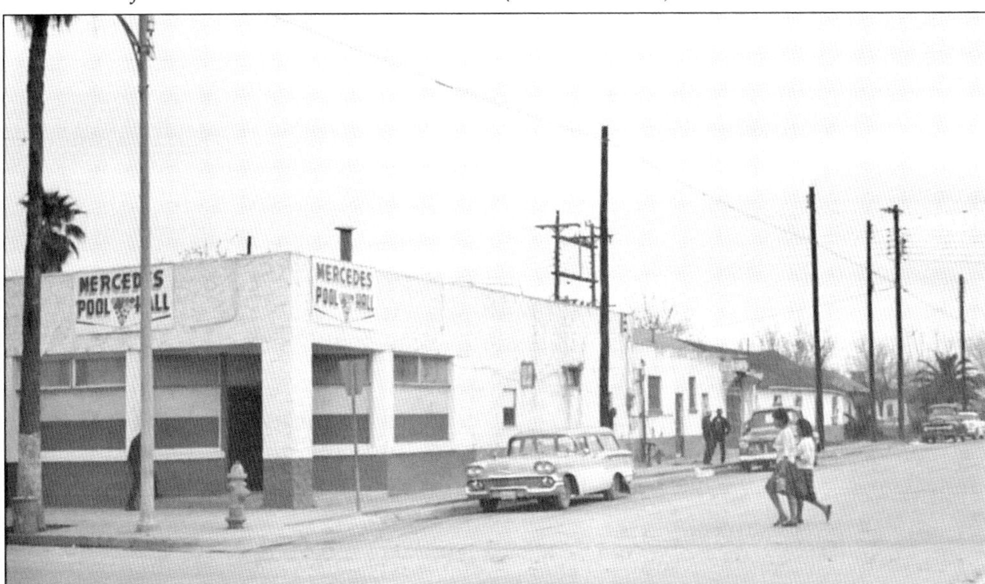

The Mercedes Pool Hall was owned by Florencio Pérez Sr., who established the business on North Texas Avenue and First Street in 1940. Later also known as the Latin American Club, it was frequented by patrons from all over the Valley. By 1948, Pérez had expanded the business to hold 14 pool tables and was also selling billiard supplies to other pool halls. (Carolyn C. López.)

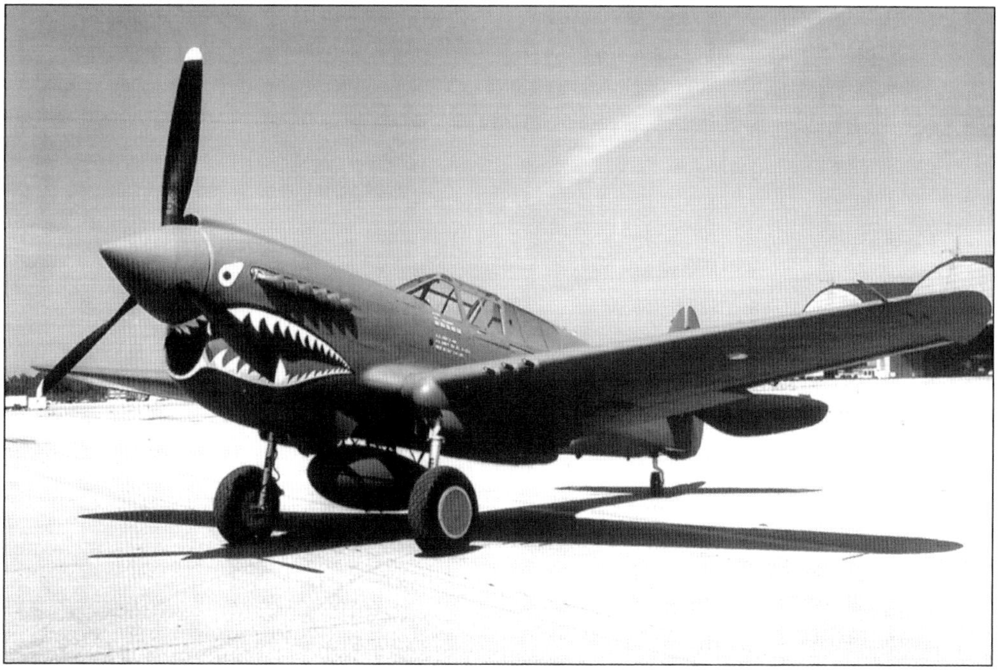

Lloyd P. Nolen acquired a P-40 Warhawk like the one shown above in 1951. The P-51 Mustang like the one shown below flew during World War II and was the second purchase by Lloyd P. Nolen and other partners in 1957 to found the Confederate Air Force, later renamed the Commemorative Air Force, flying out of the Central Valley Airport in Mercedes. The group continued to purchase, repair, and fly vintage World War II airplanes as a means of preserving aircraft that would otherwise have wound up as scrap metal. The central CAF headquarters moved to Harlingen in 1968, and later to Midland, Texas, in 1990. The Rio Grande Valley Wing of the CAF relocated to Brownsville, Texas, where they still have air shows. (Both, National Archives.)

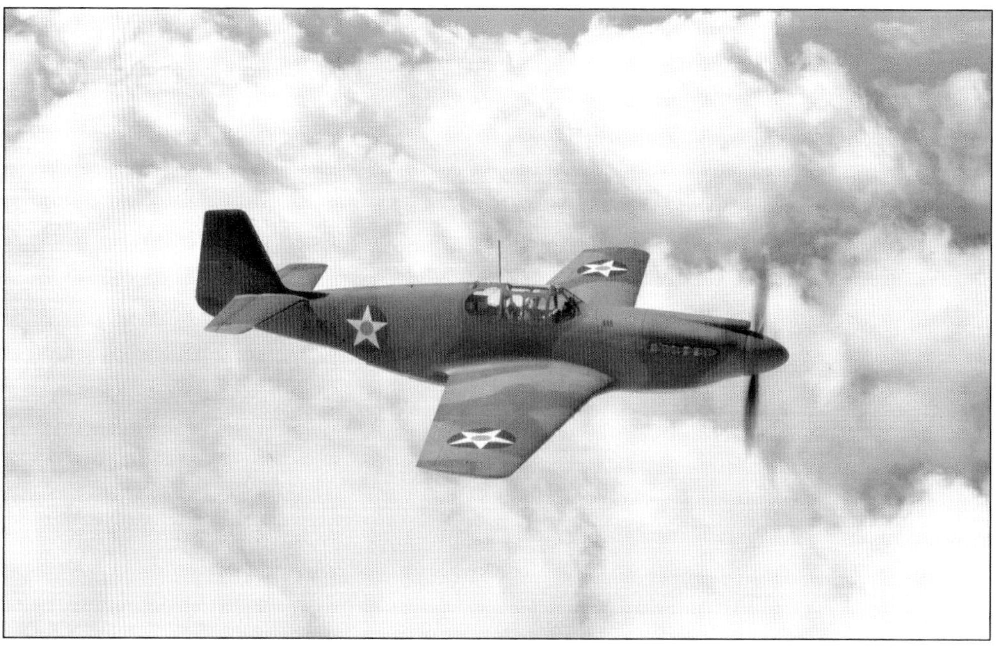

Pictured here at an event of the Confederate Air Force are, from left to right, ? Edwards, Cedric Wood, and Lloyd P. Nolen. Nolen was a World War II flight instructor who ran the Mercedes Dusting Service in the 1950s at the Central Valley Airport. All members of the CAF were called "Colonel" as an honorary title. (Weslaco Museum.)

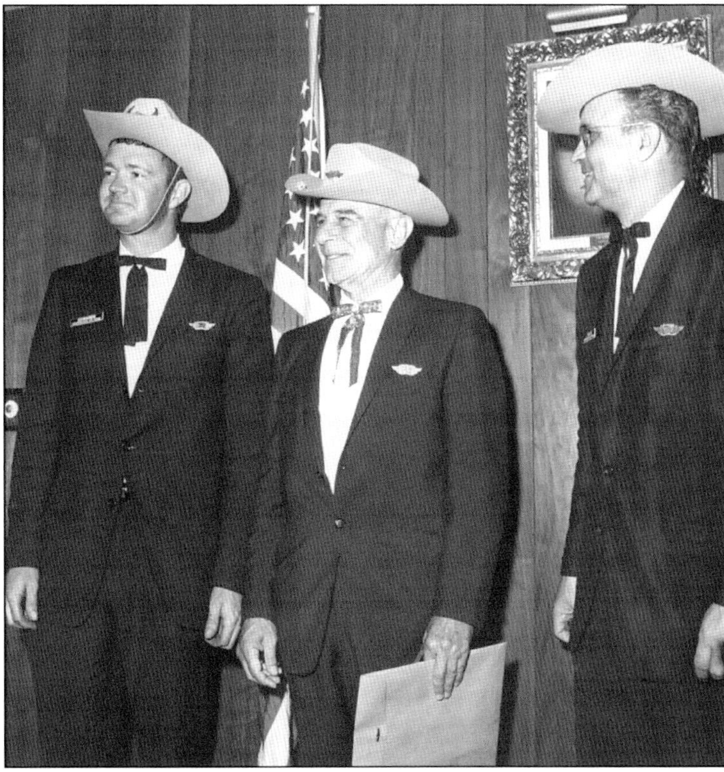

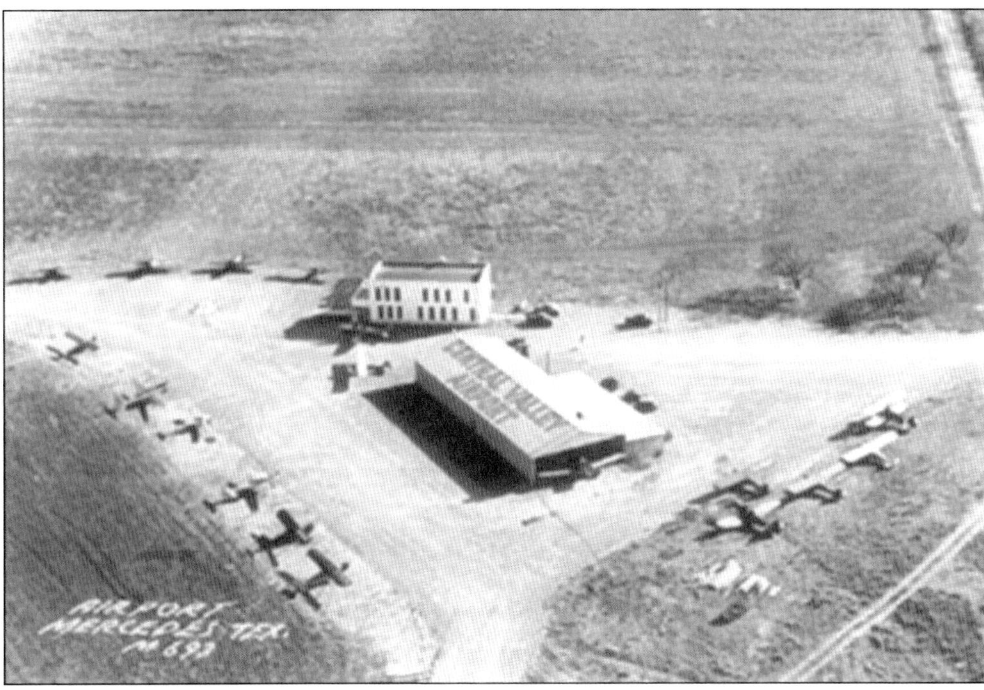

The Central Valley Airport is located on Mile 2 East, or Farm to Market Road 1425, and Mile 8 North. It is home base for crop-dusting planes since 1946. The airport was called Old Rebel Field when the Confederate Air Force began using it for air shows in the 1960s. (Vito Buenrostro.)

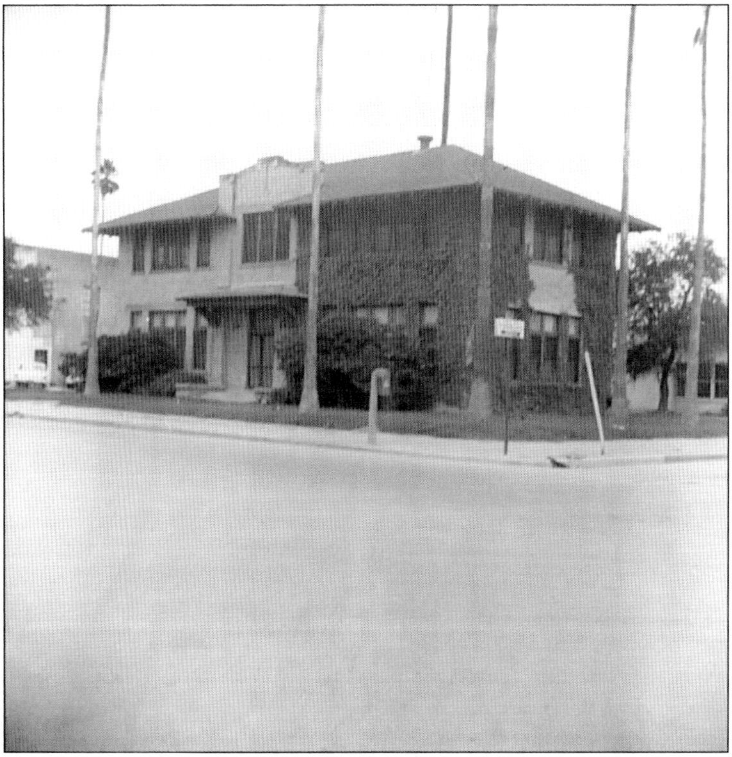

Pictured here is the Hidalgo and Cameron County Irrigation District No. 9 office building at 301 East Second Street (US Business Highway 83). This building was the second office of the American Rio Grande Land and Irrigation Company until 1927 when a group of farmers petitioned for the establishment of a regulatory group for water control and distribution, forming what became District No. 9. (Carolyn C. López.)

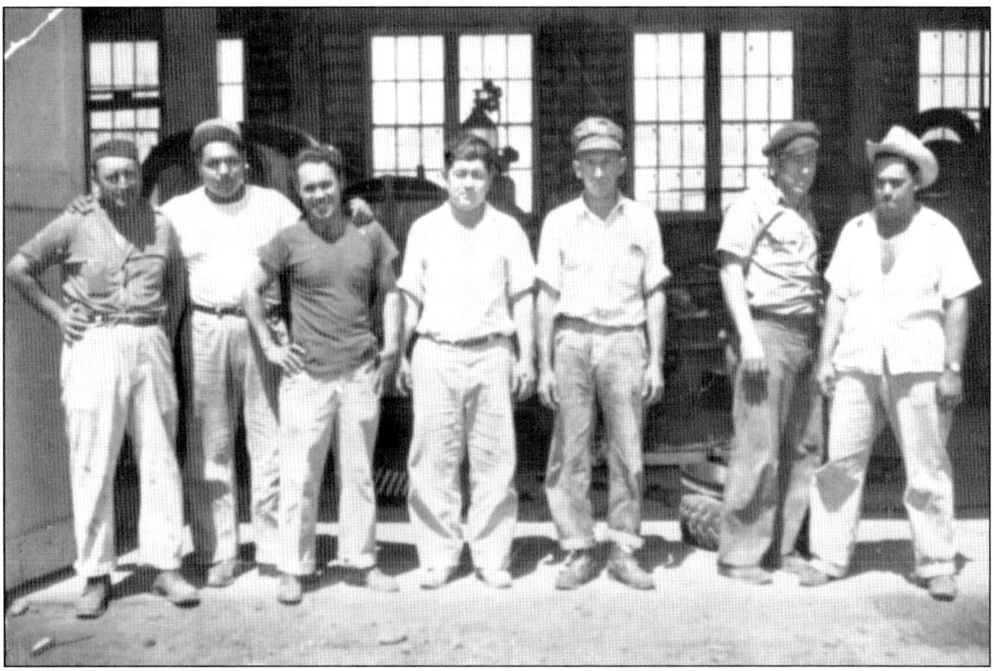

Workers at the Hidalgo and Cameron County Irrigation District No. 9 posed for this impromptu photograph taken in the 1940s. Third from left is Cato Palacios, and last on the right is his brother Juan Palacios. All others are unidentified. In 2009, District No. 9 relocated its offices to 2304 North Farm to Market Road 491. (Irma Palacios.)

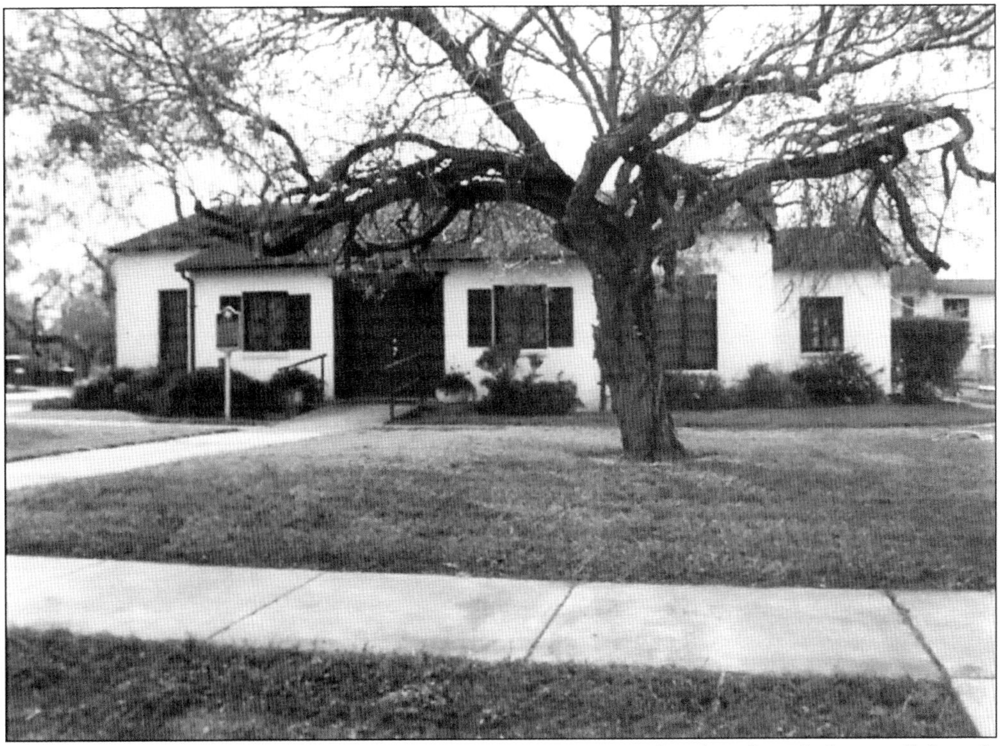

In the early 1900s, several Hidalgo and Cameron County families founded a small Jewish congregation. Lay readers led the services and the congregation met in private homes or rented space. In 1935, Temple Beth Israel pictured here was erected on the southwest corner of Tenth Street and Texas Avenue. In 1948, the congregation voted to dissolve and began attending synagogues in Harlingen or McAllen. (Hidalgo Country Historical Commission.)

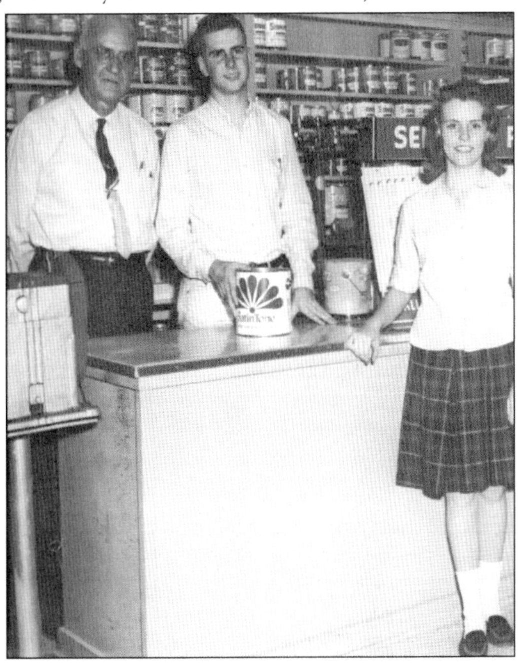

Pictured in 1964 at the counter of the Farris Paint Store are, from left to right, storeowner E. Quincy Farris, his son James Farris, and friend Rosa Mae Wheeler. Farris owned several businesses including the Farris Lumber Company. He served as president of the Valley Lumbermen's Association in the 1950s and was well known in the community. (Mercedes ISD.)

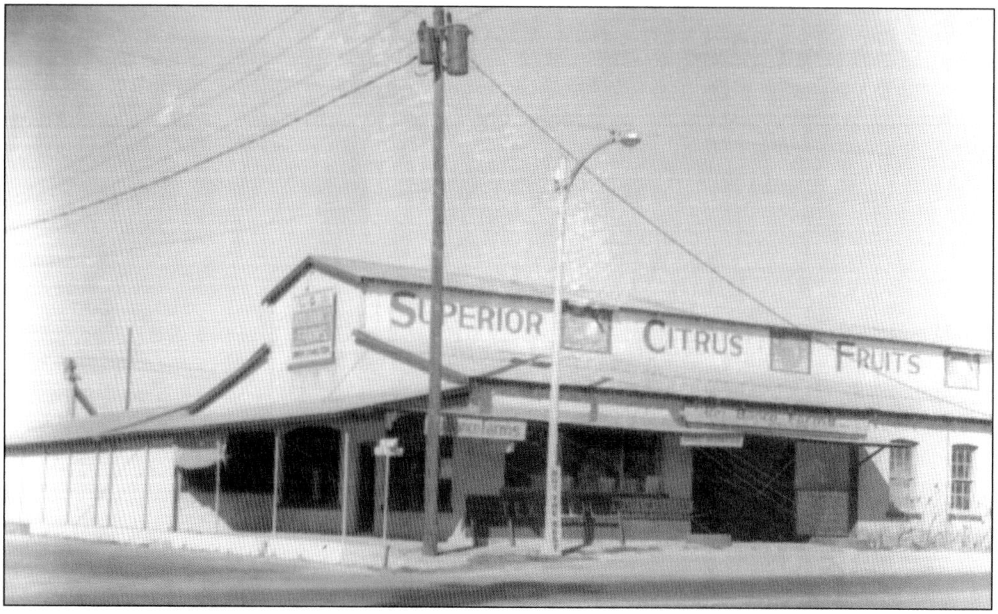

Charles P. Melton owned the Superior Citrus Fruits Packing Shed in Mercedes, shown above in 1946, to process the fruit from his Río Banco Farms. It was but one of many citrus packing sheds in Mercedes that organized through the Texas Citrus Growers Association. By 1929, this new fast-growing citrus industry was cultivated on more than 100,000 acres in Hidalgo County. (Carolyn C. López.)

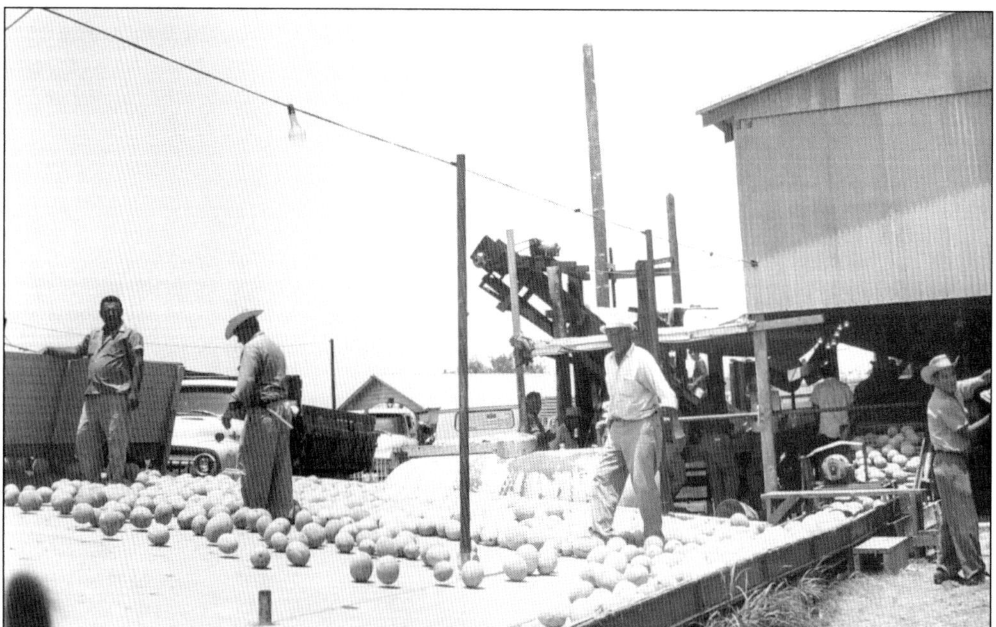

Mercedes has always been heavily involved in the citrus industry. Here, workers begin the sorting process of grapefruit at this packing shed. Grapefruit dominates the Texas citrus industry, with most of the remainder being oranges. The South Texas region is home to all Texas citrus production. Hidalgo County contains 85 percent of all citrus acres in Texas, with the remainder in Cameron and Willacy Counties. (National Archives.)

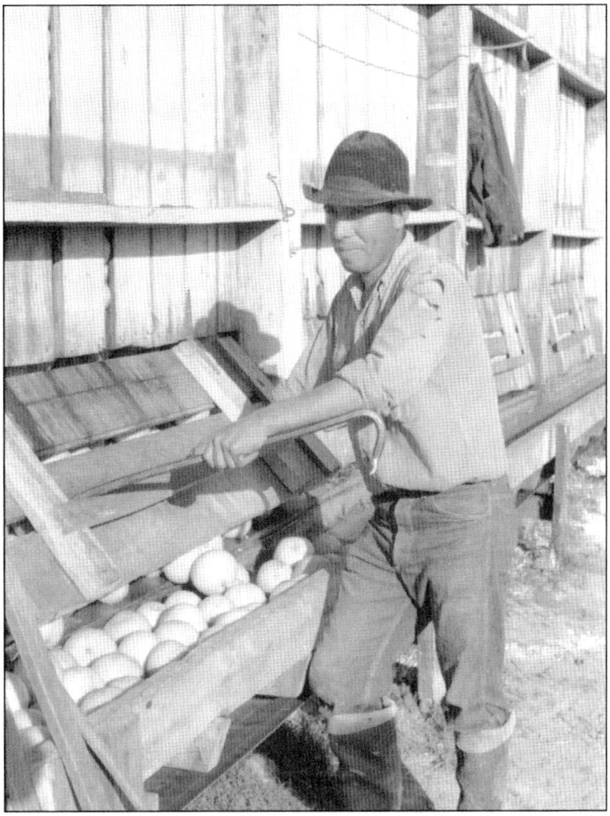

In this photograph, grapefruit is further separated for shipping whole or using it for juice processing. The earliest record of citrus in the Rio Grande Valley was seedling orange trees planted in 1882 by the Vela family at the Laguna Seca Ranch. Col. William A. Fitch was the first grower in Mercedes to plant oranges and grapefruit. The first commercial shipments from Mercedes began in 1918. (National Archives.)

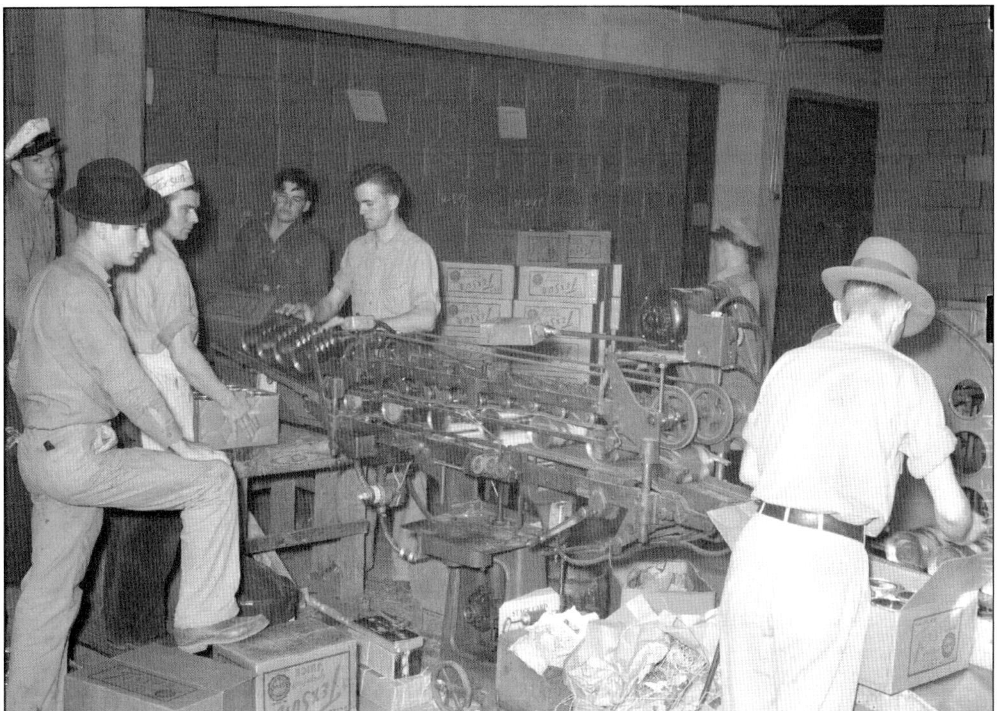

In this juicing plant, cans are prepared to be filled with grapefruit juice. During the 1930s, whole-fruit markets slowed and juice became the most profitable commodity to sell. The Texsun canning plant in neighboring Weslaco was often used by Mercedes growers to process their oranges and grapefruit. (National Archives.)

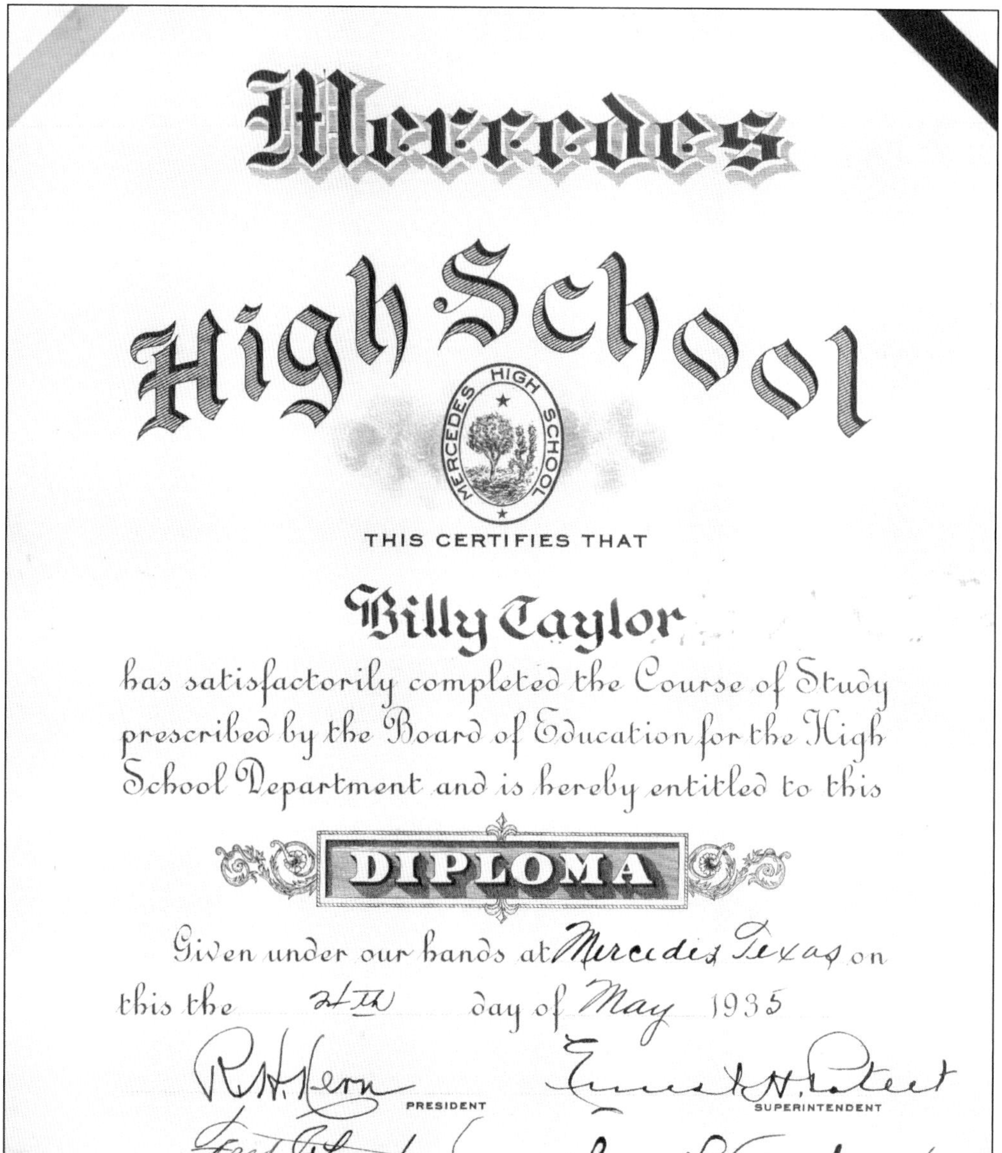
Mercedes High School

THIS CERTIFIES THAT

Billy Taylor

has satisfactorily completed the Course of Study prescribed by the Board of Education for the High School Department and is hereby entitled to this

DIPLOMA

Given under our hands at Mercedes Texas on this the 24th day of May 1935

R. H. Kern PRESIDENT

Ernest H. Poteet SUPERINTENDENT

Fred Johnston SECRETARY

Leon R. Graham PRINCIPAL

Shown here is a Mercedes High School diploma from 1935 given to graduate William "Billy" Taylor. It is signed by Robert H. Kern, president of the school board; Fred Johnston, school board secretary; Ernest H. Poteet, superintendent of schools; and Leon R. Graham, principal of the Mercedes high school. The format shown here has changed little over the years. In 1935, the number of credits required to graduate from high school was 18. By 1968, the number of credits required had increased to 24. The number of years of schooling it took to graduate also changed. Up until 1941, only 11 years of school were required; from 1942 on, 12 years of schooling were required for graduation. (Mercedes ISD.)

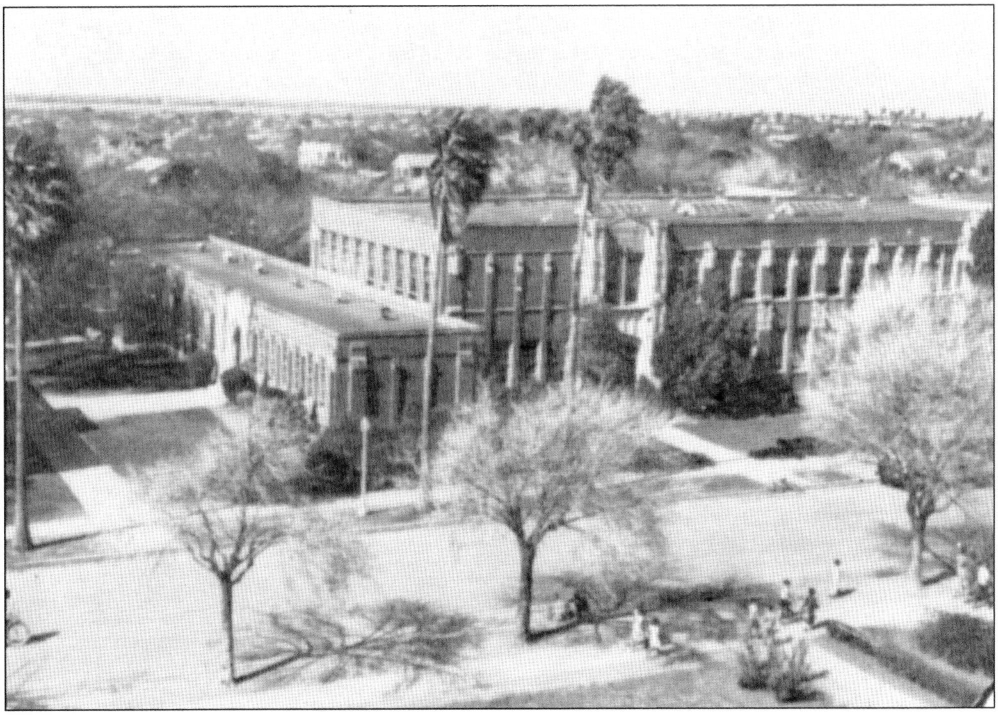

R. Newell Waters was the architect for the redbrick Mercedes High School that was completed and occupied in 1932 on the west side of Ohio Avenue and Eighth Street. It continued to be used as the high school until 1967, when a new high school was built east of the Main Canal at 1200 South Florida Avenue. (Mercedes ISD.)

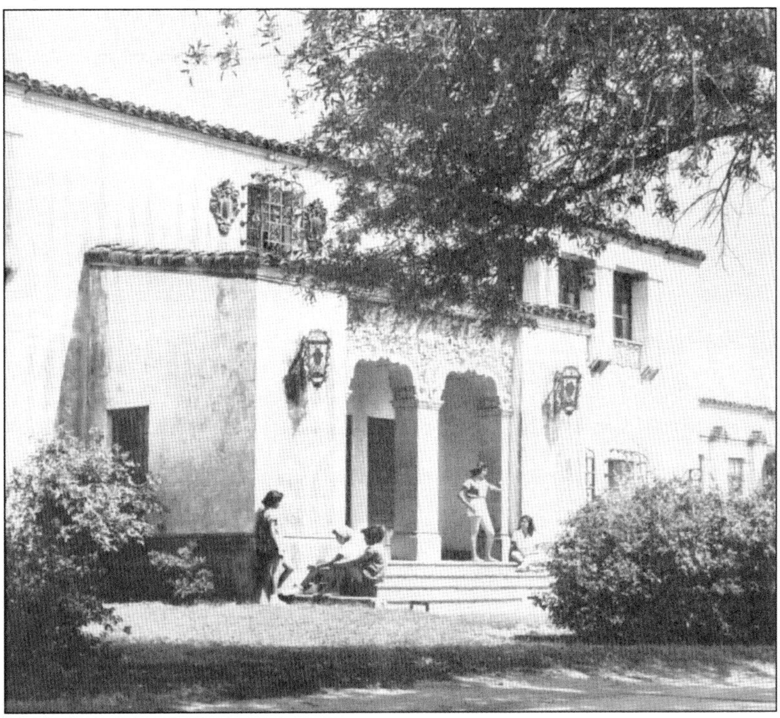

The photograph here shows the building used as the high school gymnasium from 1940 to 1967. It was built together with the cafeteria in a Spanish revival style and was located at the same complex where the high school and junior high were on South Ohio Avenue. (Mercedes ISD.)

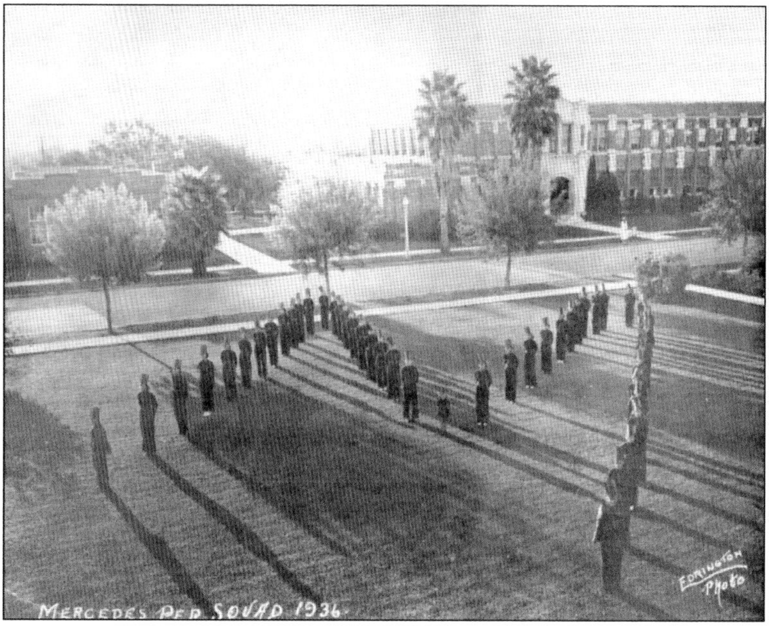

Shown here posing in front of the Mercedes High School on the right and the Mercedes Junior High School on the left is the 1936 Mercedes High School Pep Squad. The Pep Squad was formed to assist cheerleaders in generating enthusiasm from the fans at sports events, particularly football games. (Vito Buenrostro.)

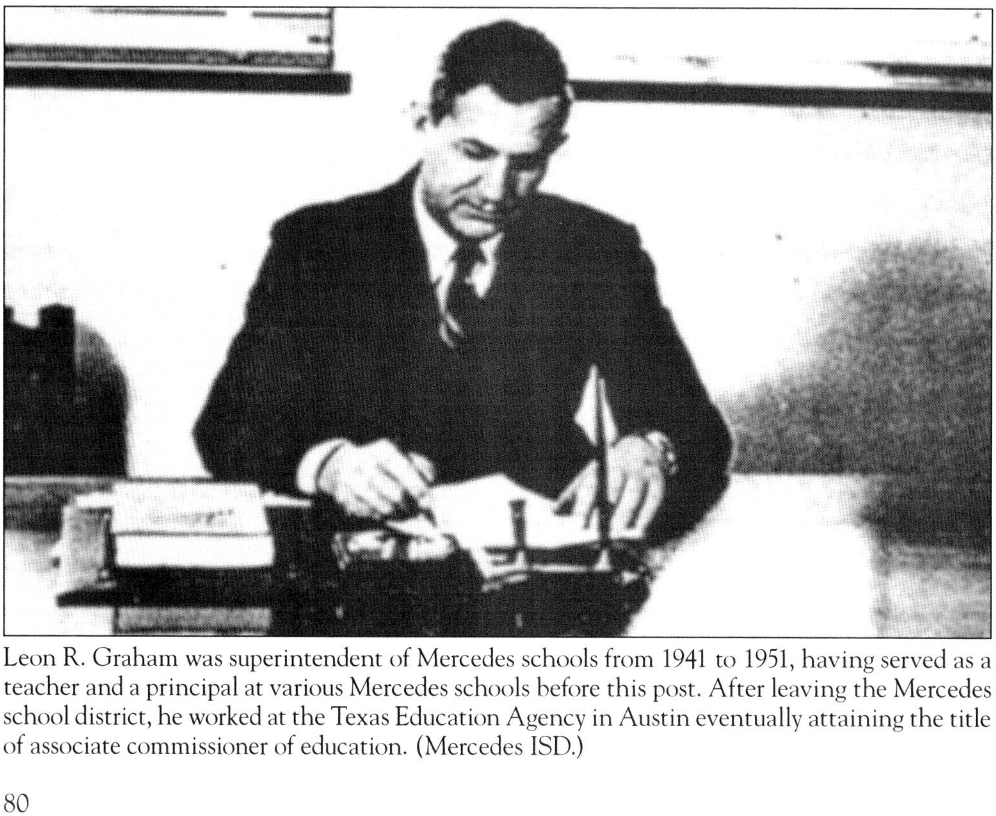

Leon R. Graham was superintendent of Mercedes schools from 1941 to 1951, having served as a teacher and a principal at various Mercedes schools before this post. After leaving the Mercedes school district, he worked at the Texas Education Agency in Austin eventually attaining the title of associate commissioner of education. (Mercedes ISD.)

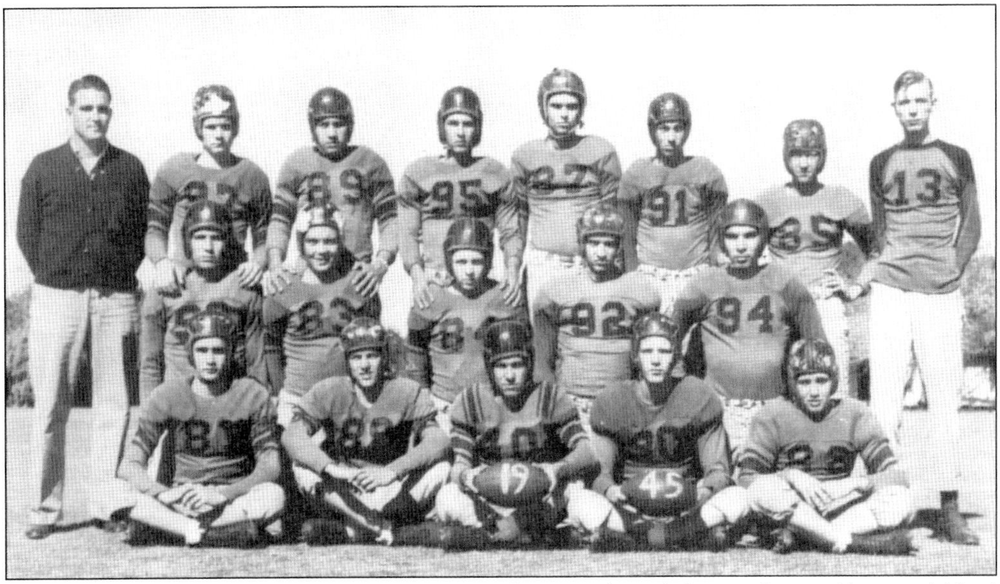

Posing here is the 1945 Mercedes Tiger Football Team: from left to right are (first row) Noel Caldeira, Angel González, Louis E. Drawe, James B. Taylor, and Anthony Caldeira; (second row) Ismael González, Bob Steer, Charles Eldridge, Kenneth Clarke, and Rudy Garza; (third row) coach Henry D. Crawford, Ernest Newmann, Senobio Uresti, Luis Garibay, Roy T. Pinkerton, Elmo Wade, Derald Hentrich, and Robert Crenshaw. (Mercedes ISD.)

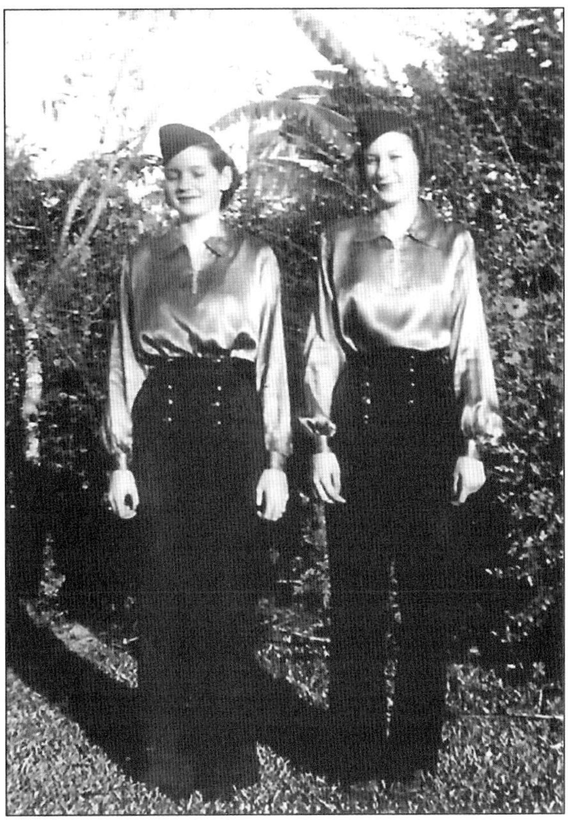

Kathleen Twenhafel (left) and her sister Helen Twenhafel pose in 1937 in their orange and black Mercedes high school band uniforms, worn that year for the first time. Their father, Albert F. Twenhafel, came to Mercedes from Illinois in 1914 with a land party and purchased 52 acres on which he raised vegetables, citrus, cotton and corn. Helen married Herbert Vogel and is still active in Mercedes where the family continues the farming and ranching tradition. (Helen Vogel.)

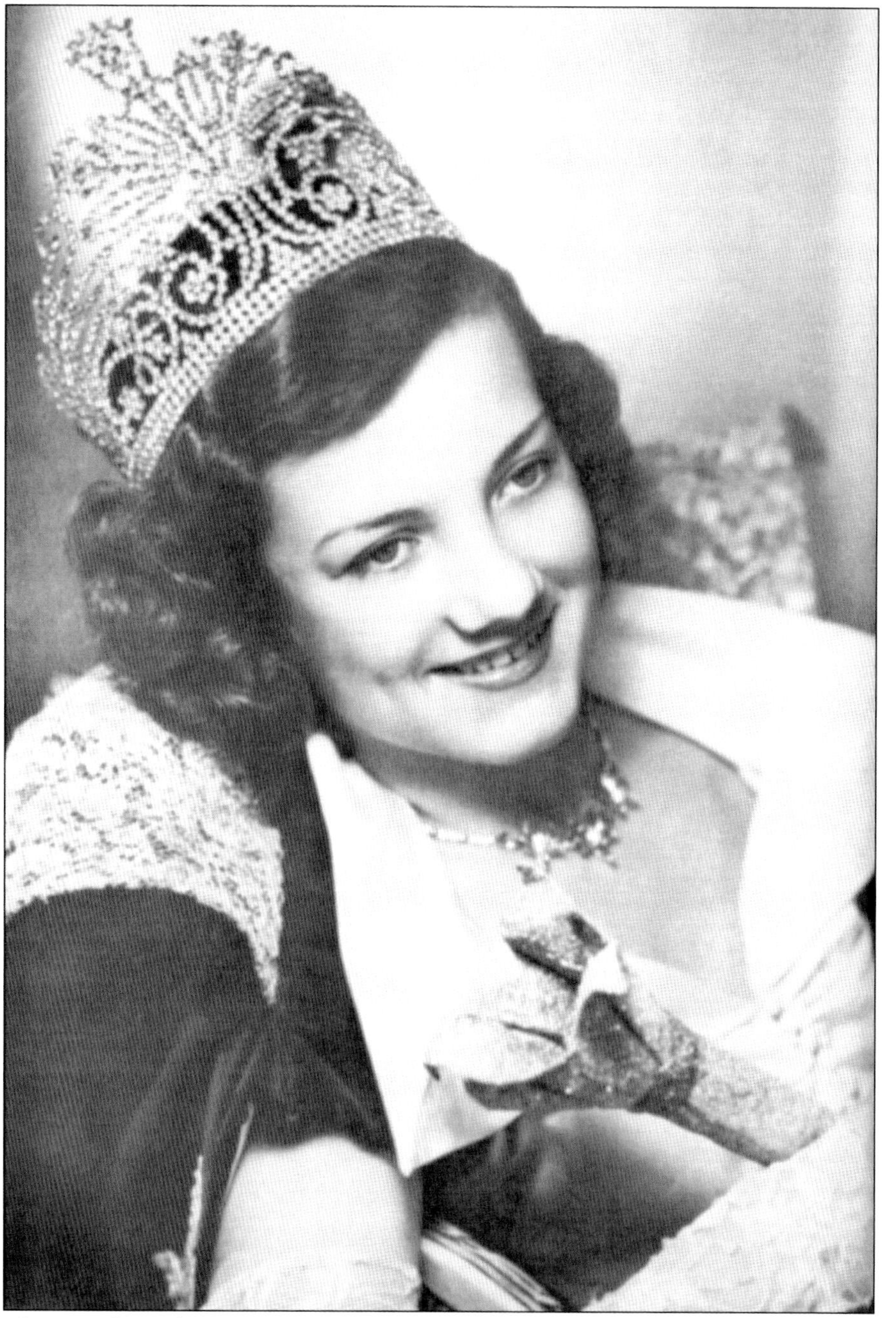

Alicia García is shown here in 1951 winning the title of "Fiestas Patrias Queen" at an annual event sponsored by Our Lady of Mercy Catholic Church celebrating Mexican Independence Day. The daughter of Jesús and Enriqueta Salinas García, she was crowned on September 16, 1951, by Lauro Izaguirre, the Mexican Consul based in McAllen, at the Mercedes High School Auditorium on Ohio Avenue. Tragically, García was diagnosed with leukemia just weeks after the celebration, and by December of that year she had died, leaving her family and friends stunned by her loss. This photograph appeared in the 1952 Bengal yearbook, which was dedicated to her memory by the Mercedes High School students and staff. (Mercedes ISD.)

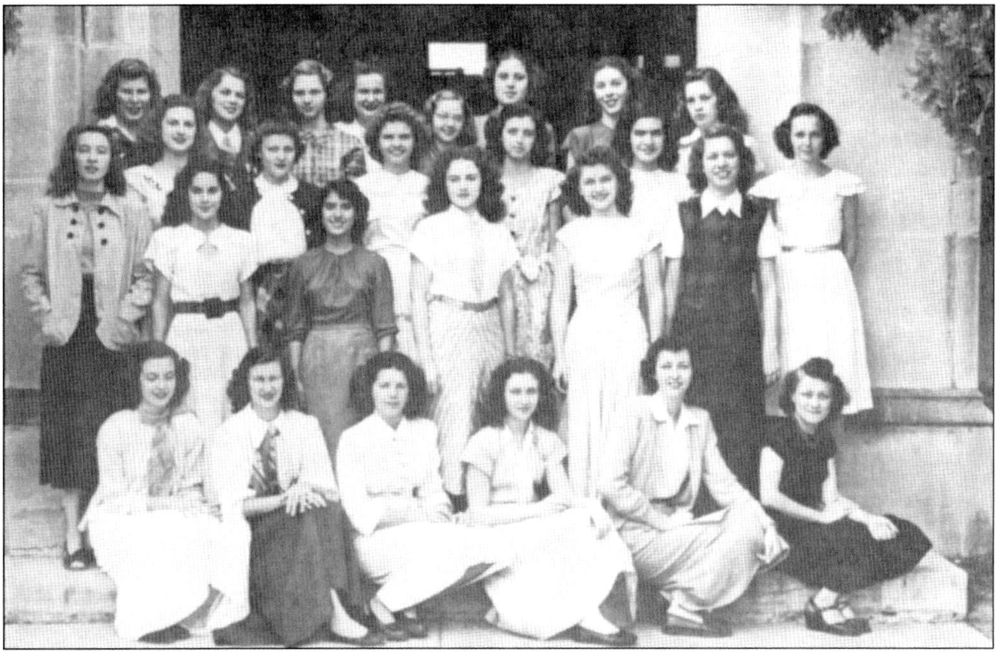

The all-female members of the Zeta Eta Sigma organization of the Mercedes High School pose here in this 1949 photograph in the Bengal yearbook. The club honors girls who are scholastically outstanding. Members must have made the honor roll to qualify for the organization. (Mercedes ISD.)

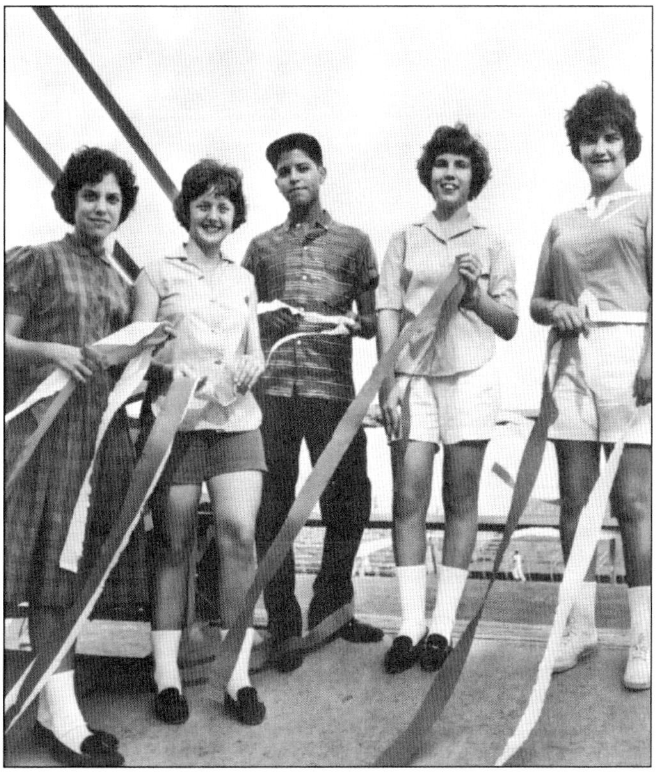

Mercedes High School 1962 freshman class officers stop to pose for a photograph as they prepare to decorate the football stadium on a Friday afternoon for a game later that night. From left to right are Stella Marroquín, Lillian Billings, Vito Buenrostro, Cynthia Hoverson, and Joan Wilt. (Mercedes ISD.)

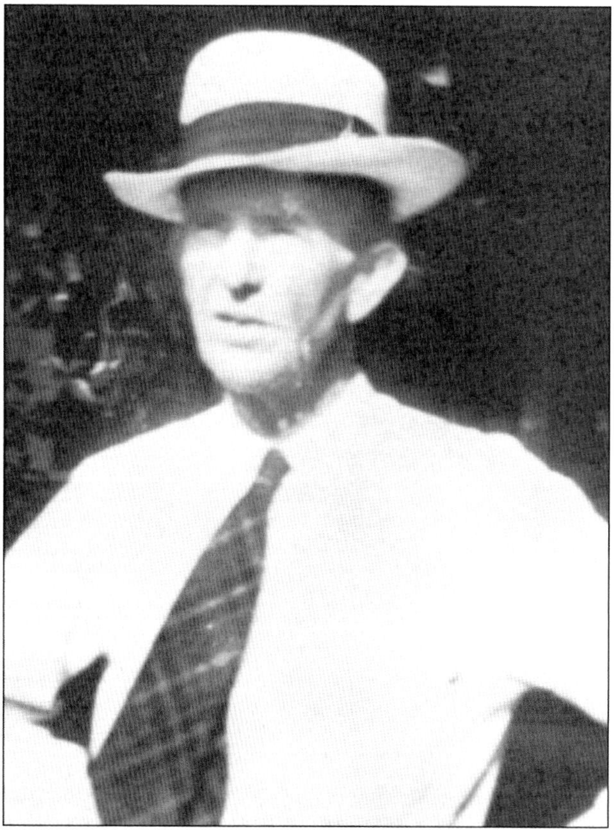

Frederick L. Johnston was involved in Mercedes education all his life. By the age of 15 he was already teaching children at a ranch school. In 1908, he and Agapita Tijerina were the first teachers at North School. That year, they taught English to 189 Mexican American students in a two-room frame schoolhouse. Johnston also served many years as secretary to the Mercedes ISD School Board. (Mercedes ISD.)

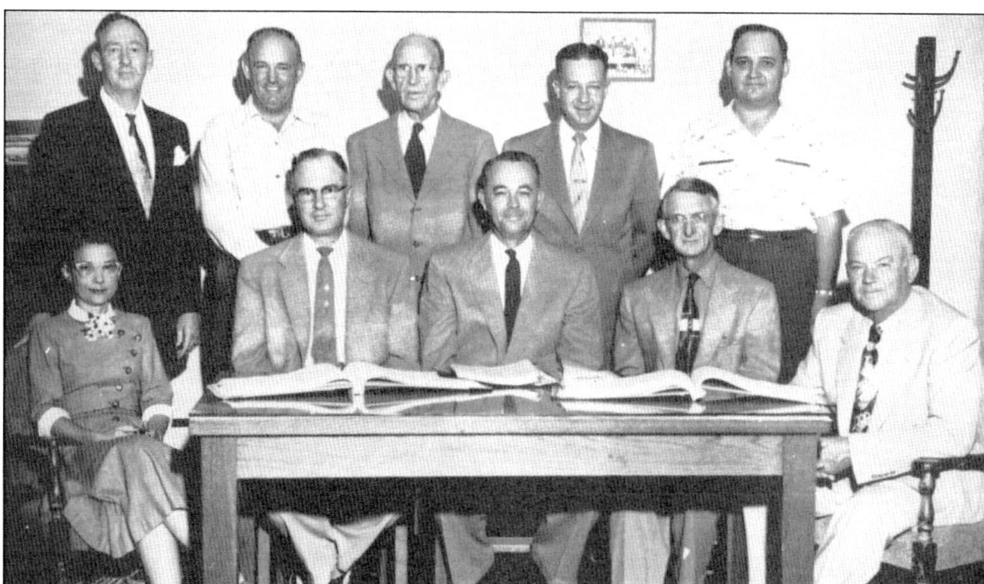

The 1954 Mercedes Independent School District Board of Trustees is pictured here. Seated from left to right are Helen M. Watson, Dr. Thomas G. Edwards, Joe Winston, superintendent of schools Lawrence W. St. Clair, and Clyde Hollon. Standing are Ernest E. Marchant, Thomas B. Ewing, Frederick L. Johnston, James McElyea, and Joaquín Fernández. (Mercedes ISD.)

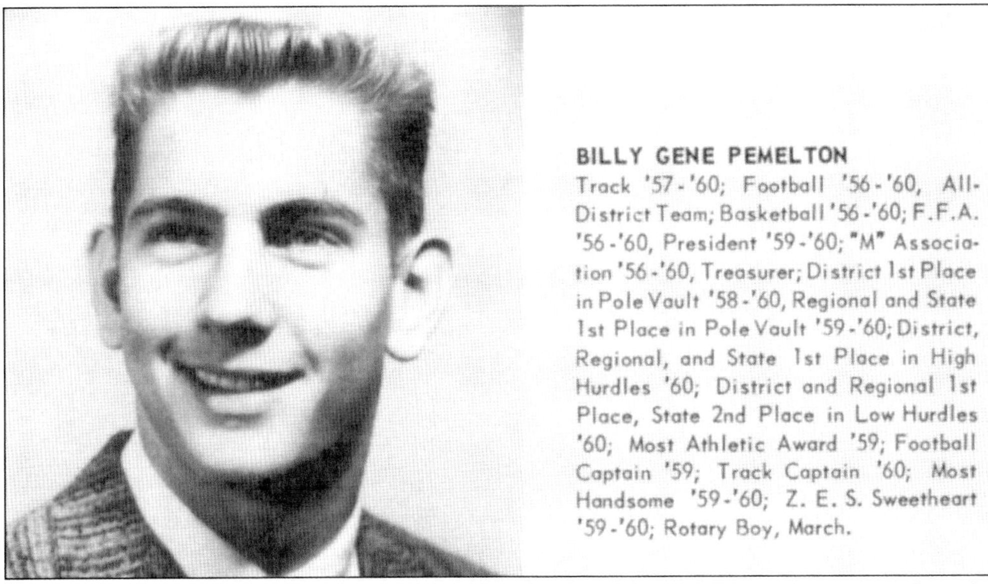

BILLY GENE PEMELTON
Track '57-'60; Football '56-'60, All-District Team; Basketball '56-'60; F.F.A. '56-'60, President '59-'60; "M" Association '56-'60, Treasurer; District 1st Place in Pole Vault '58-'60, Regional and State 1st Place in Pole Vault '59-'60; District, Regional, and State 1st Place in High Hurdles '60; District and Regional 1st Place, State 2nd Place in Low Hurdles '60; Most Athletic Award '59; Football Captain '59; Track Captain '60; Most Handsome '59-'60; Z. E. S. Sweetheart '59-'60; Rotary Boy, March.

Billy Gene Pemelton, 1960 Mercedes graduate and outstanding athlete, participated in the 1964 Summer Olympics in Tokyo, Japan, placing in the top 10 in the men's pole vault. For the Mercedes Tigers, he won the Texas state class 2A title in the pole vault (1959–1960) and in the high hurdles (1960). (Mercedes ISD.)

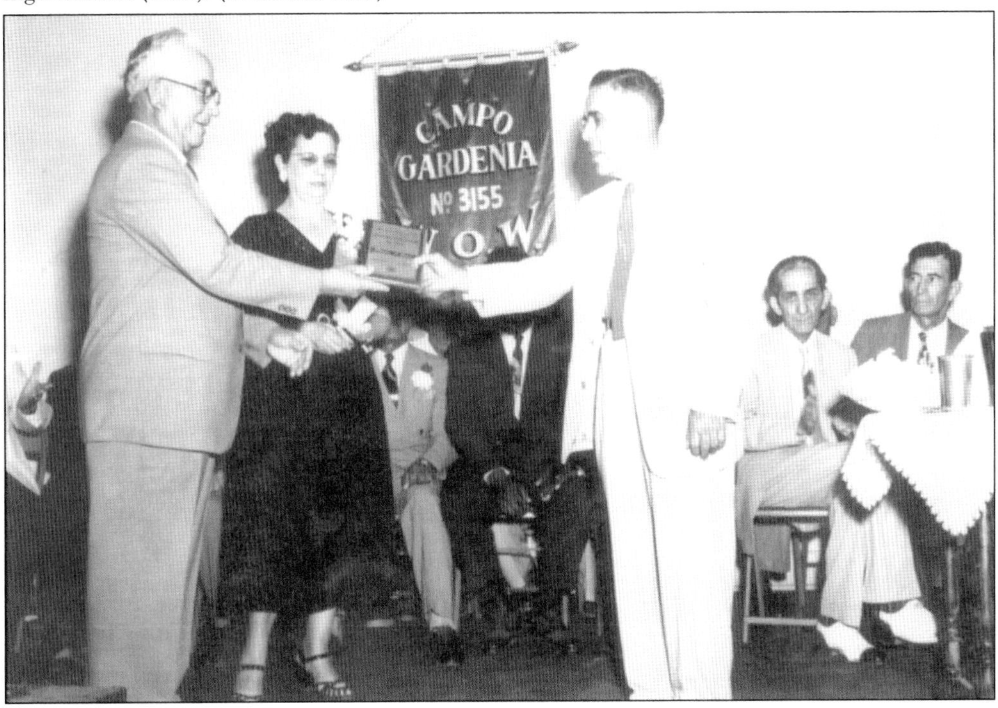

Pictured at this 1954 Campo Gardenia No. 3155 Woodmen of the World (WOW) award ceremony are, from left to right, (standing) Florentino Zamora, Amalia Zamora, and Juventino de León Sr.; (seated) José "Pepe" Díaz and Severo Díaz. The WOW organization was very active in Mercedes, sponsoring events for schoolchildren, fundraising for scholarships, and taking part in patriotic events such as flag presentations. (Delia de León.)

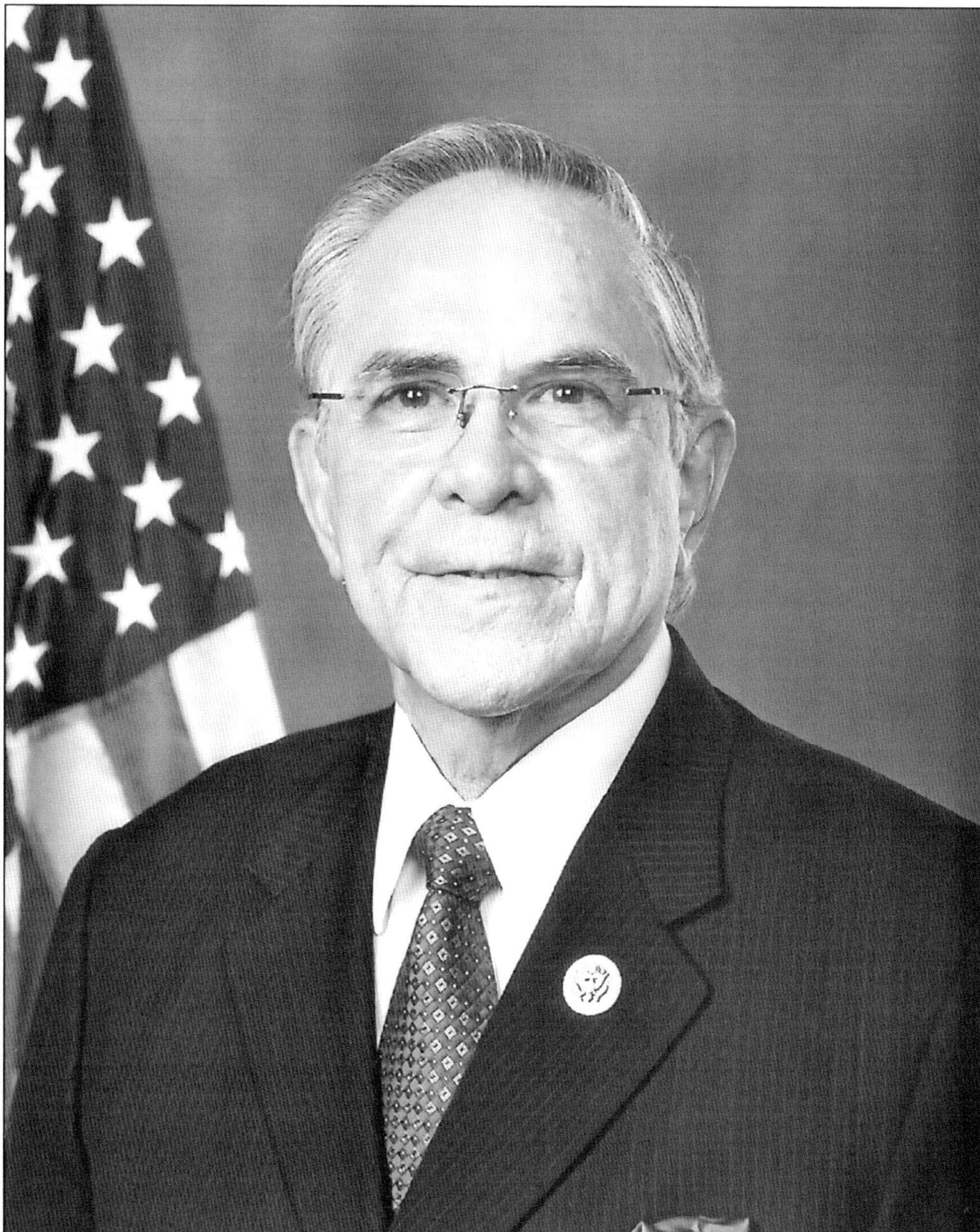

The Honorable Rubén Hinojosa graduated from Mercedes High School in 1958, having demonstrated early leadership abilities. After earning business degrees from the University of Texas at Austin, he served 20 years as president and chief financial officer of the family business H&H Foods. He was elected to Congress in 1996 and is currently serving his ninth term as representative of the 15th District of Texas. He serves on the House Committee on Education and the Workforce and the Committee on Financial Services. He serves as ranking member of the Subcommittee on Higher Education and Workforce Training as well as serving on the Subcommittee on Health Employment Labor and Pensions. By popular acclamation, he was selected in 2012 to be chairman of the Congressional Hispanic Caucus for the 113th Congress (2013–2015). (Rubén Hinojosa Congressional Office.)

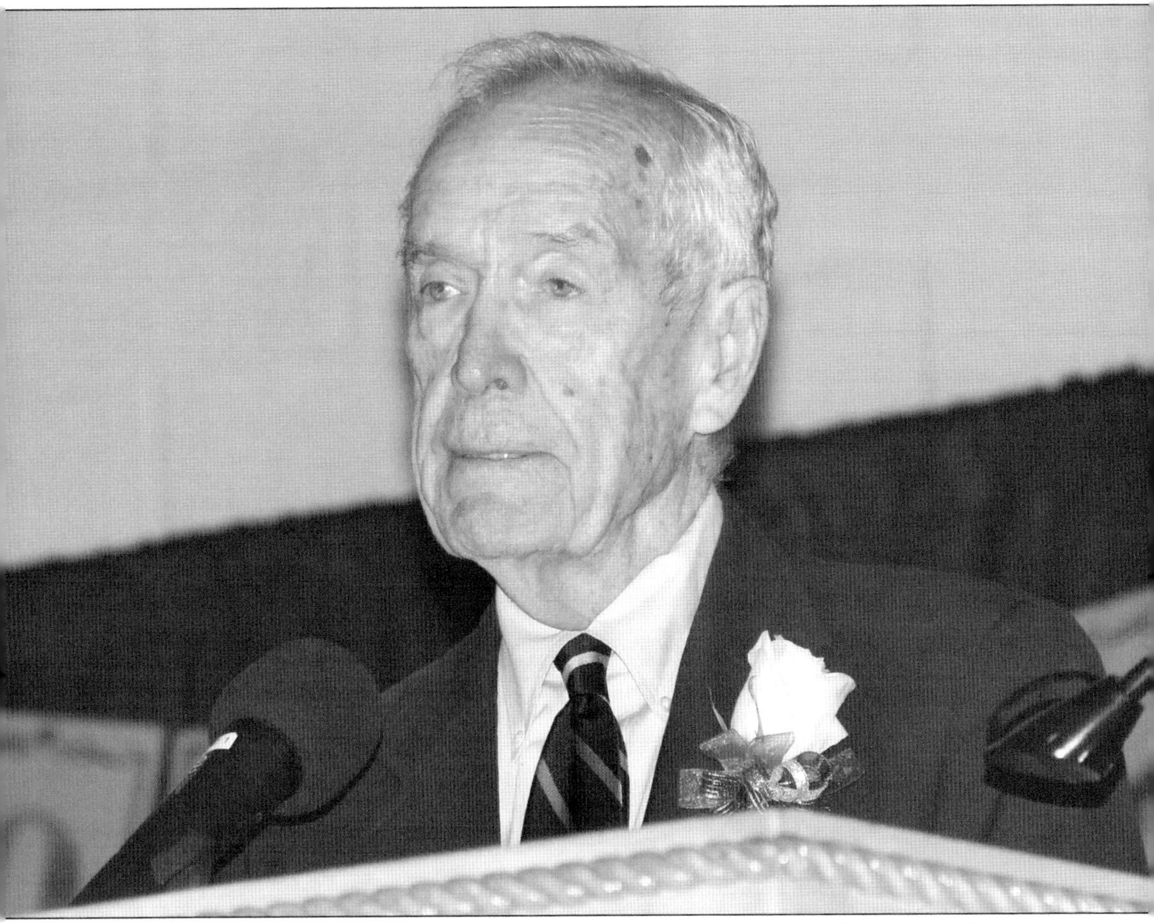

Dr. Rolando Hinojosa-Smith is a 1946 graduate of Mercedes High School. He is an award-winning novelist of the *Klail City Death Trip Series*, which comprises 15 volumes to date and for which he has received two prestigious awards: the Premio Casa de las Américas and the Premio Quinto Sol. After serving in the Korean conflict and then completing a doctorate in Spanish literature, he held several teaching assignments, including Chairman of Chicano Studies at Minnesota. In the early 1980s he switched academic departments to become a professor of English and Creative Writing at the University of Texas at Austin. Currently, he holds the Ellen Clayton Garwood Chair in the English department at the University of Texas at Austin. He focuses on American literature, specializing in life and literature of the Southwest. He continues to teach and travels extensively. He has visited more than 250 colleges and universities in the United States and abroad, where he reads from his books and gives classes. In March 2014, Dr. Hinojosa-Smith received the Ivan Sandrof Lifetime Achievement Award given by the National Book Critics Circle. (Debbie Winslow.)

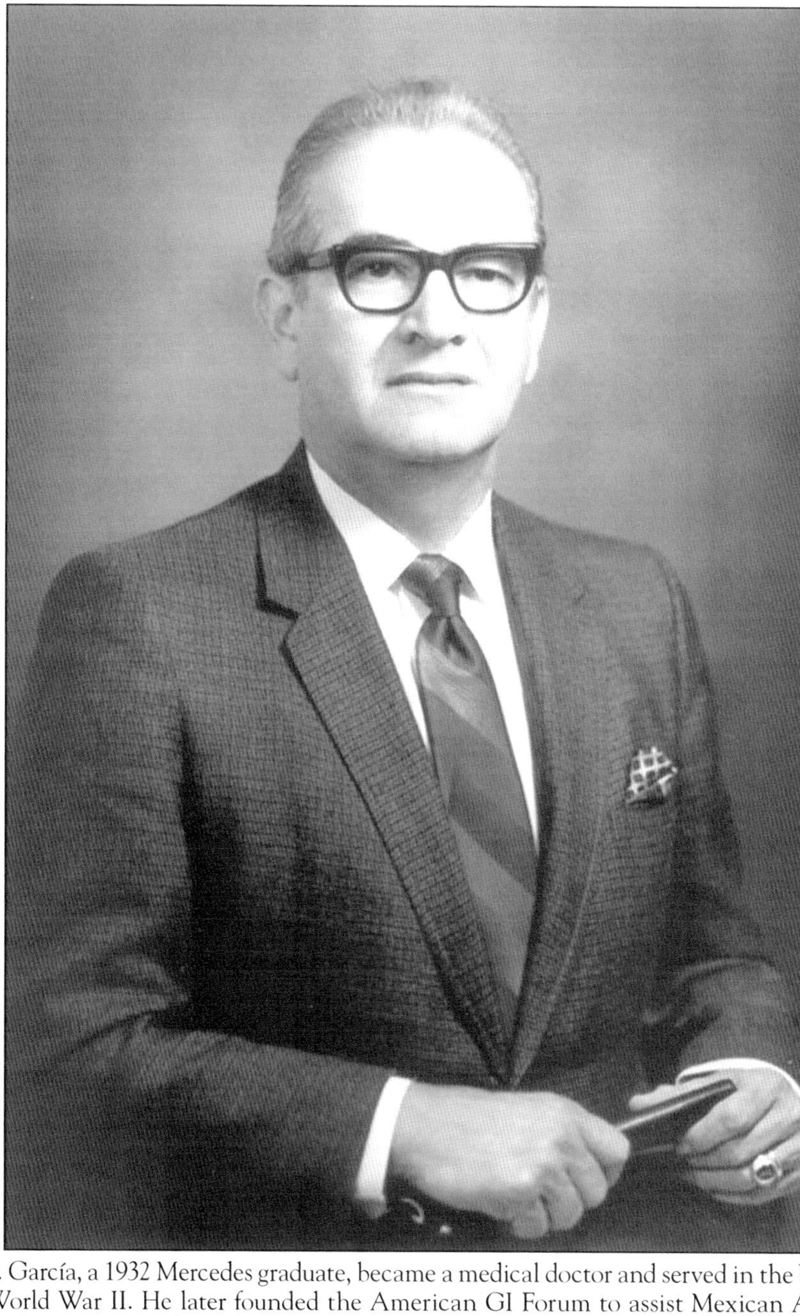

Hector P. García, a 1932 Mercedes graduate, became a medical doctor and served in the US Army during World War II. He later founded the American GI Forum to assist Mexican American veterans who were struggling with discrimination and being denied veterans' benefits. He was named alternate ambassador to the United Nations in 1967; was appointed to the United States Commission on Civil Rights in 1968; was awarded the Presidential Medal of Freedom, the nation's highest civilian honor, in 1984; and was named to the Order of Saint Gregory the Great by Pope John Paul II in 1990. In 1998, he was posthumously awarded the Aguila Azteca, or Aztec Eagle, Mexico's highest award for foreigners, in a ceremony in Corpus Christi, Texas. Mercedes has honored him by naming its library for him—the Dr. Hector P. García Memorial Library. (Hector P. García family.)

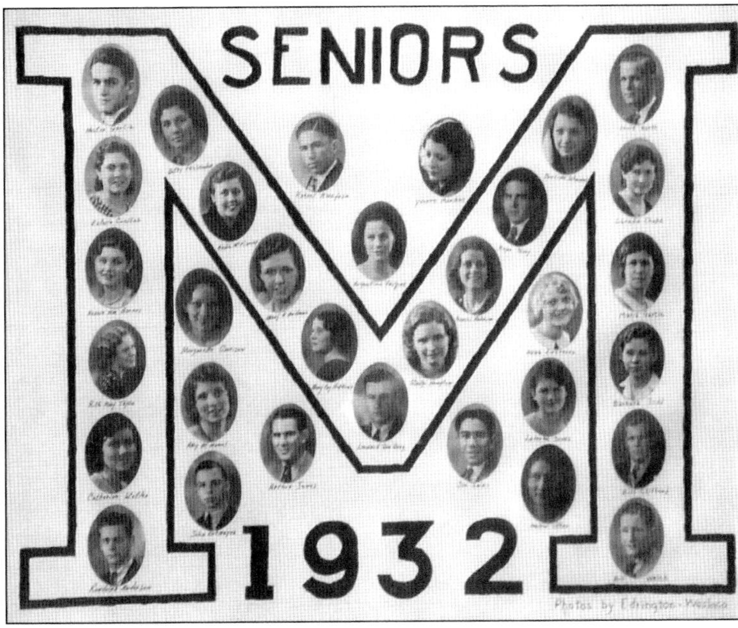

This image of the Mercedes High School Class of 1932 hangs on the "Wall of Fame" at the newest Mercedes High School Cafeteria along with all graduates since 1914. In the upper left corner of this class is Hector P. García. Only seven of the 32 graduates were Mexican American, although they were the majority population of the city at that time. (Mercedes ISD.)

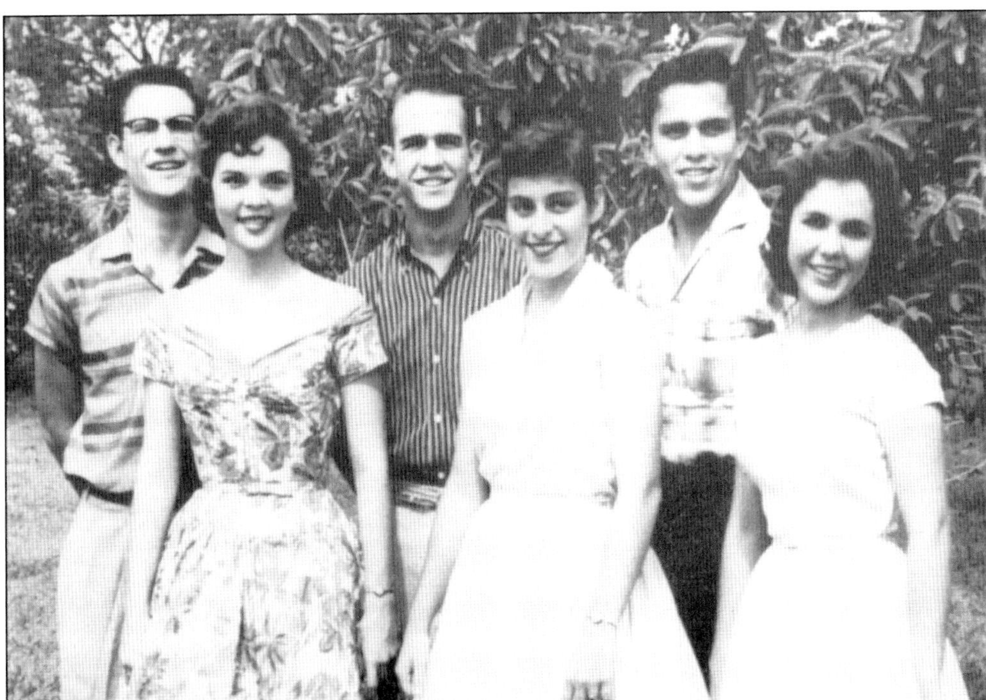

Posing for Bengal yearbook pictures are the 1957 Mercedes High School "class favorites." From left to right are (first row) Marie Watson, Patsy O'Shea, and Nancy Archer; (second row) Joseph Fernández, Bud Terry, and Rubén Hinojosa. (Mercedes ISD.)

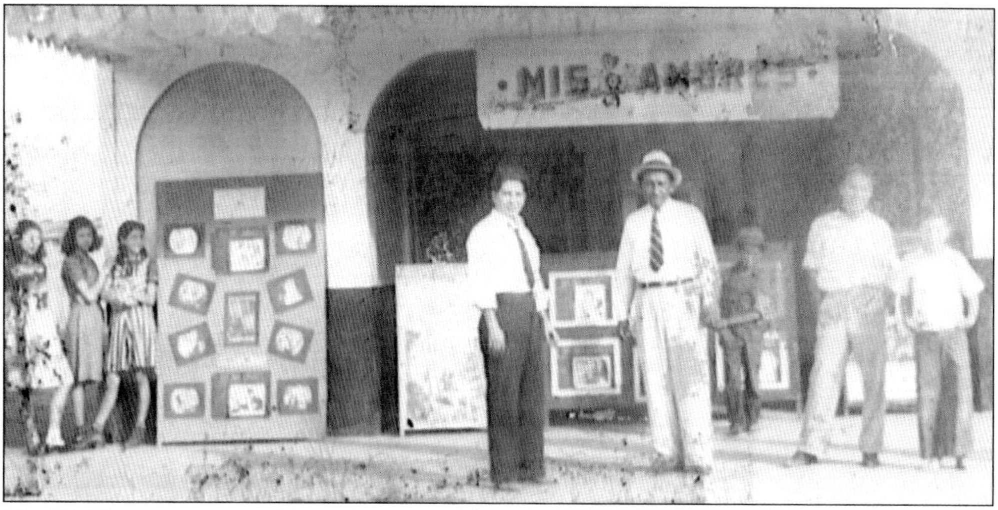

The Río Theater was one of three theaters in Mercedes. The other two were the Rex and the State. The State was previously the Capitol and the Empire. This 1940 photograph shows the first Río Theater before it was remodeled. Standing in front are, from left to right, Mary Guerrero, Mary Zamora, Olga Ochoa, Raul Galván, Carlos "Chale" Leal, Cato Palacios, and two unidentified young boys (at right and in back). (Irma Palacios.)

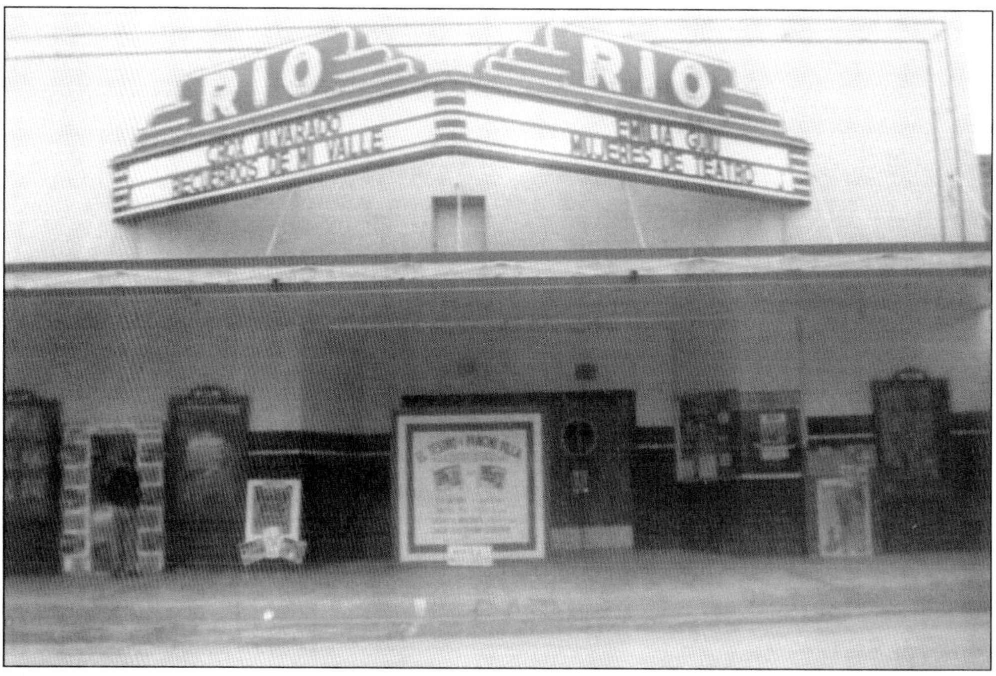

The Río Theater was remodeled in 1946 with a brand new marquee, as shown in this photograph, and a capacity of 639 seats. The Rio Theater specialized in Spanish-language movies, while the Rex showed Westerns, and the State showed first-run movies. Alberto Arteaga worked at the Río since 1935, eventually becoming the manager. (Sylvia Arteaga Calles.)

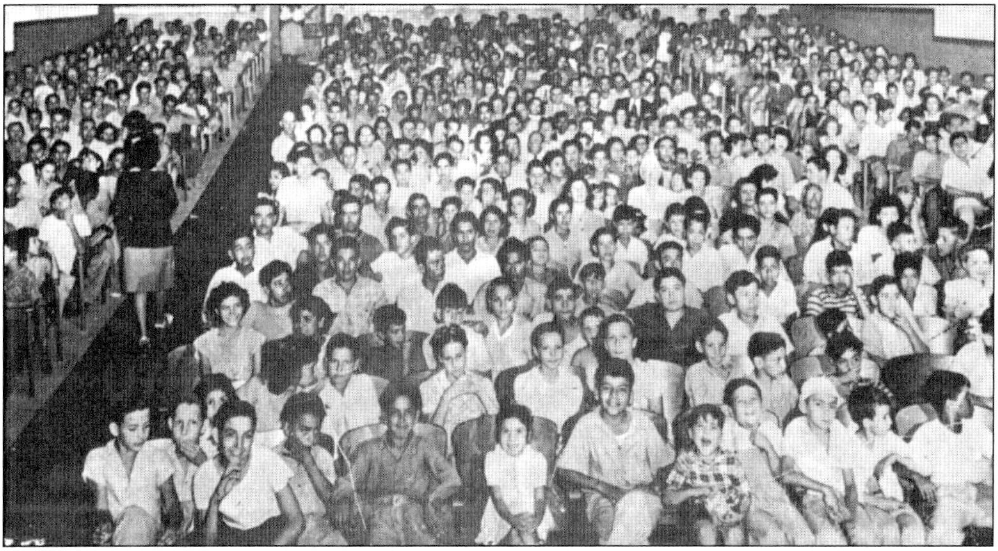

The Río Theater often had a capacity crowd such as this one gathered for opening night of the remodeled theater on May 17, 1946. The Río was located on North Texas Avenue near Hidalgo Street; the Rex was located on South Texas Avenue on the 200 block; and the State was also located on South Texas Avenue next to the First National Bank on the 300 block. (Sylvia Arteaga Calles.)

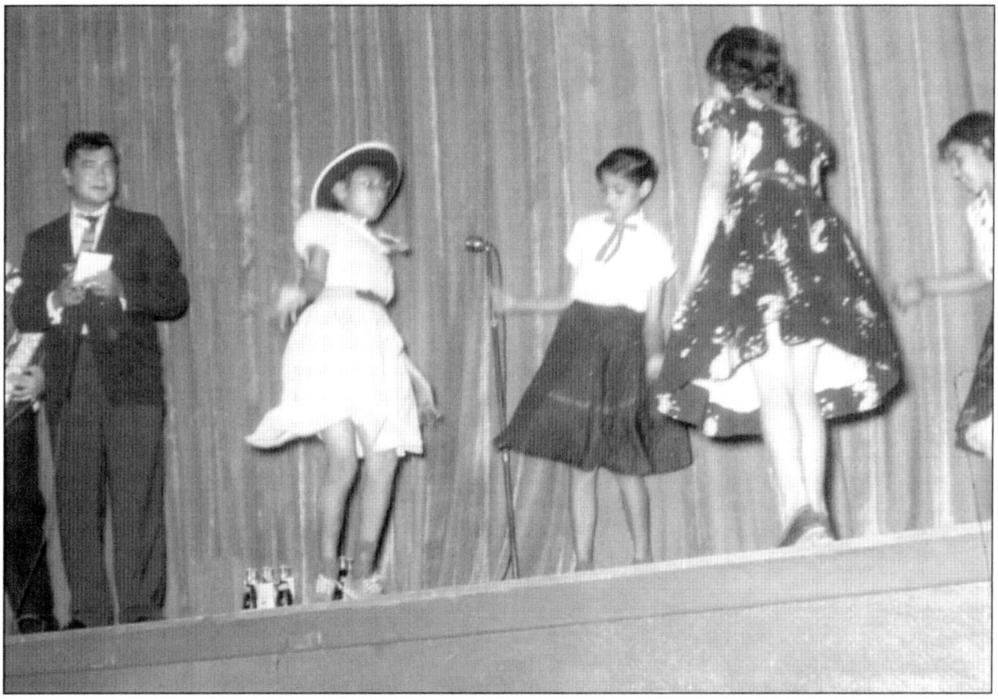

The Río Theater did not just show movies, it also featured "Amateur Night," during which local talent could perform for prizes. Pictured here in this 1955 photograph are, from left to right, announcer Martín Rosales, Carlota Cantú (in the white dress), Olga Rodríguez (with the black skirt), and two unidentified girls. Competitors mostly sang and danced, but some did specialty acts such as juggling or gymnastic tumbling. (Sylvia Arteaga Calles.)

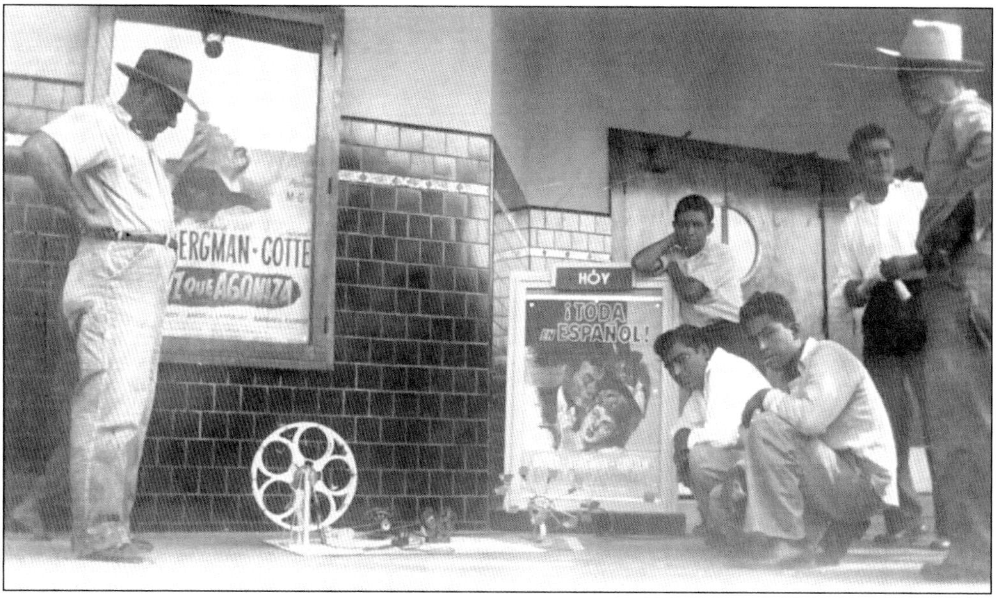

Projectionist Emilio Ybarra Sr. (standing at left) explains how it all works to several unidentified men who are interested in movie theaters in this 1954 photograph. Ybarra worked for all of the Mercedes Theaters: the Rex, the State, the Río, and the Wes-Mer Drive-In Theater west of town. (Sylvia Arteaga Calles.)

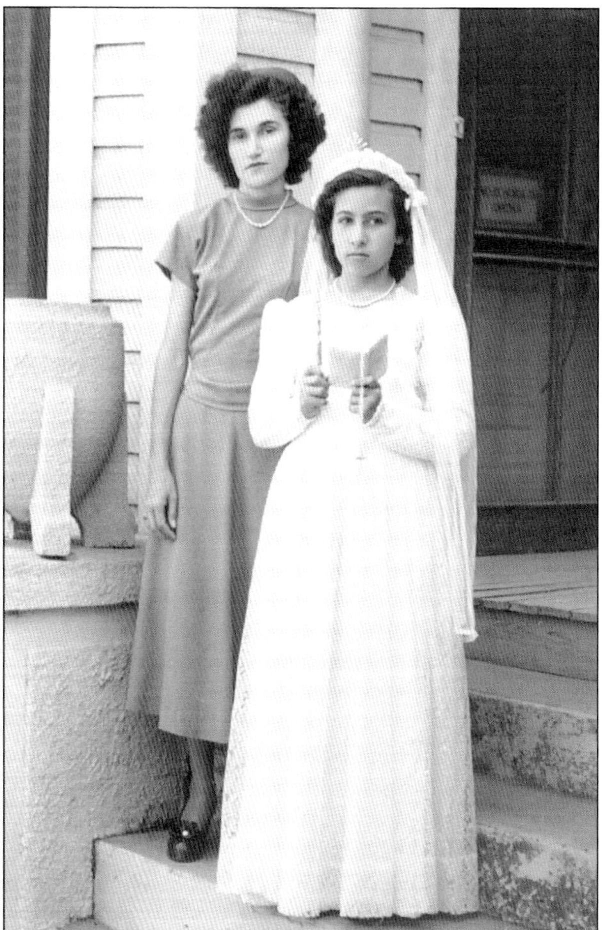

Raquel Gonzales Palacios (left) stands in as *madrina*, or female sponsor, for Emilia Marroquín as she makes her first communion at Our Lady of Mercy Catholic Church on May 21, 1949. *Padrinos* and *madrinas* agreed to assist parents with the responsibility for a child's religious upbringing in the Catholic faith. (Irma Palacios.)

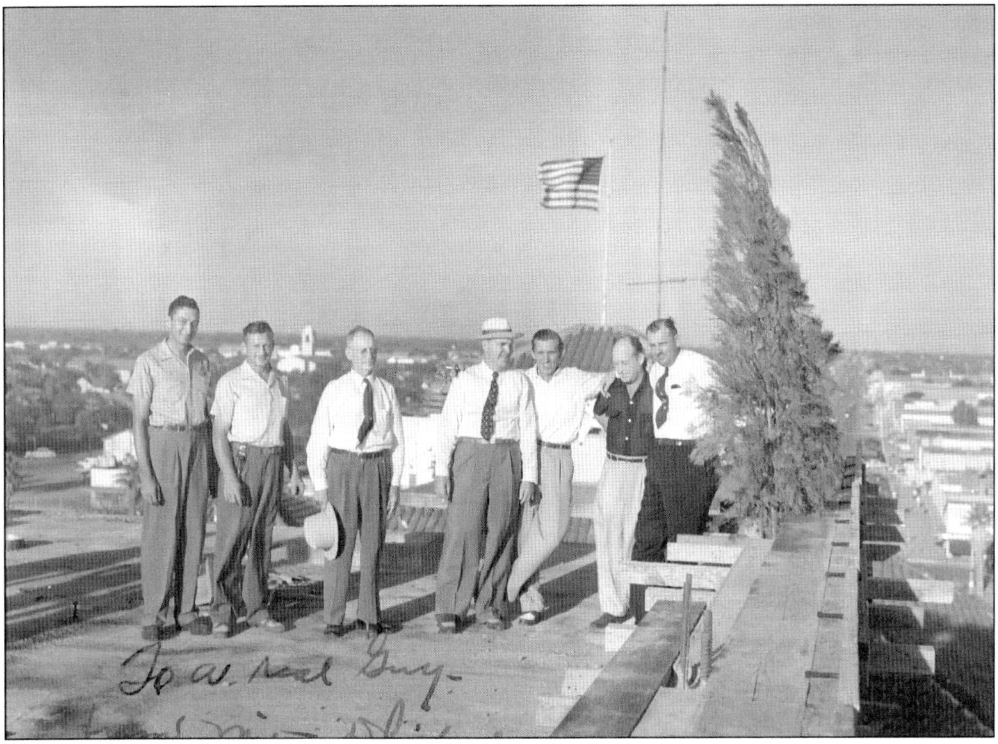

In the center wearing a hat is architect Roscious Newell Waters with unidentified friends or associates. He designed many Mercedes businesses and residences, including, among many others, city hall, the Llano Grande Clubhouse, and the Mercedes High School and auditorium on Ohio Street. Waters's architectural styles changed over the years and included Spanish, Gothic, Princeton, and Early Modern designs. (Hidalgo County Historical Commission.)

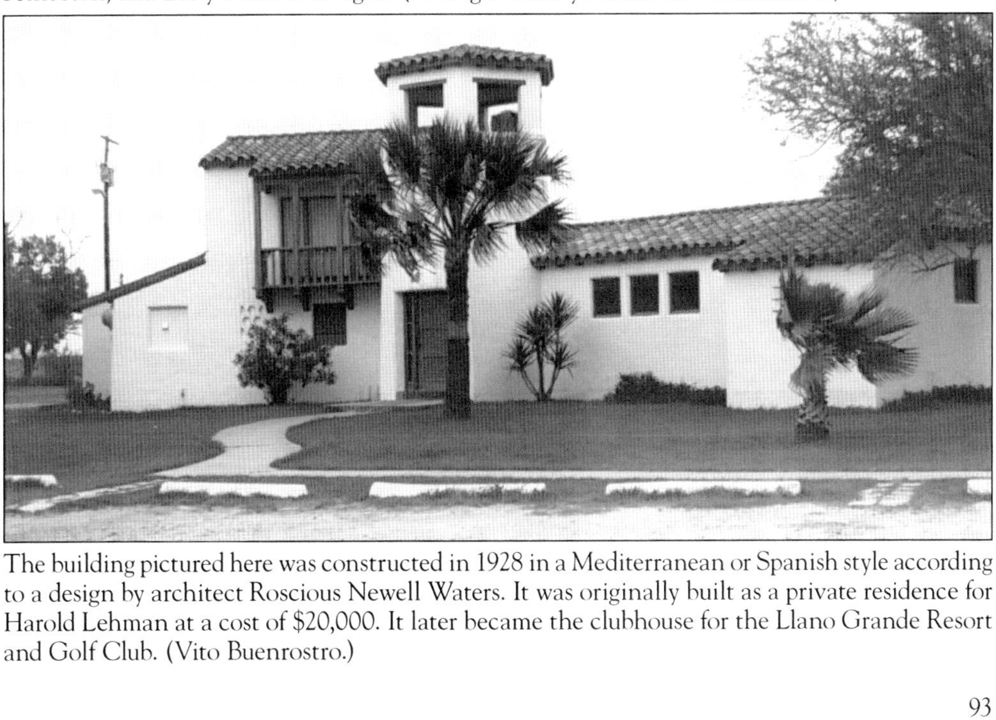

The building pictured here was constructed in 1928 in a Mediterranean or Spanish style according to a design by architect Roscious Newell Waters. It was originally built as a private residence for Harold Lehman at a cost of $20,000. It later became the clubhouse for the Llano Grande Resort and Golf Club. (Vito Buenrostro.)

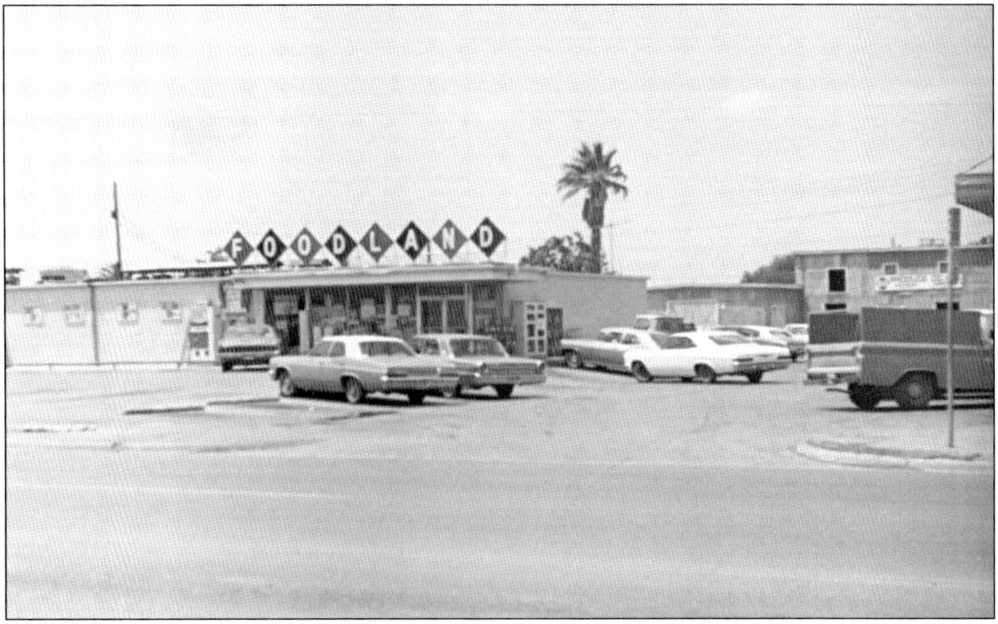

Ferguson "Ferg" Wood was the owner and manager of Ferg's Foodland, a popular grocery store located at 425 Second Street, also known as US Business Highway 83. Wood learned the grocery business from Robert H. Kern, working at Kern's grocery store from 1928 to 1958. In 1972, Wood retired and sold the store to Wendel Drefke. (Carolyn C. López.)

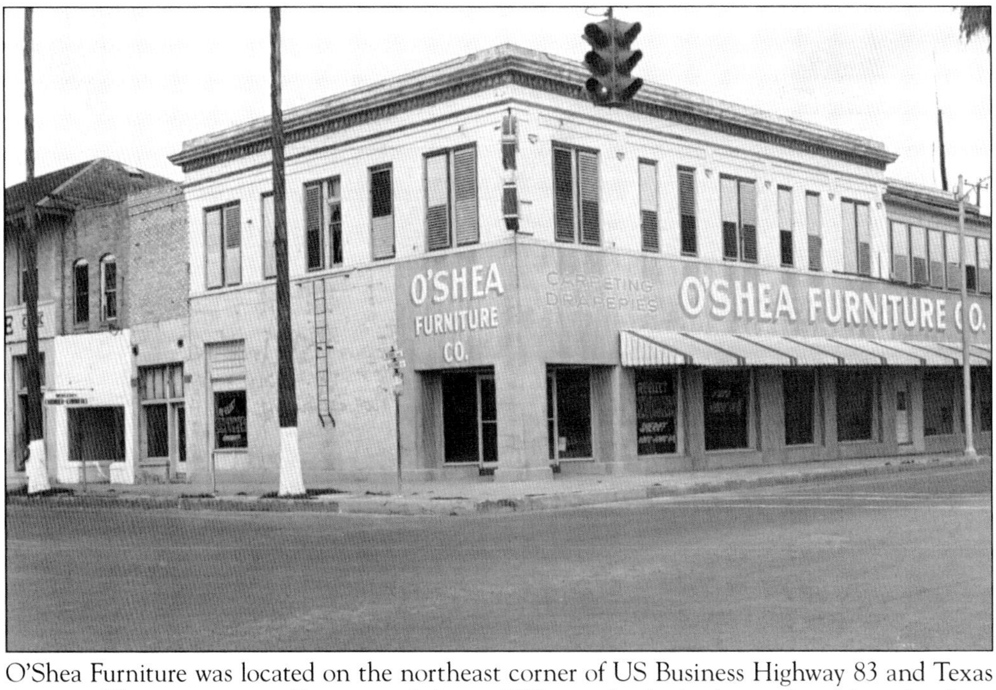

O'Shea Furniture was located on the northeast corner of US Business Highway 83 and Texas Avenue. The owners were Eugene and Anne O'Shea, who had relocated to Mercedes from Arkansas in the 1940s. The building was later demolished in the 1960s to make way for other businesses. (Carolyn C. López.)

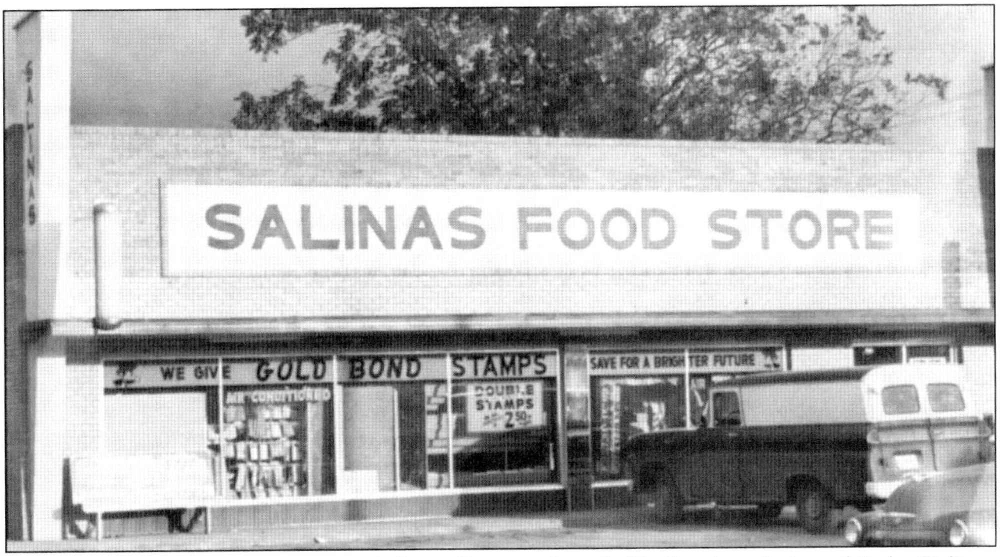

Another popular grocery store was Salinas Grocery, founded by brothers Luis and Pedro Salinas and Luis's son Rigoberto in 1946. In 1957, they expanded to the larger building seen here and renamed the business Salinas Food Store. Don Luis and his son Rigoberto were very involved citizens and remembered by their patrons for excellent service. (Carolyn C. López.)

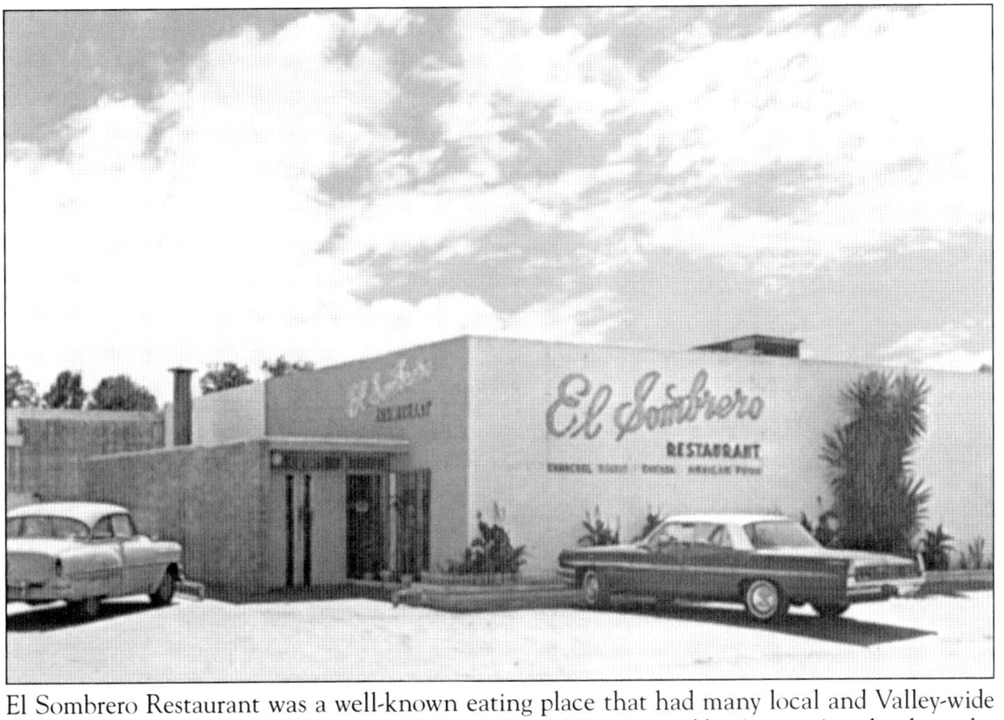

El Sombrero Restaurant was a well-known eating place that had many local and Valley-wide clients. It was located on US Business Highway 83 and first opened by Arturo Arredondo in the 1940s. It was later purchased by Wayne and Mary Love. Many prom attendees may recall having dined there after the junior-senior prom at their high school. (Carolyn C. López.)

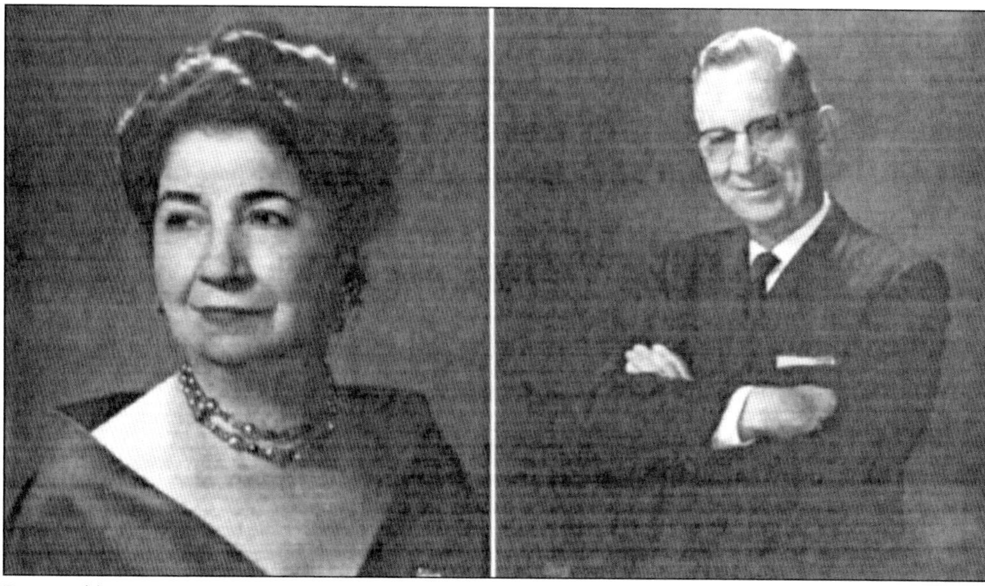

Pictured here are Marguerite (left) and Shelley H. Collier Sr. Collier was well known in banking circles and came to work at the First National Bank in 1923. An active and involved citizen in Mercedes, he stayed with the bank until 1972 when he retired. Personally as well as through the bank, Collier supported educational ventures through scholarships and gifts to students and often made charitable contributions to many organizations. (Mercedes Centennial Committee.)

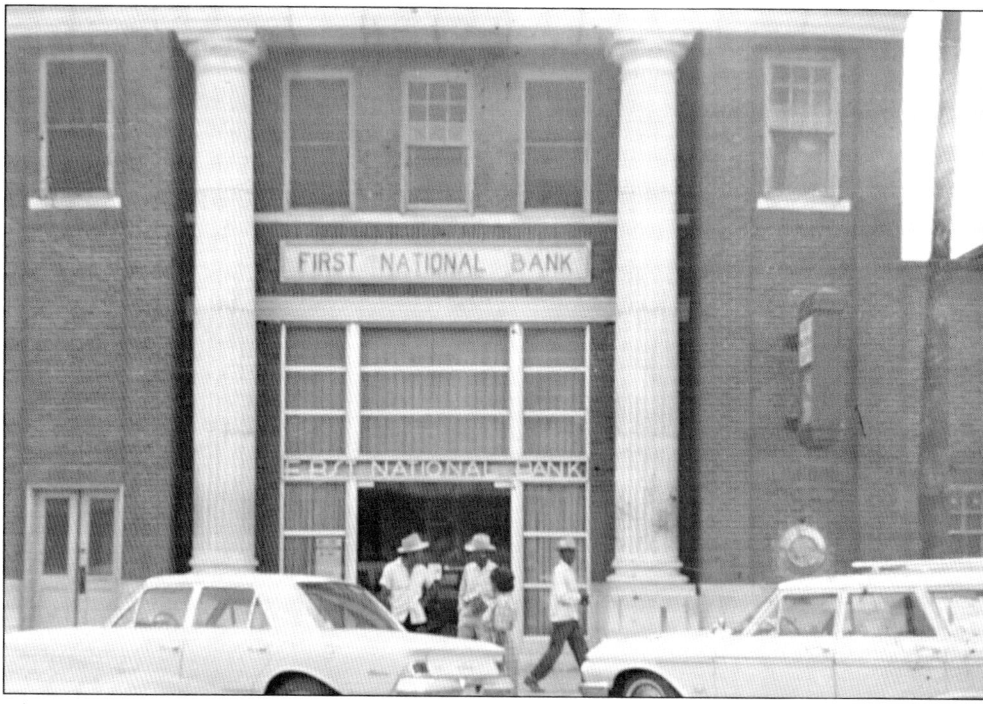

The second building used by the First National Bank was designed by Austin architect Hugo Franz Kuehne and was occupied by the end of 1921. Chatting in front of the building in this 1960 photograph are, from left to right, Daniel Barrientos, Domingo Buenrostro, and Cristina C. Buenrostro with an unidentified man walking by. (Vito Buenrostro.)

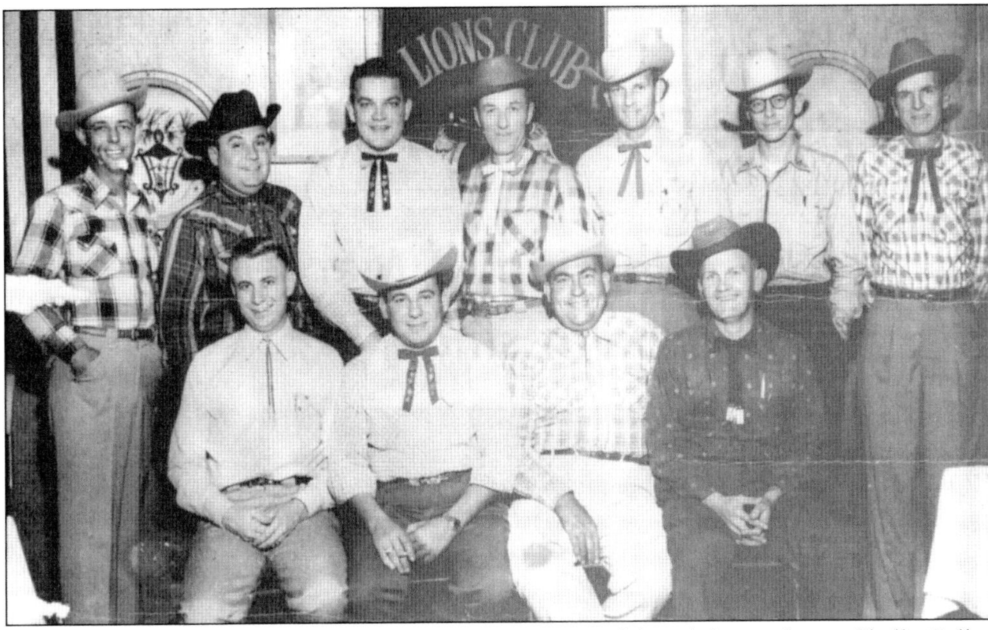

Lion's Club members pose in Western dress in 1957. Seated from left to right are Shelly Collier Jr., Eli Ríos, Adán Longoria, and Fleet S. Lentz. Standing are Bill Basinger, Joe Adame, Dennis Clifford, Gordon Leonard, James Van Burkleo, William B. "Dub" Lauder, and James Kirber. (*Mercedes Enterprise.*)

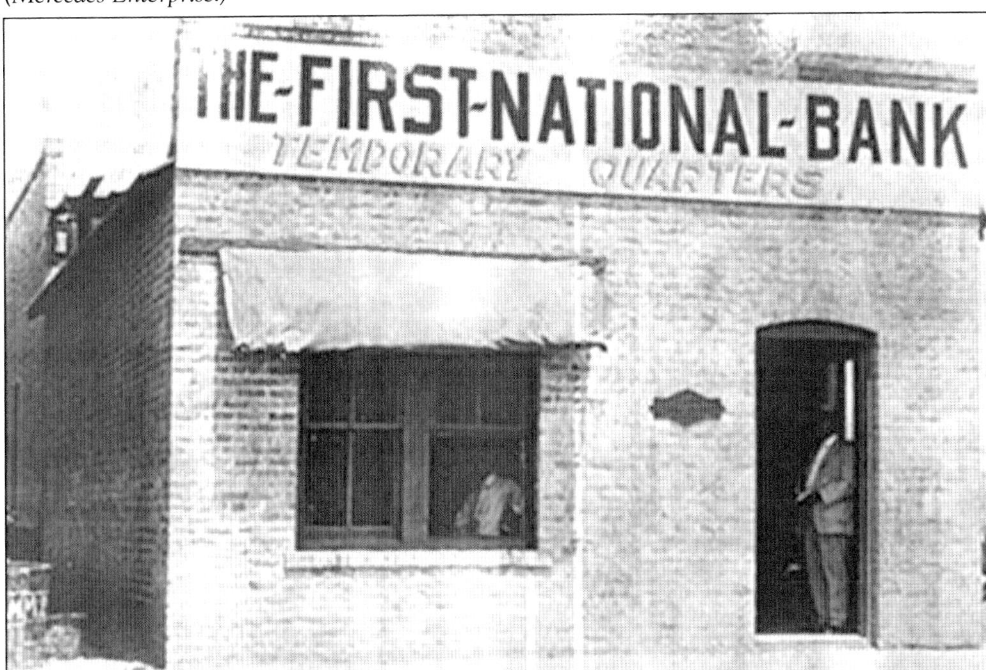

The temporary location of the First National Bank when it first opened in January 1921 was in this building. Under the direction of Pres. John Hackney, the bank moved that same year into a beautiful new brick building on South Texas Avenue. Today, the bank is on the corner of Texas Avenue and US Business Highway 83 as the Texas National Bank. (*Mercedes Enterprise.*)

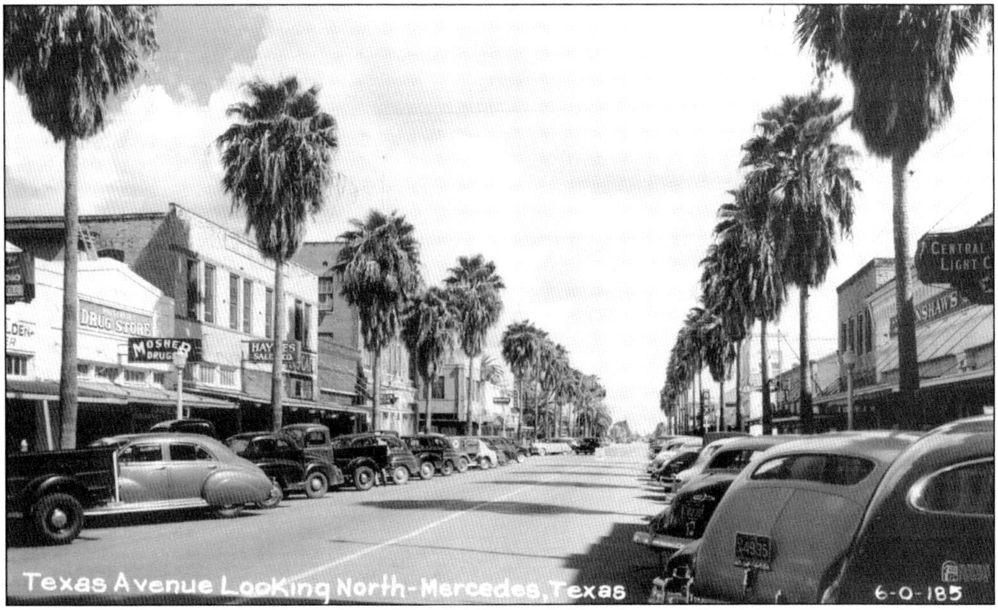

The 1940s and 1950s were some of the most prosperous years for Mercedes. Many businesses had recovered from the Depression of the 1930s, and the post–World War II boom was at its highest point. In 1940, the population was 7,624, but by 1950 it had grown to 10,065. In this downtown scene of Mercedes, every building is occupied by a thriving business. (MSTH.)

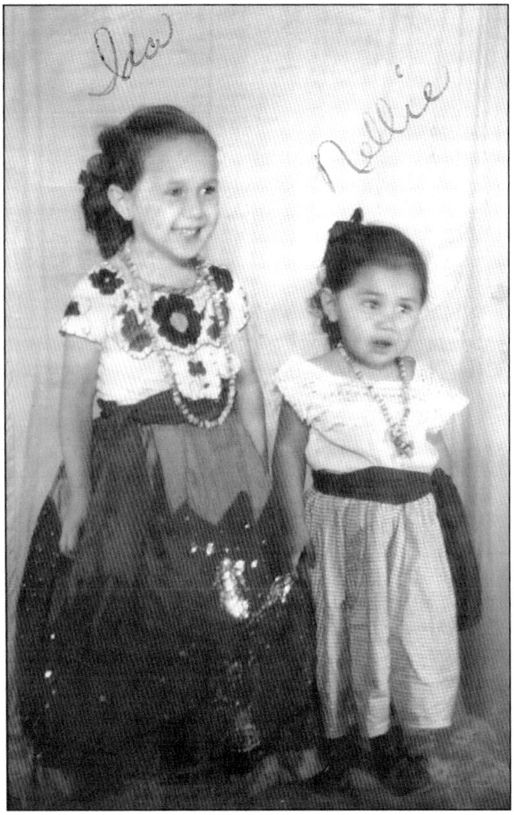

Sisters Ida (left) and Irma "Nellie" Palacios dress up in their Fiestas Patrias costumes in 1954. The celebrations recognize the area's Mexican heritage and recall the independence won by Mexico from Spain in 1821. In earlier days, the city sponsored the celebrations but later the Catholic churches became sponsors of the event. (Irma Palacios.)

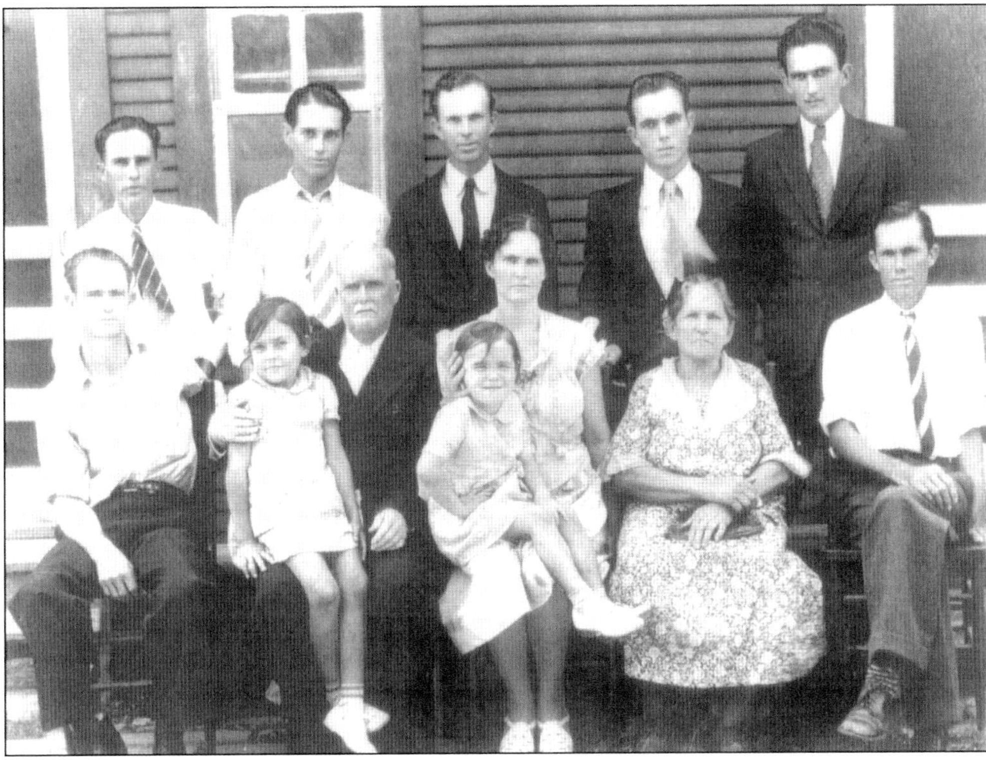

Howell family members are pictured here in a late 1940s photograph. From left to right are (seated) Jacinto Howell, Joseph Henry Howell Sr., Pauline Howell Gorena, María Escobedo Howell, and Casimiro Howell; (standing) William Howell, Henry Joseph Howell, Albert Howell, Charles Howell, and Joseph Henry Howell Jr. Children in arms are Beatriz Gorena (left) and Edna Gorena, Pauline's children. (Eddie Howell Sr.)

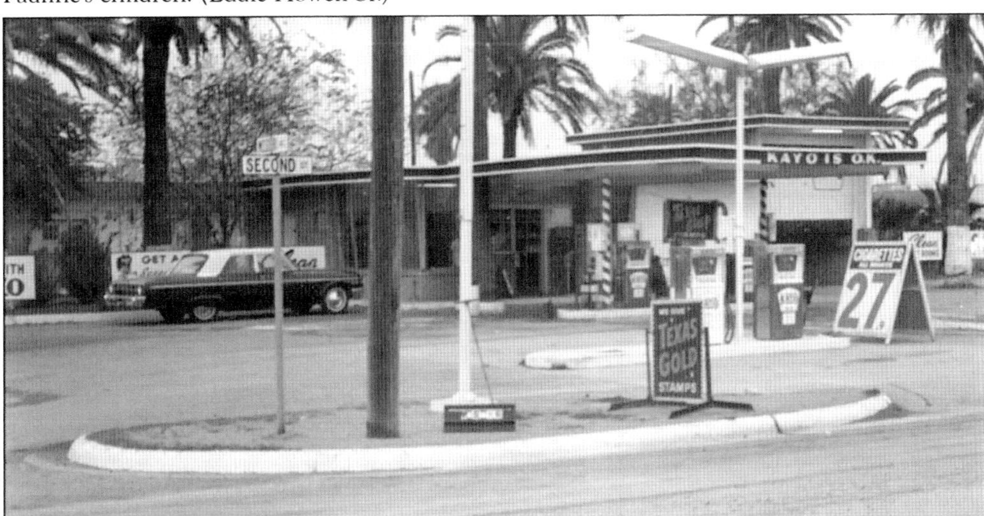

Many Mercedes residents remember the good old days when gasoline was 27¢ a gallon in the 1960s. This Kayo Is O.K. gas station was located on the northeast corner of US Business Highway 83 and Missouri Avenue. By then, gasoline stations were "self-serve," although the pumps were still not accepting credit cards. (Carolyn C. López.)

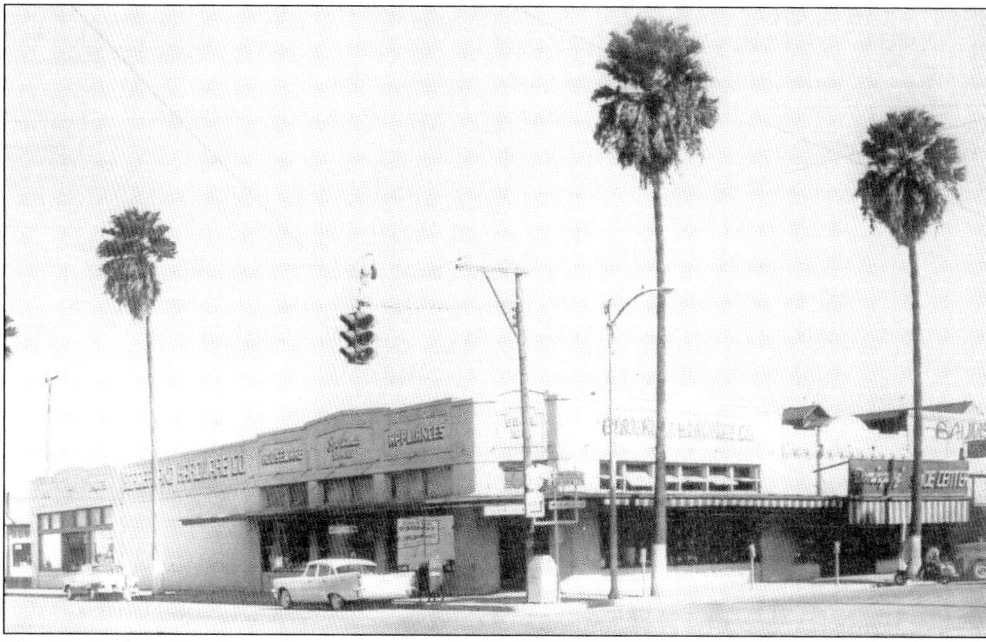

The Borderland Hardware Company, now in its 95th year, is the oldest hardware store in the Rio Grande Valley. It was first opened for business by owner Ellery E. "Jack" Johnson in 1919 on the southeast corner of US Business Highway 83 and Texas Avenue, as pictured above. Robert Eilers, pictured below at a Rio Grande Valley Livestock Show display in 1955, moved to Mercedes after serving in the US Army and began working at Borderland in 1949. He became Mercedes manager in 1955 and bought the store in 1969. In 1999, the family built a completely new 25,000-square-foot store on the northeast corner of US Business Highway 83 and Ohio Avenue, occupying almost the complete block. Robert and his wife, Loretta, along with their son Kenneth and his wife, Debbie, remain very active today in the family-owned operation. (Both, Eilers family.)

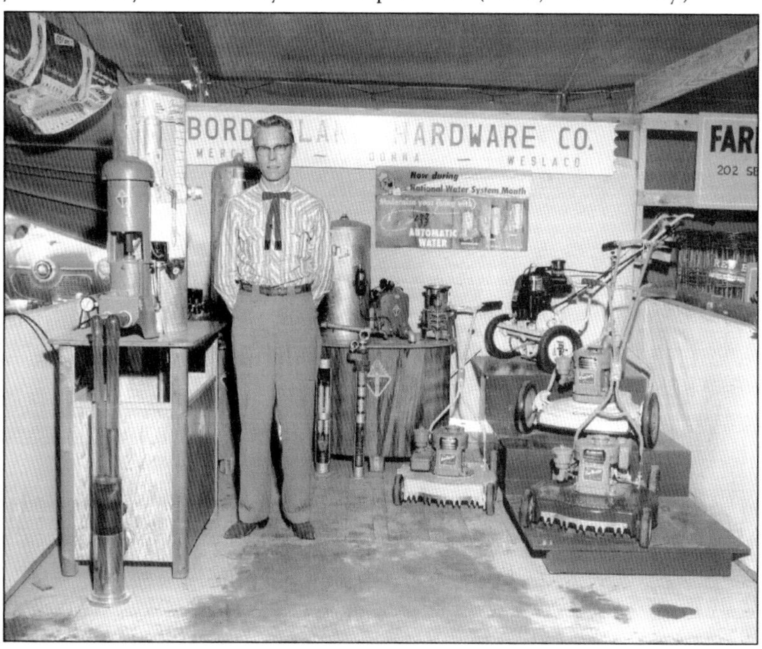

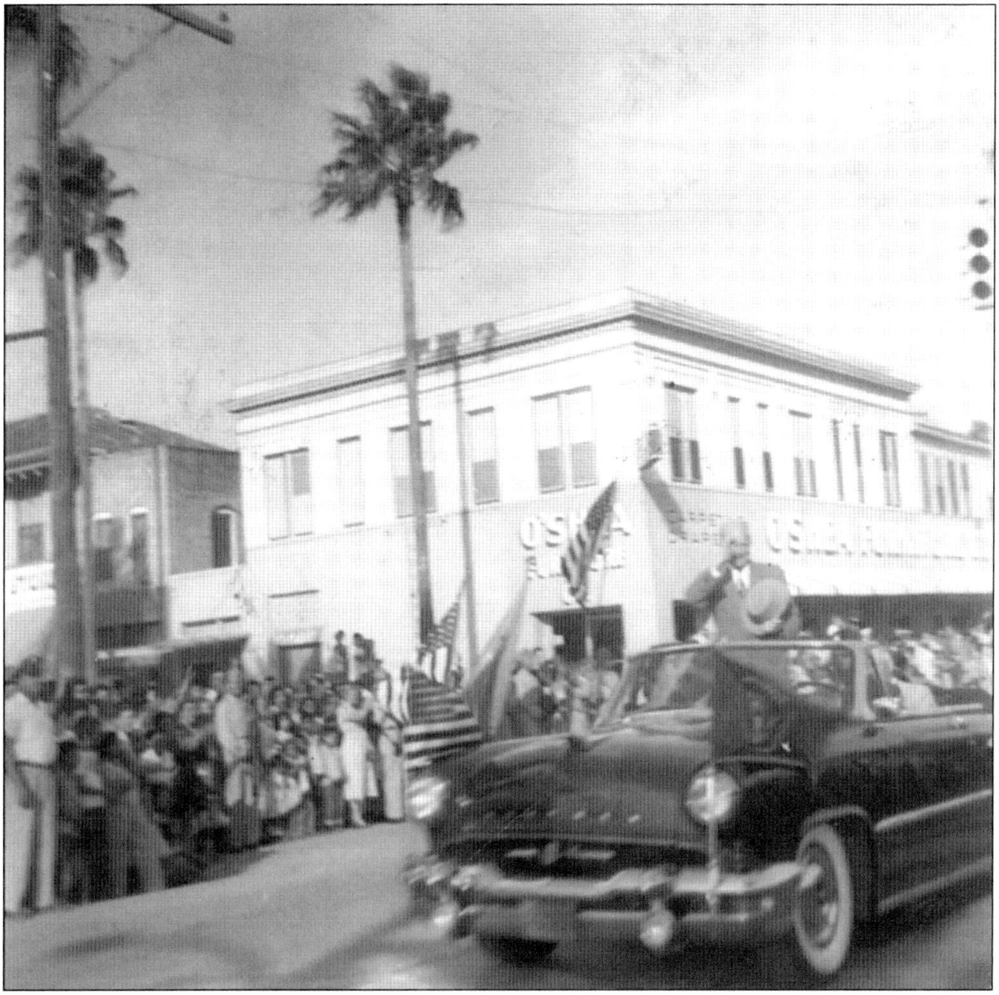

In October 1953, Pres. Dwight D. Eisenhower rode through Mercedes on his way to the dedication of Falcon Dam in neighboring Starr County. Hundreds of Mercedes citizens turned out to line US Business Highway 83 to get a glimpse of the president as he rode by in a red 1953 Lincoln Capri convertible. (Delia de León.)

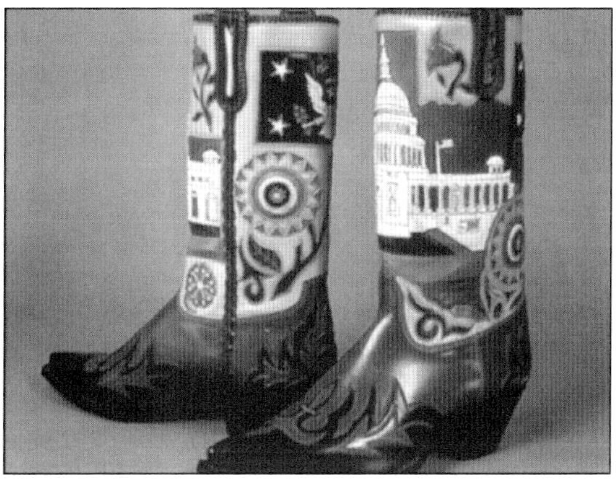

Zeferino and Eli Ríos, custom boot makers in Mercedes since 1935, presented these boots to President Eisenhower in 1954 to commemorate his visit to the Rio Grande Valley the year before. Their design includes the Capitol, the Great Seal of the United States, sunflowers from Eisenhower's home state of Kansas, and "Ike," the president's nickname. They are currently housed at the National Archives in Washington, DC. (National Archives.)

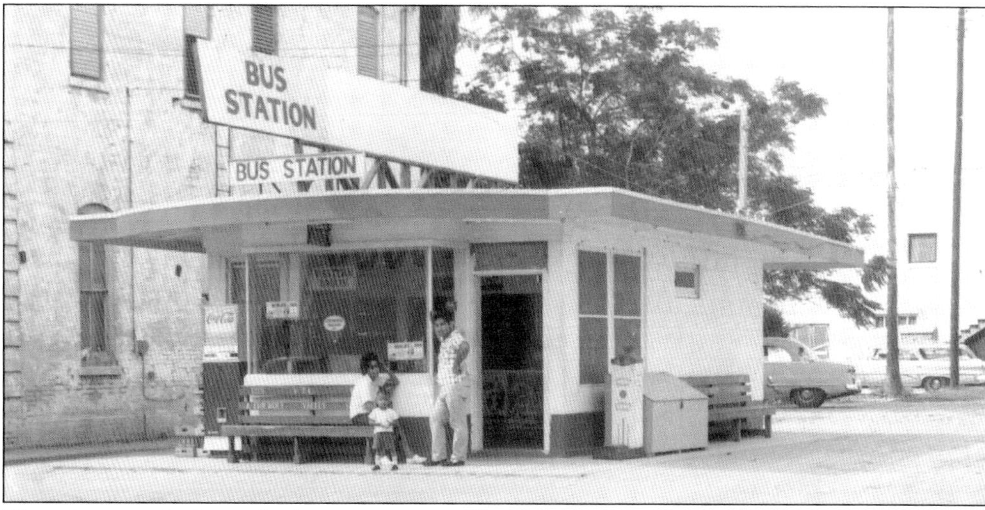

This photograph shows the bus station once located between the McAfee Insurance Building and the Hidalgo and Cameron County Water District No. 9 Building on US Business Highway 83. Valley Transit Company and Greyhound buses stopped here to pick up passengers traveling up and down the Valley as well as out-of-state. (Carolyn C. López.)

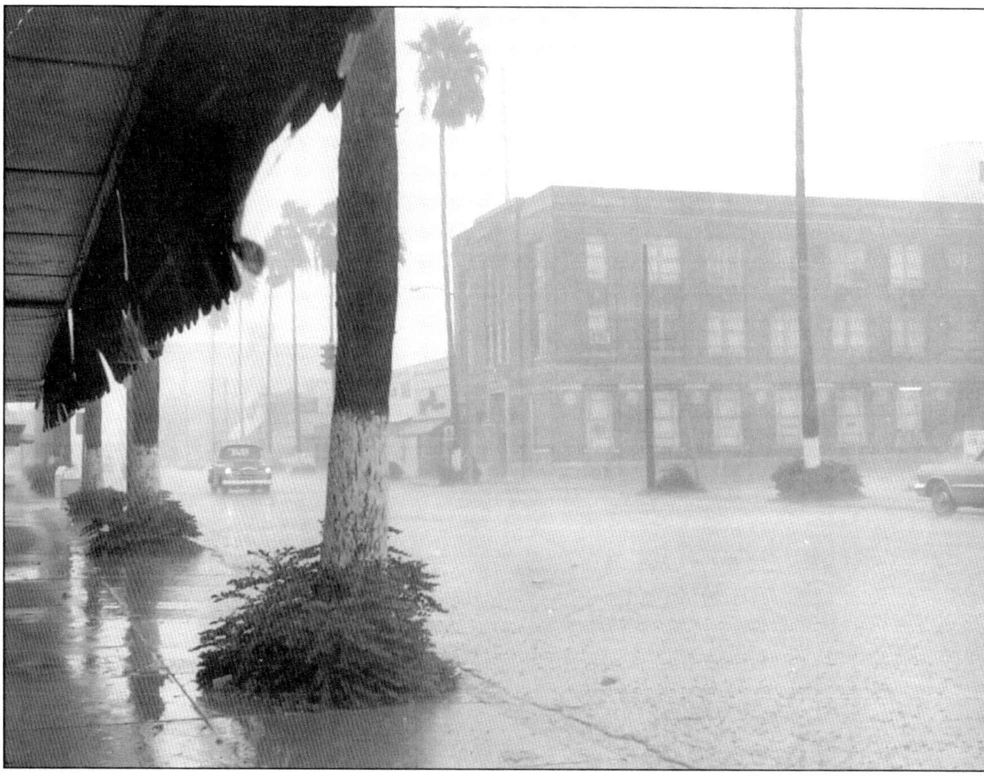

By the middle of the 20th century, Mercedes had nearly 11,000 inhabitants and was a busy, prosperous city. In addition to the surrounding thriving farms and ranches, the downtown area on both the north and the south side boasted many shops and businesses. But Mercedes did not always experience sunny days. This photograph captures the rains that accompanied Beulah, the 1967 hurricane that caused widespread flooding in the Valley. (*Mercedes Enterprise*.)

Four

Wars and Natural Disasters

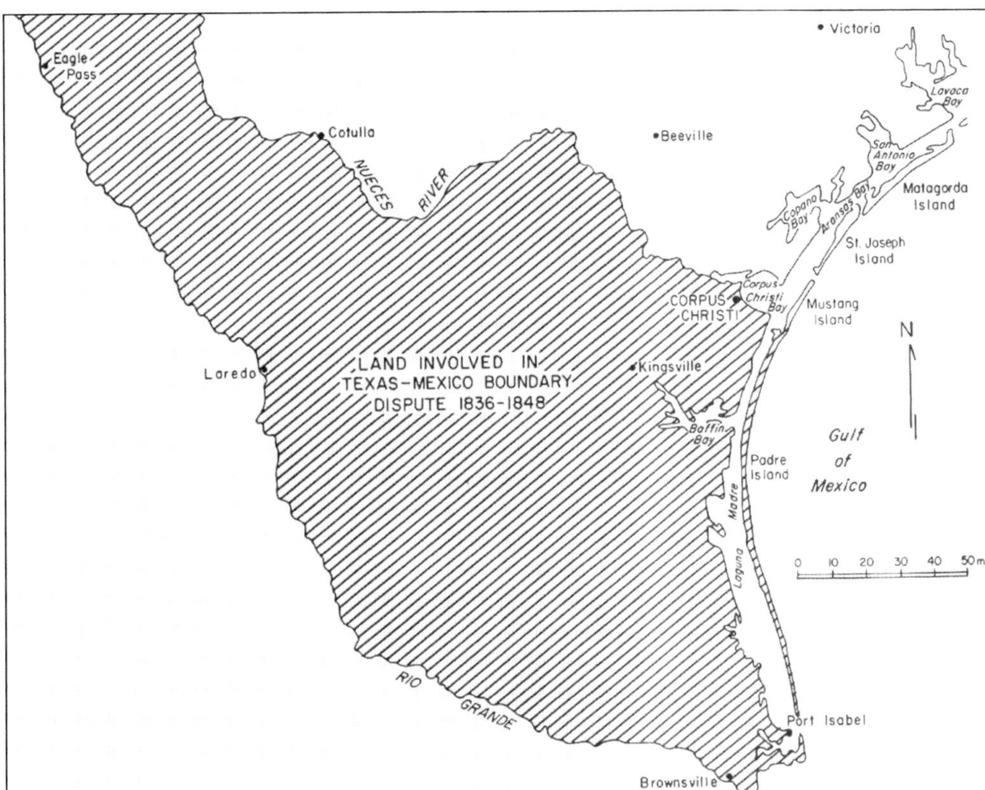

The map here shows the disputed territory called the Nueces Strip that resulted from Texas Independence in 1836 and led to the Mexican–American War. The land was claimed by both Mexico and the United States after it annexed Texas in 1845. People living in the Rio Grande Valley at that time were caught in a dangerous situation, particularly when the United States sent troops to secure the area. (National Archives.)

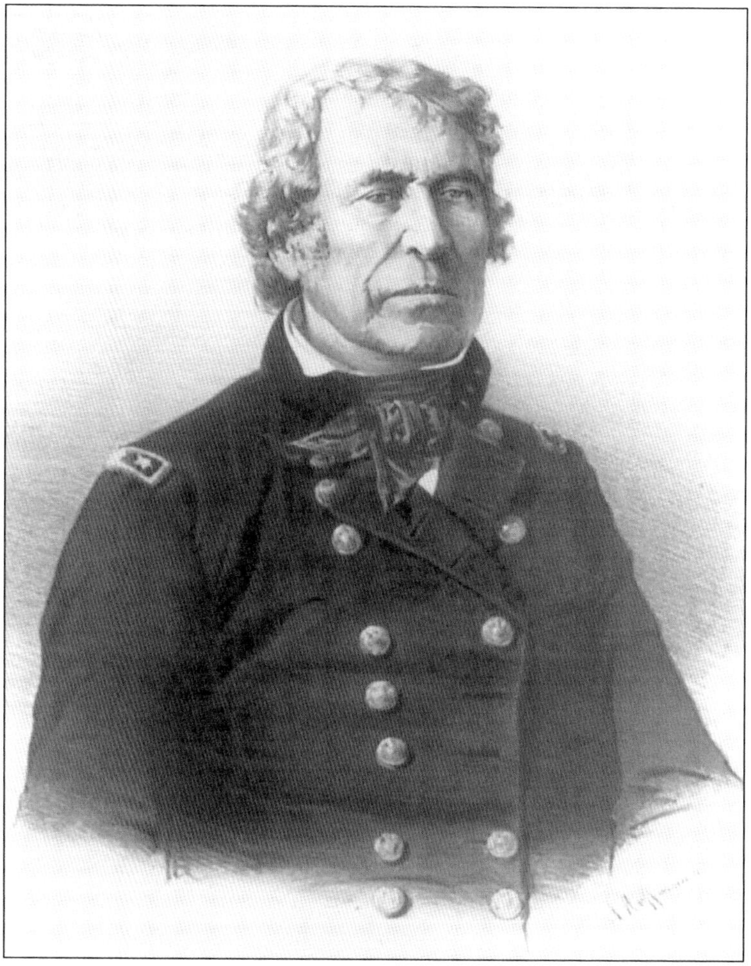

Gen. Zachary Taylor, pictured here, was sent to Texas by Pres. James K. Polk. In March 1846, Taylor marched to the Rio Grande, a move that was interpreted by Mexican forces as an invasion of their country. The Battle of Palo Alto near Brownsville in May 1846 was the first official battle of the Mexican–American War, followed soon after by the nearby Resaca de la Palma engagement. (National Archives.)

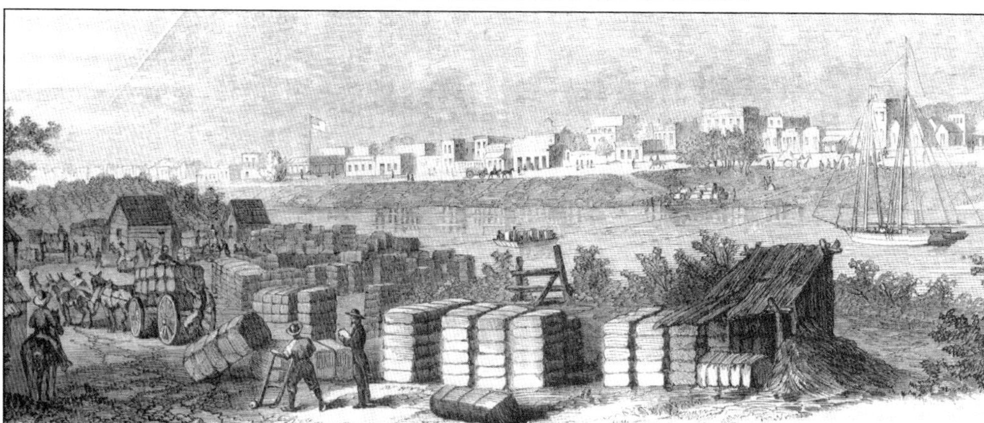

The lower Rio Grande became important during the Civil War in 1863 as the only waterway available for the export of Confederate cotton. This sketch by L. Avery in *Frank Leslie's Illustrated Newspaper* shows the cotton being ferried across to Mexico for transport to British ships trading arms for cotton. Involvement in trade by Anglo-Americans during this time caused increased interest in the Rio Grande Valley. (Library of Congress.)

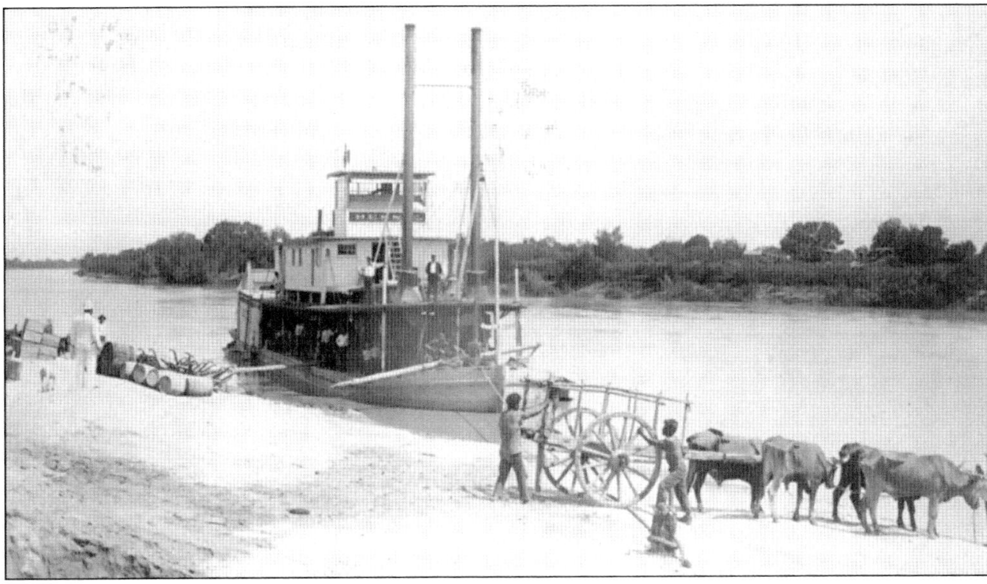

In the late 1800s, steamboats became important to the Valley in conducting trade with Mexico and with European countries. They provided another means of transporting goods up and down the Rio Grande Valley besides by mule train. Steamboat *Bessie*, pictured here, was the last of the Mifflin Kenedy–Richard King Rio Grande shipping fleet. It made its final trip on the river in 1902. (National Archives.)

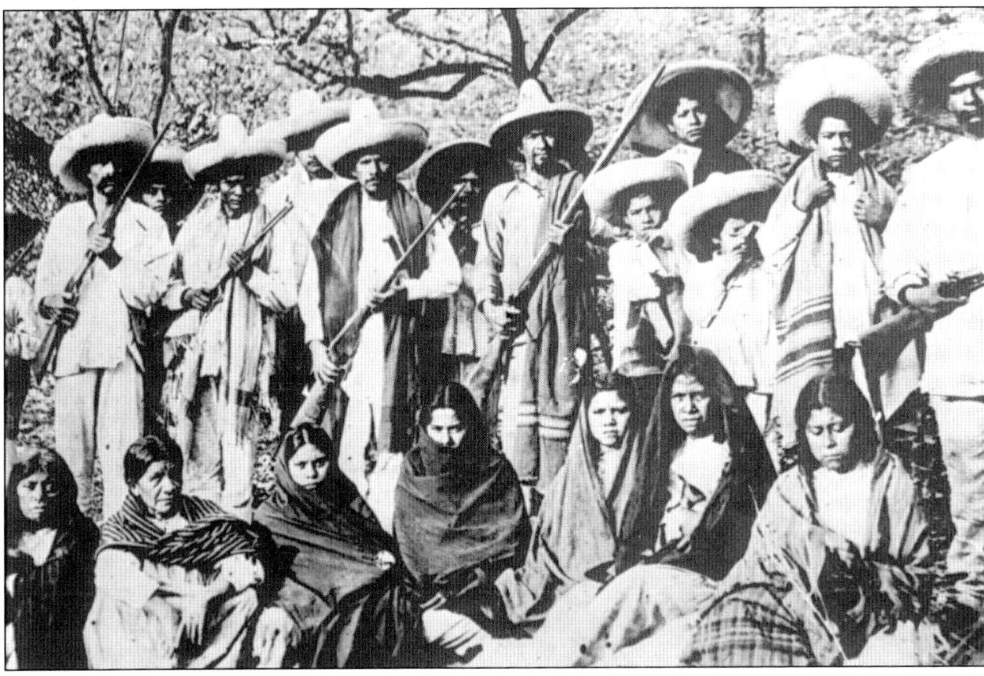

After years of social turmoil in Mexico, the Mexican Revolution broke out in 1910. By then, the Rio Grande Valley had established several towns, including Mercedes, founded in 1907. Between 1914 and 1918, various Mexican revolutionary factions raided on the US side, usually attempting to get food and other supplies needed to conduct their war. Many Mercedes and other Valley residents lived in terror of spillover violence from Mexico. (National Archives.)

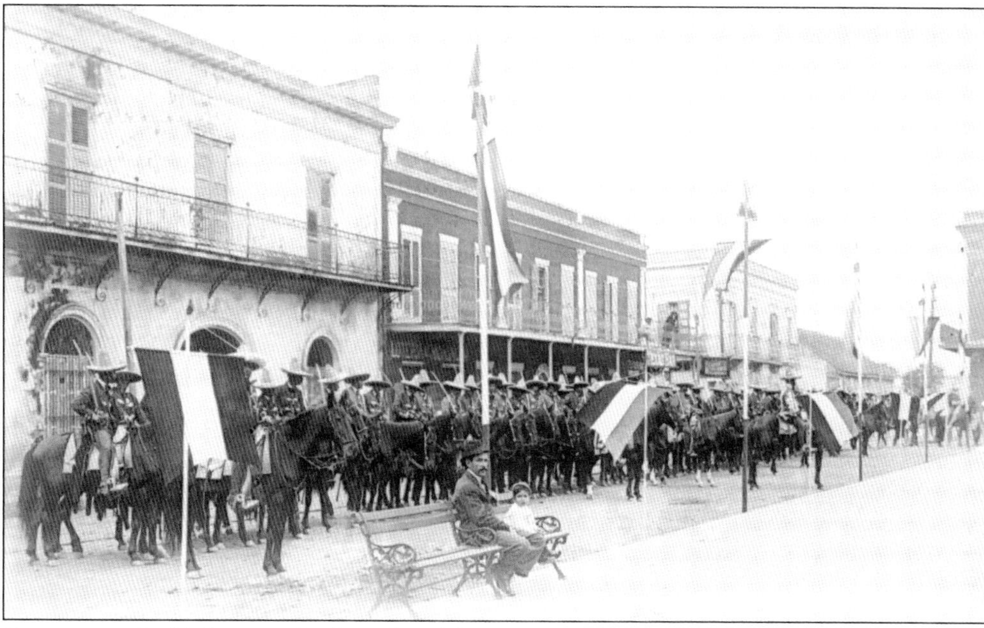

Tensions in the Valley grew higher when Mexican general Lucio Blanco's revolutionaries took Matamoros on June 4, 1913, just across the river from Brownsville and only 39 miles away from Mercedes. Some Mercedes residents wrote memoirs later describing their trip to Matamoros to see the executions by firing squad of the captured federal soldiers. Many people fled Mexico and came to the Valley seeking refuge from the war. (National Archives.)

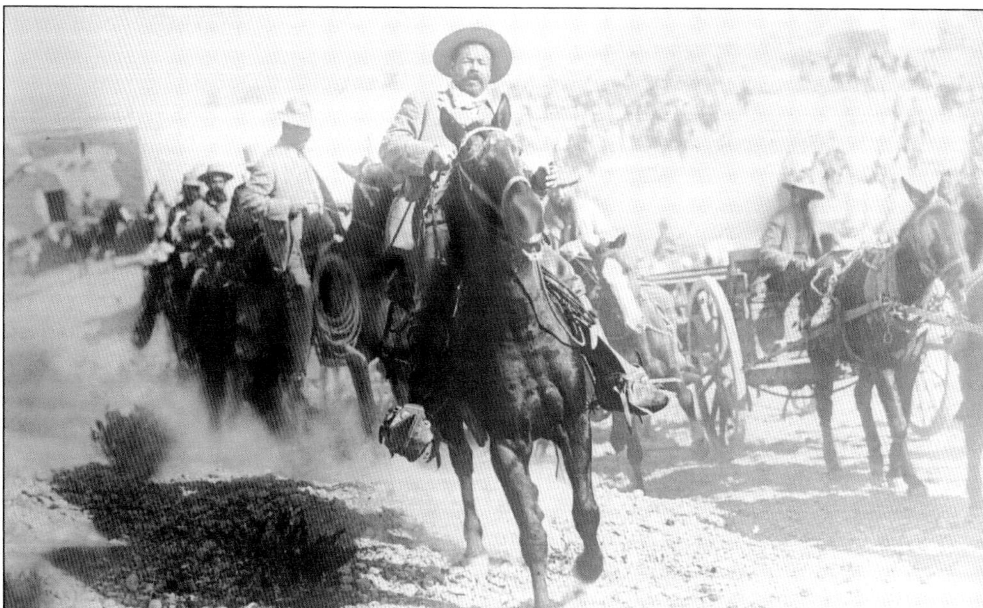

When Mexican revolutionary caudillo Pancho Villa crossed into US territory in March 1916 and attacked Columbus, New Mexico, over an arms deal gone bad, US residents along the southern border began clamoring Washington to send troops for their protection. By August 1916, an estimated 117,000 national guardsmen were stationed along the border in Texas, New Mexico, Arizona, and California. (National Archives.)

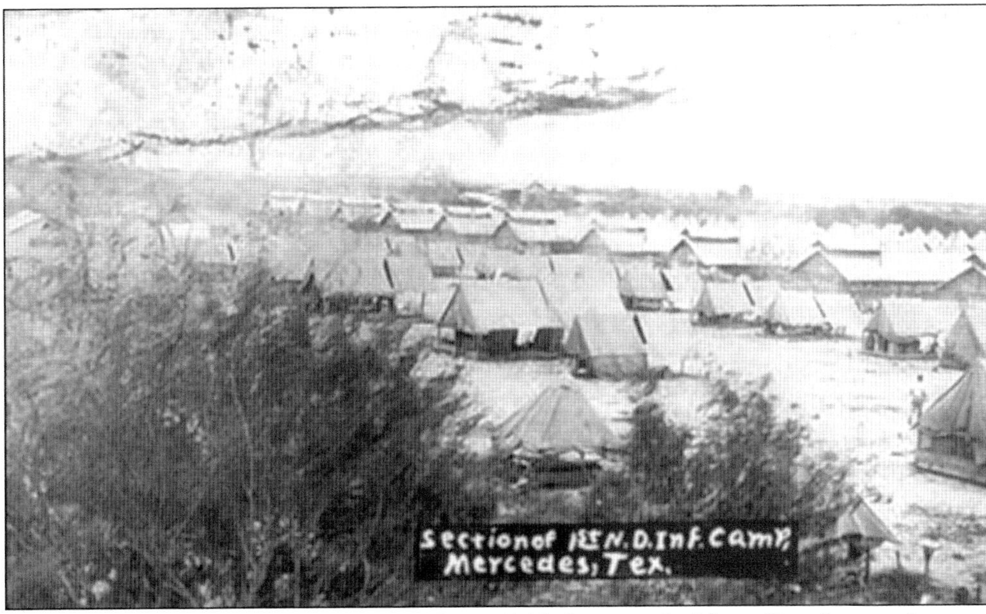

Two Army camps were set up near Mercedes in 1916. One was the Llano Grande camp between Weslaco and Mercedes on both north and south sides of now US Business Highway 83. The other was Camp Mercedes, shown in this photograph, the large bulk of which was located east of the Mercedes Main Canal and south of Tenth Street. (Library of Congress.)

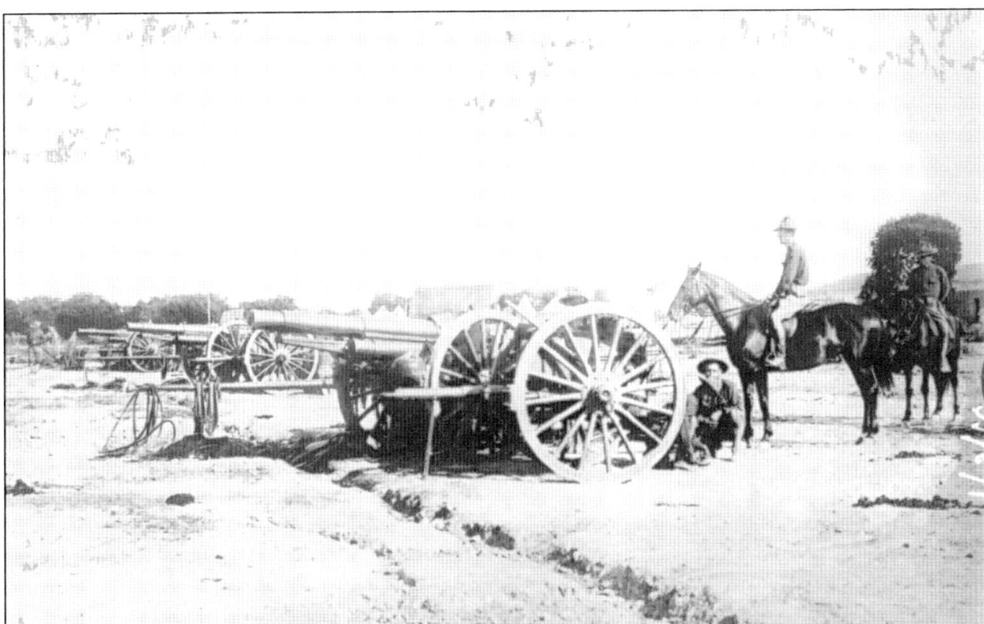

The guardsmen assigned to the Valley camps trained in all aspects of warfare available at that time including artillery fire as seen here, something which would serve them well when the United States entered World War I in Europe in 1917. During this time of the Mexican Border Service, motor vehicles and aircraft were first used in the US military forces. (National Archives.)

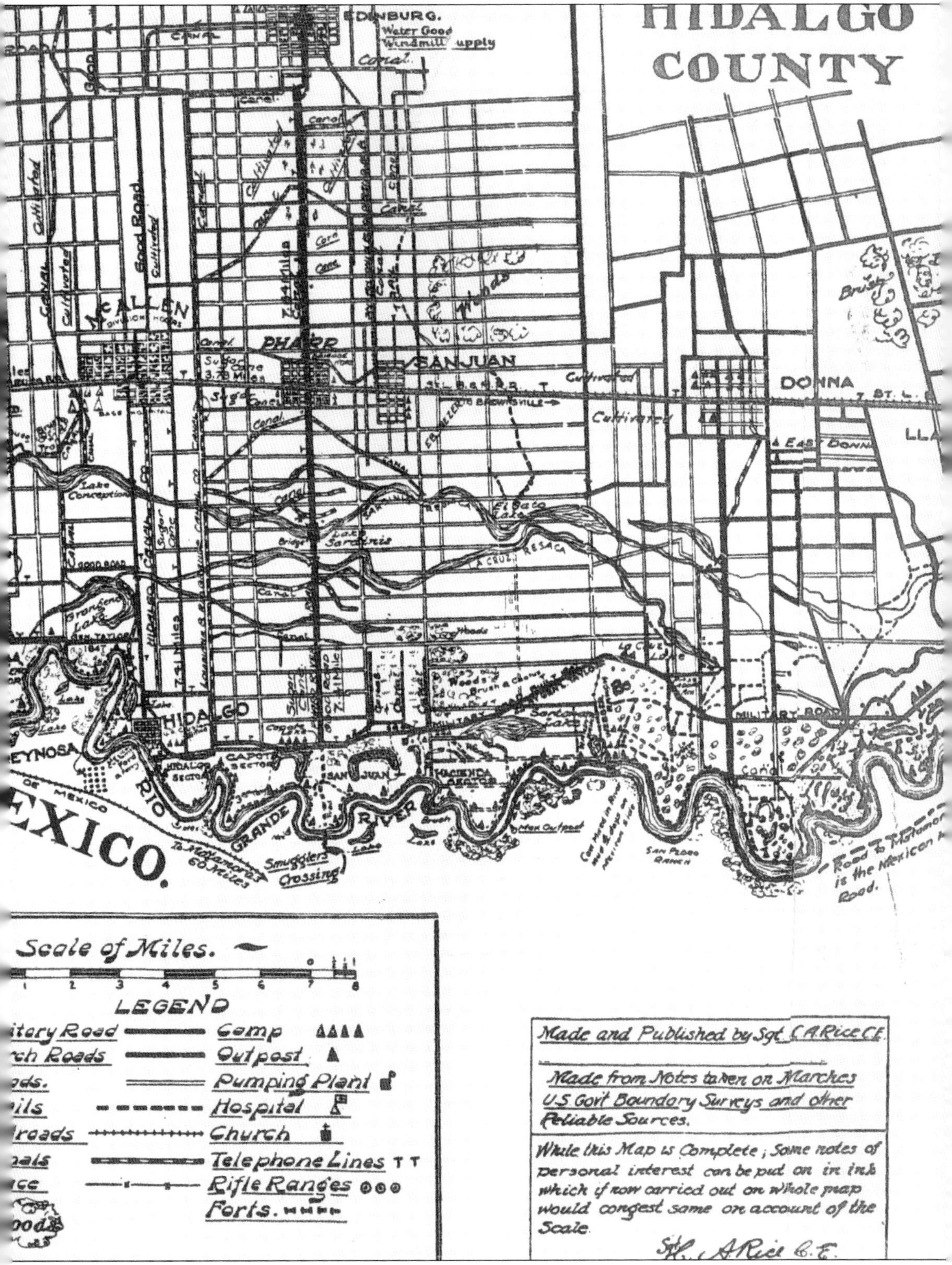

HIDALGO COUNTY
EDINBURG.
Water Good Windmill supply
McALLEN
PHARR
SAN JUAN
DONNA
HIDALGO
EAST DONNA
Lake Conception
Lake Sardinis
El Gato Lake
La Cruz Resaca
La Cruz Lake
Bridge
MILITARY ROAD
HIDALGO SECTOR
CAPOTE SECTOR
SAN JUAN
HACIENDA SECTOR
RIO GRANDE RIVER
Smugglers Crossing
Mex Outpost
SAN PEDRO RANCH
To Matamoras 60 Miles
Road to Matamoras is the Mexican Road.
EXICO.
Woods
Brush
Cultivated
Good Road
Canal
Sugar Cane
7.41 Miles
Scale of Miles.
1 2 3 4 5 6 7 8
LEGEND
Camp
Outpost
Pumping Plant
Hospital
Church
Telephone Lines
Rifle Ranges
Forts.
Made and Published by Sgt. C.A.Rice C.E.
Made from Notes taken on Marches U.S. Gov't Boundary Surveys and other Reliable Sources.
While this Map is Complete; Some notes of personal interest can be put on in ink which if now carried out on whole map would congest same on account of the Scale.

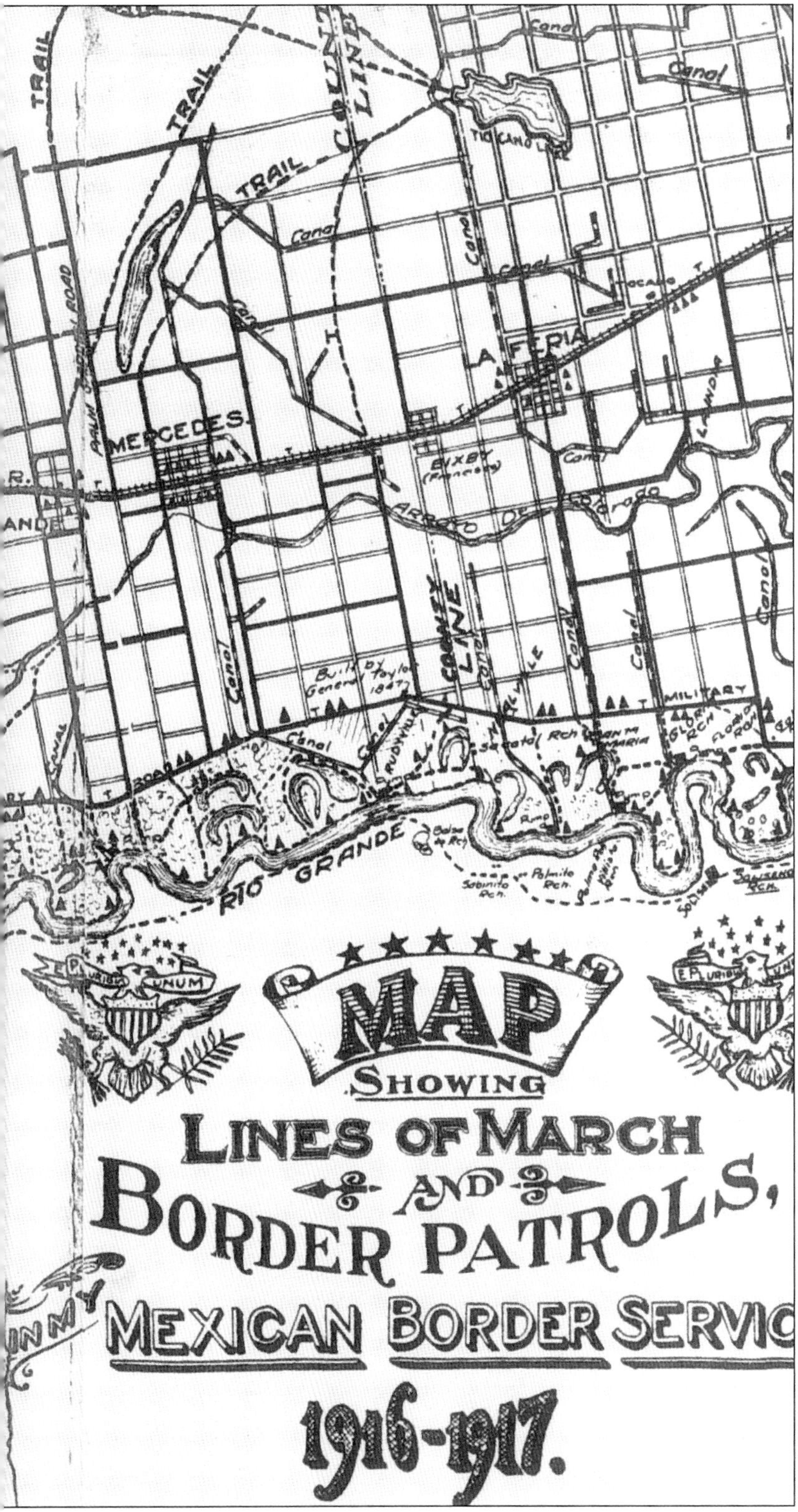

Shown here is part of a 1917 hand-drawn map prepared by Sgt. Charles A. Rice based on field notes taken while out on patrol with the US Army while stationed in the Rio Grande Valley. The map shows the winding Rio Grande forming the boundary between Mexico and the United States. The present-day towns of McAllen, Pharr, San Juan, Donna, Mercedes, and La Feria can be seen along the track of the St. Louis, Brownsville and Mexico Railway. The Military Highway is labeled as having been built by Gen. Zachary Taylor in 1847, but many historians dispute this statement due to lack of documented evidence. In his Valley campaign during the Mexican–American War, Taylor used steamships and the road running south of the river to transport his troops and supplies upriver to Camargo. (Hidalgo County Historical Society.)

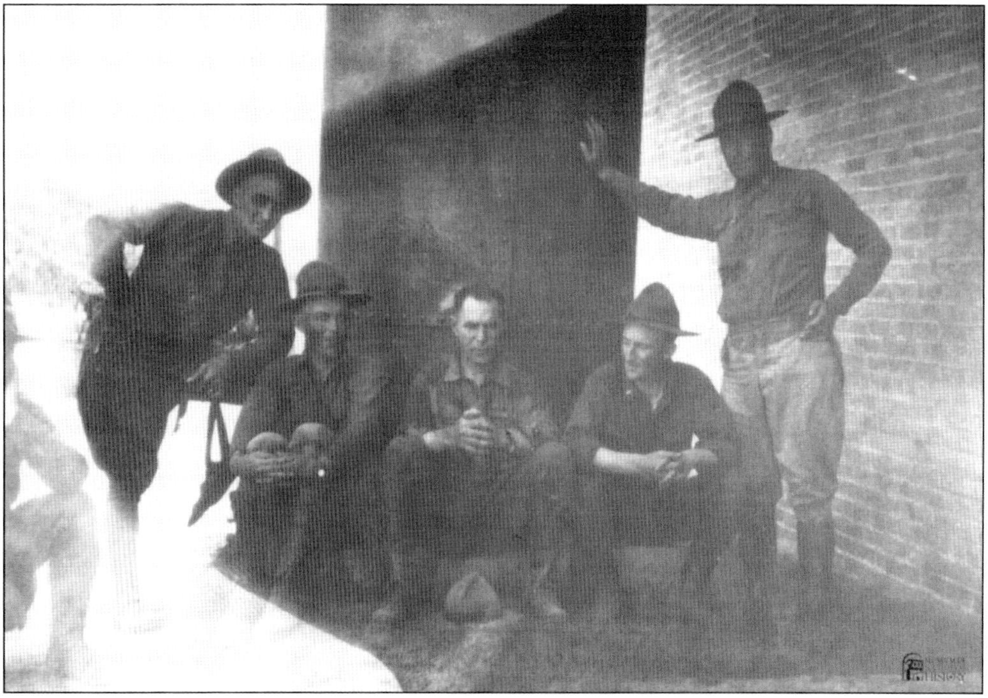

Soldiers from Camp Mercedes are pictured stationed at the Toluca Ranch. The Toluca Ranch south of Mercedes was considered a likely target for a Mexican raid during that era, and it was raided on four separate occasions. There were several skirmishes with Mexican "bandits" in the Valley in the early 1900s, but no major invasions by Mexicans ever occurred. (MSTH.)

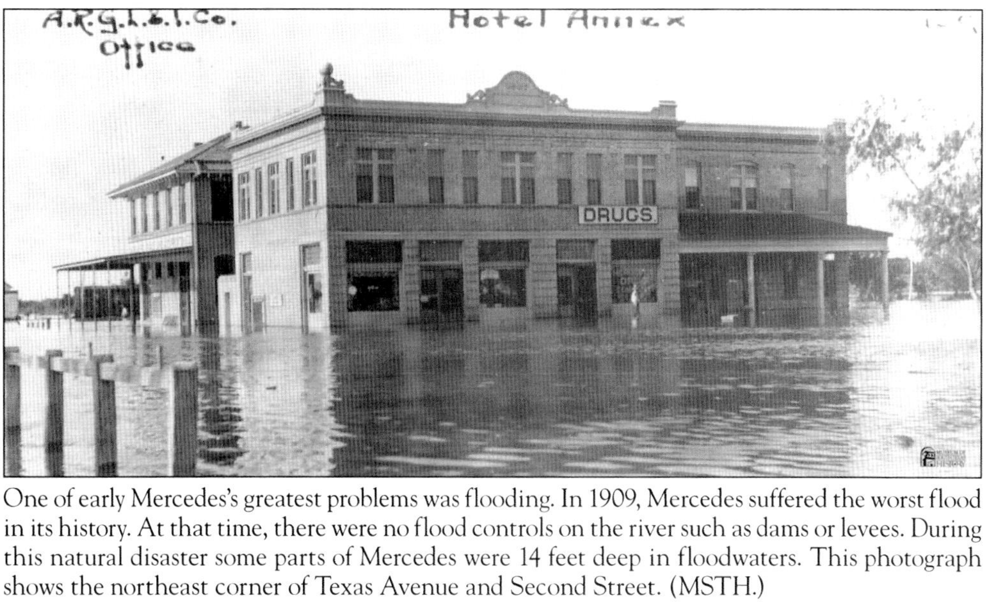

One of early Mercedes's greatest problems was flooding. In 1909, Mercedes suffered the worst flood in its history. At that time, there were no flood controls on the river such as dams or levees. During this natural disaster some parts of Mercedes were 14 feet deep in floodwaters. This photograph shows the northeast corner of Texas Avenue and Second Street. (MSTH.)

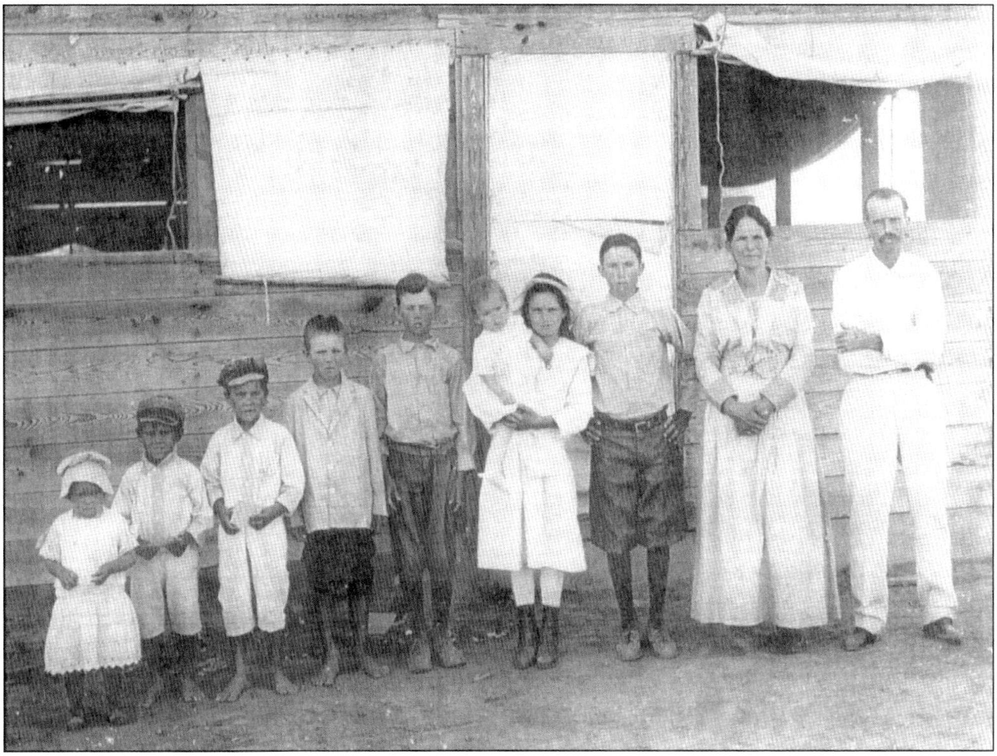

The Howell family is pictured in 1916 standing outside a community building on North Missouri Avenue that was used for church services. From left to right are Mary, Henry Joseph, William, Albert, Jacinto, Joseph Henry Jr. (in arms), Pauline, Casimiro, María Howell, and Joseph Henry Howell Sr. Tragically, little Mary died in 1918 during an influenza pandemic. Both influenza and smallpox took a deadly toll in the Valley during the early 1900s. (Eddie Howell Sr.)

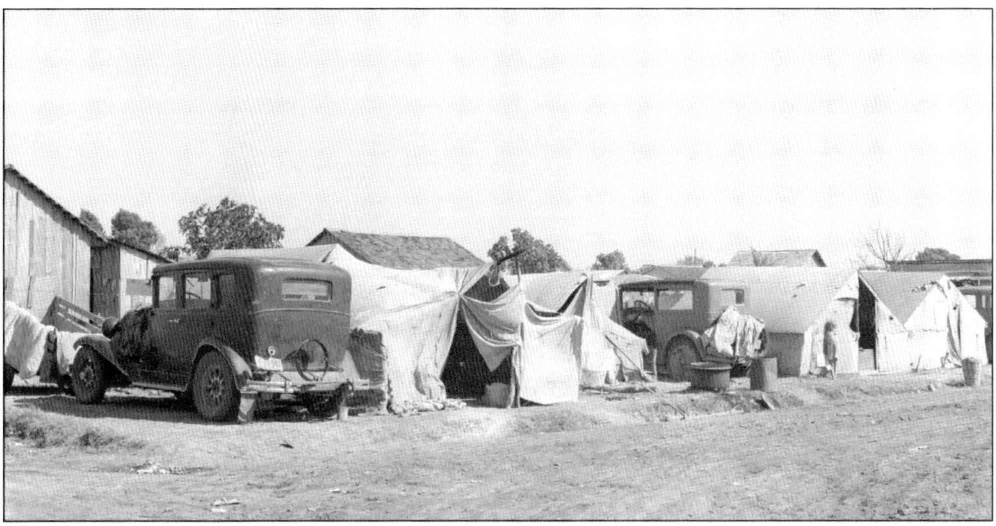

The Great Depression hit the Rio Grande Valley with a vengeance. In Mercedes, many businesses failed and farmers went broke. Many people from other states came to the Valley looking for work and often clashed with locals that also needed work. Tent cities like this one in Mercedes in 1939 could be found all over the Valley. (Library of Congress.)

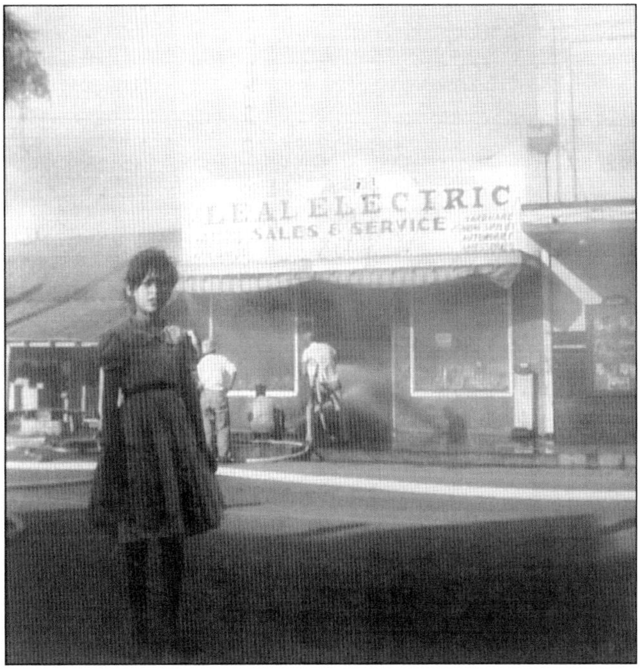

Mercedes businesses also suffered devastating fires such as this one on North Texas Avenue when Leal's Electric business burned down in 1954. The girl is unidentified, but Alberto Arteaga, manager of the Rio Theater next door to Leal's Electric, captured her frightened look in this photograph. (Sylvia Arteaga Calles.)

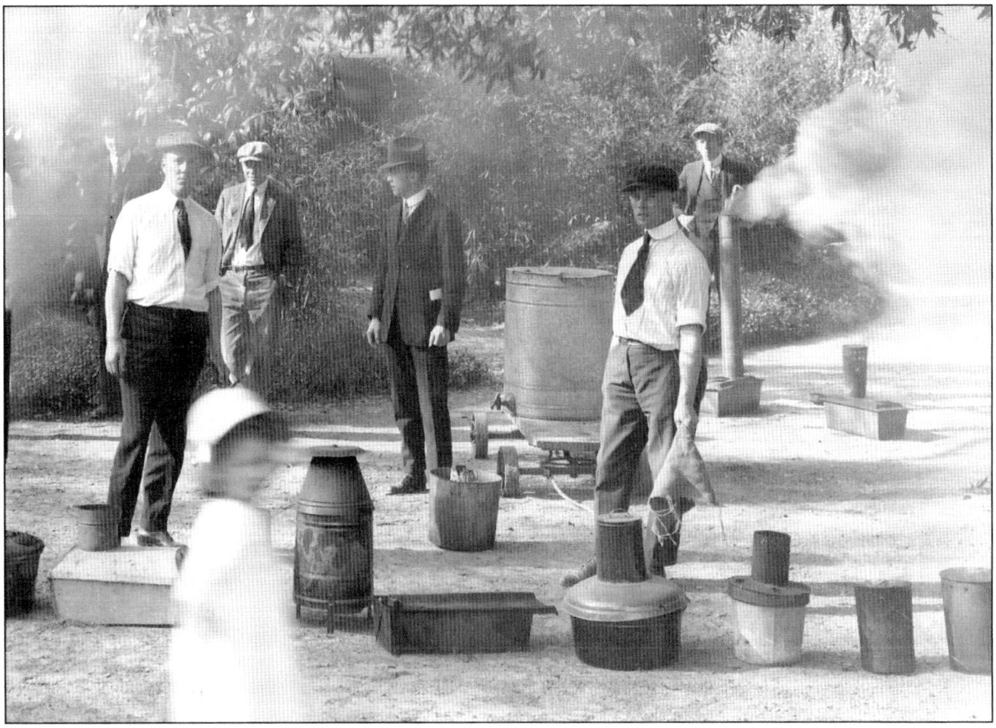

Unidentified persons in this photograph prepare smoke pots to protect a citrus crop during an anticipated hard freeze in 1920. Smoke pots contained kerosene and were placed between the rows of grapefruit or orange trees to keep them warm during nights of low temperatures. A severe freeze could destroy the citrus crop and ruin agricultural investments in a single night of low temperatures. (Weslaco Museum.)

Five

The Rio Grande Valley Livestock Show

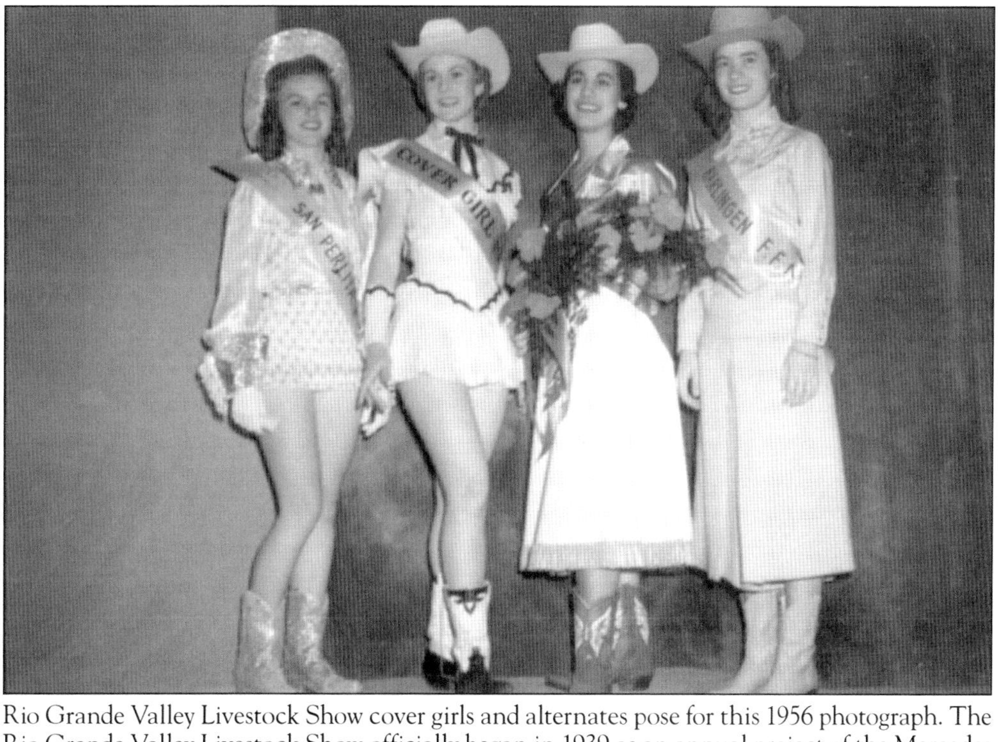

Rio Grande Valley Livestock Show cover girls and alternates pose for this 1956 photograph. The Rio Grande Valley Livestock Show officially began in 1939 as an annual project of the Mercedes Chamber of Commerce in efforts to promote livestock and poultry production. Although the livestock show began in Mercedes, it quickly included Cameron, Willacy, Starr, and Hidalgo Counties in the project. (Rio Grande Valley Livestock Show Museum.)

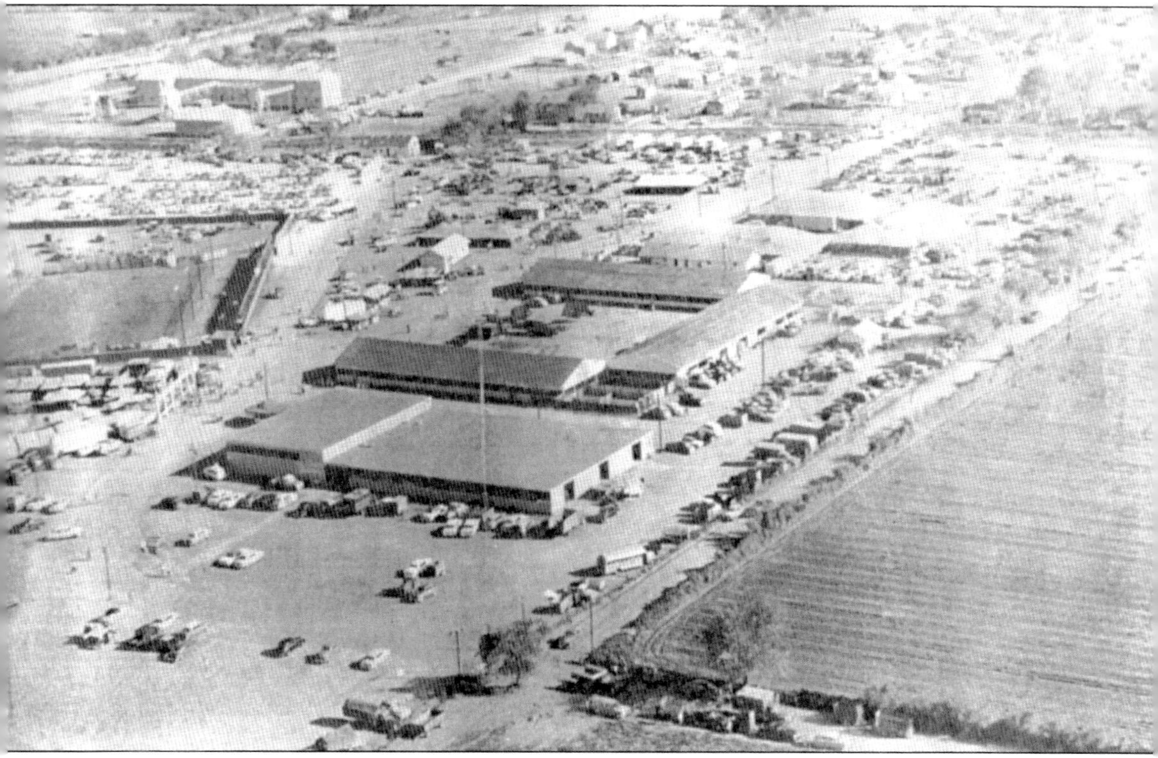

An aerial view of the Rio Grande Valley Livestock Show grounds covering more than 100 acres at the north end of Texas Avenue was taken in 1955 when many metal and wood buildings were used to replace tents and other less durable structures. With more than 1,000 volunteers and 4,000 exhibitors expected, the 2014 show was a far cry from the earliest shows. The earliest documented show was a one-day affair in 1913 held at the Mercedes Power Plant, a two-story building located on Second Street (US Business Highway 83) and the Main Canal. It was so popular that the next year, in 1914, it was a three-day event with many exhibits of livestock and agricultural products, lectures, a US Cavalry sham battle, and boat rides on the Main Canal. It did not become an annual event, however, until 1939. Unfortunately, in 1965, a fire destroyed much of the early records of the show, and photographs such as this one have slowly been recovered from other sources. (Mercedes ISD.)

Sun Valley Horse Show Queen Pip Setter and her horse Rex pose for a photograph in 1964. The Rio Grande Livestock Show grounds host many events other than the annual March livestock show. The Sun Valley Horse Show is a Mercedes High School FFA Club fundraiser that accepts Valley-wide competitors in various events. Many other horse shows are held annually at the livestock show grounds. (Weslaco Museum.)

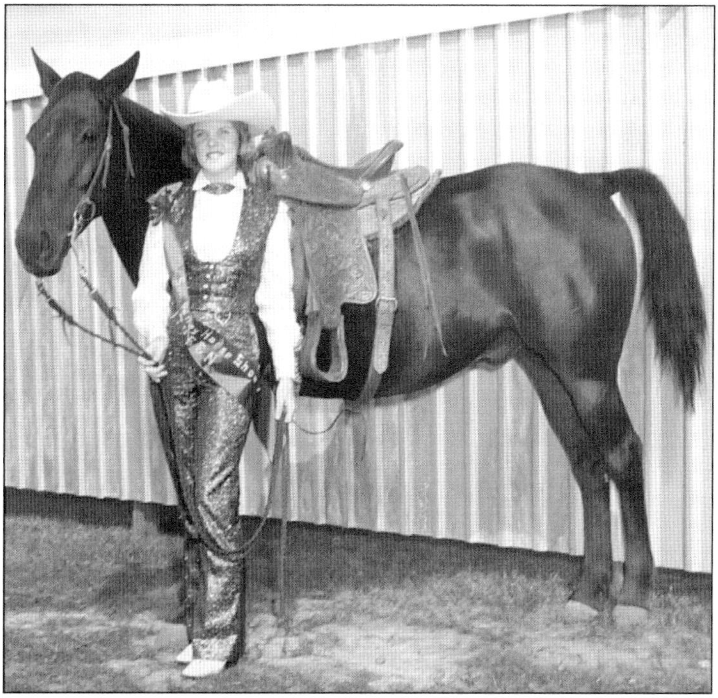

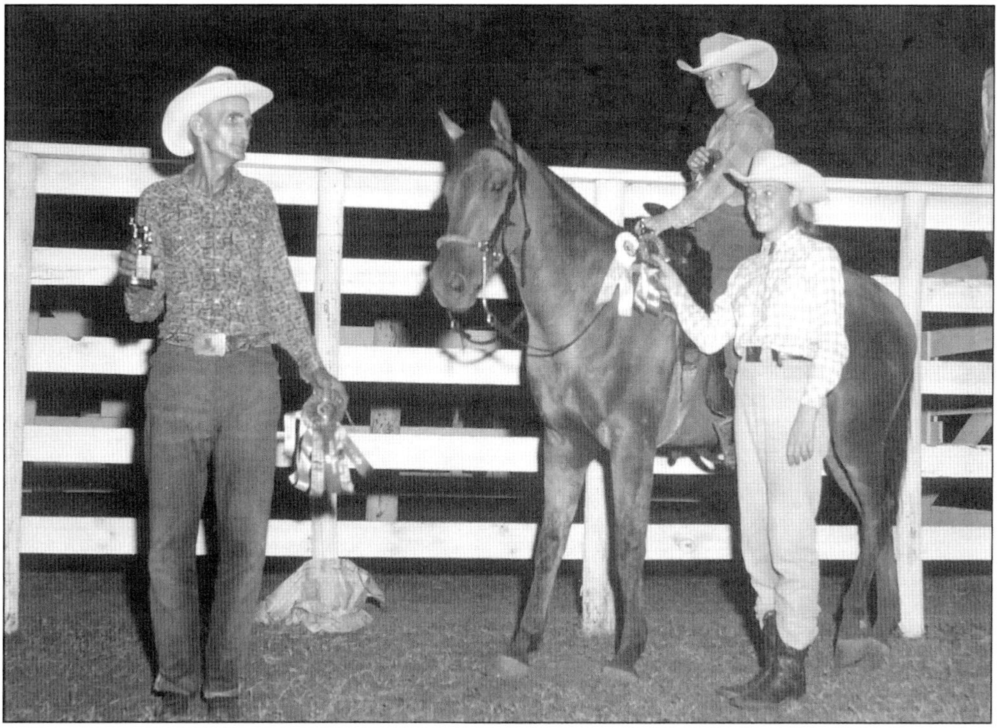

Thomas Treasure (left) awards the "Best Cowboy Trophy" to 12-year-old Kenny Reger mounted on his horse Mr. Red, which is held by an unidentified girl, in the Sun Valley Horse Show held October 1964 at the Rio Grande Valley Livestock Show grounds. Competitive events included barrel races, stake races, pole bending races, and children's showmanship. (Weslaco Museum.)

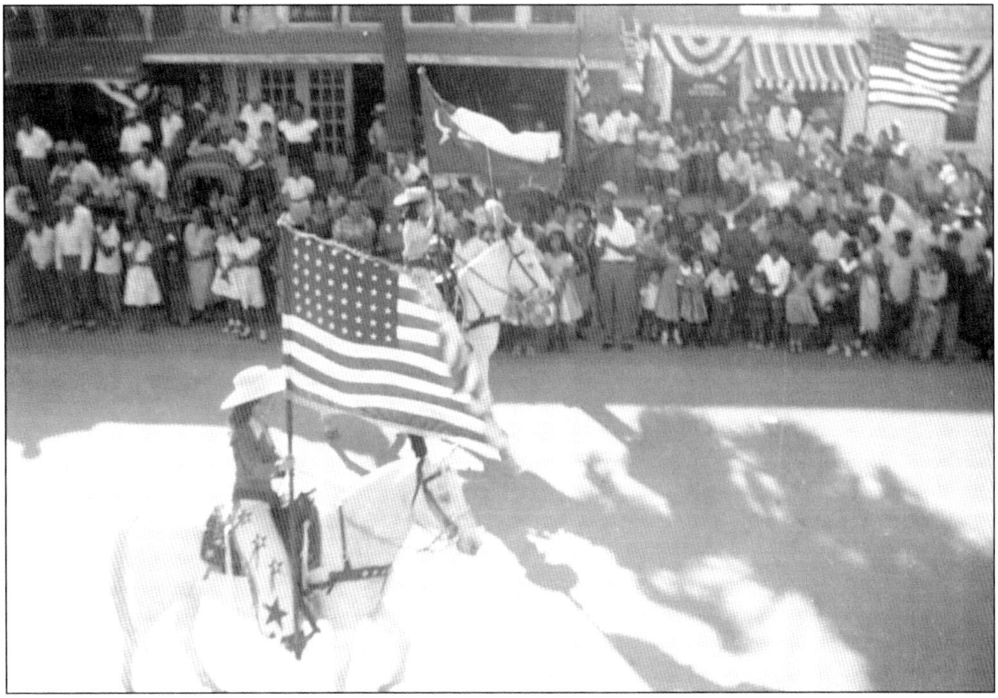

The traditional opening of the Rio Grande Valley Livestock Show is the parade held on the first day of the show. It always includes decorated floats, trail riders from various horseman's associations, marching school bands, cover girl candidates, show officials, city officials, local clubs and organizations either walking or riding floats, and singing or acting stars invited to perform. (Sylvia Arteaga Calles.)

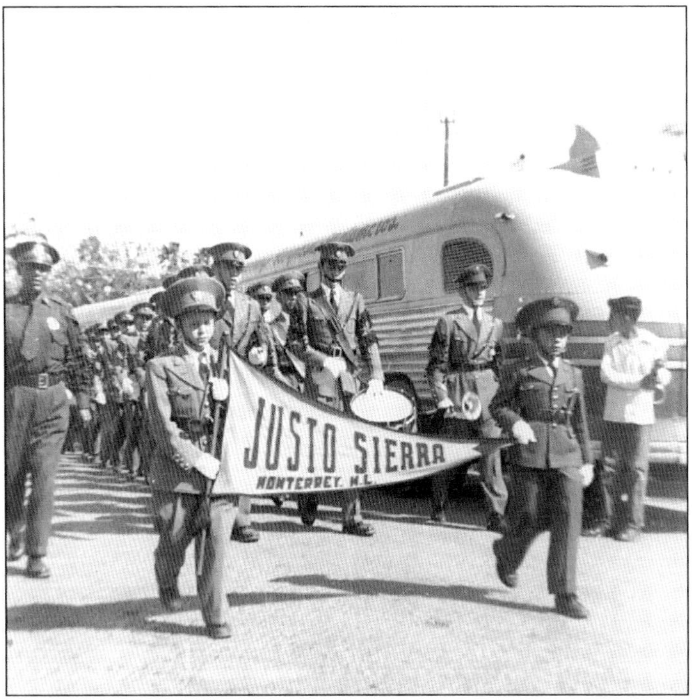

A guest band from the Justo Sierra Boy's Orphanage and Military School in Monterrey, Nuevo Leon, Mexico marches in the Rio Grande Valley Livestock Show Parade in March 1956. Special arrangements were made to allow members of the school to attend the livestock show, and local families agreed to house the younger students in order to help defray lodging costs. (Sylvia Arteaga Calles.)

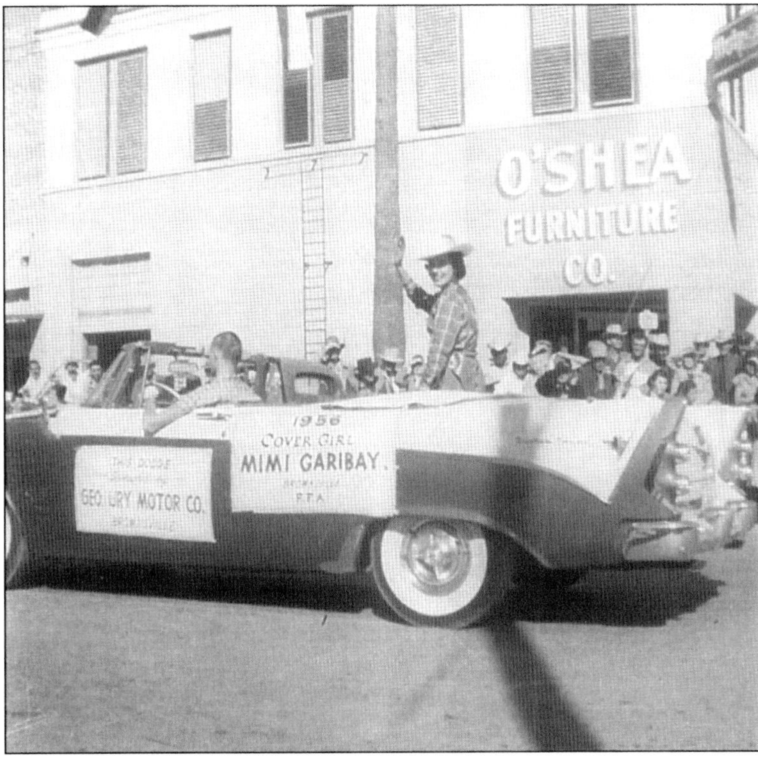

Mimi Garibay, 1956 cover girl winner sponsored by the Brownsville FFA organization rides in a 1956 Dodge convertible in the Rio Grande Valley Livestock Show Parade as it wends its way up Texas Avenue to end at the show grounds on North Texas Avenue. (Sylvia Arteaga Calles.)

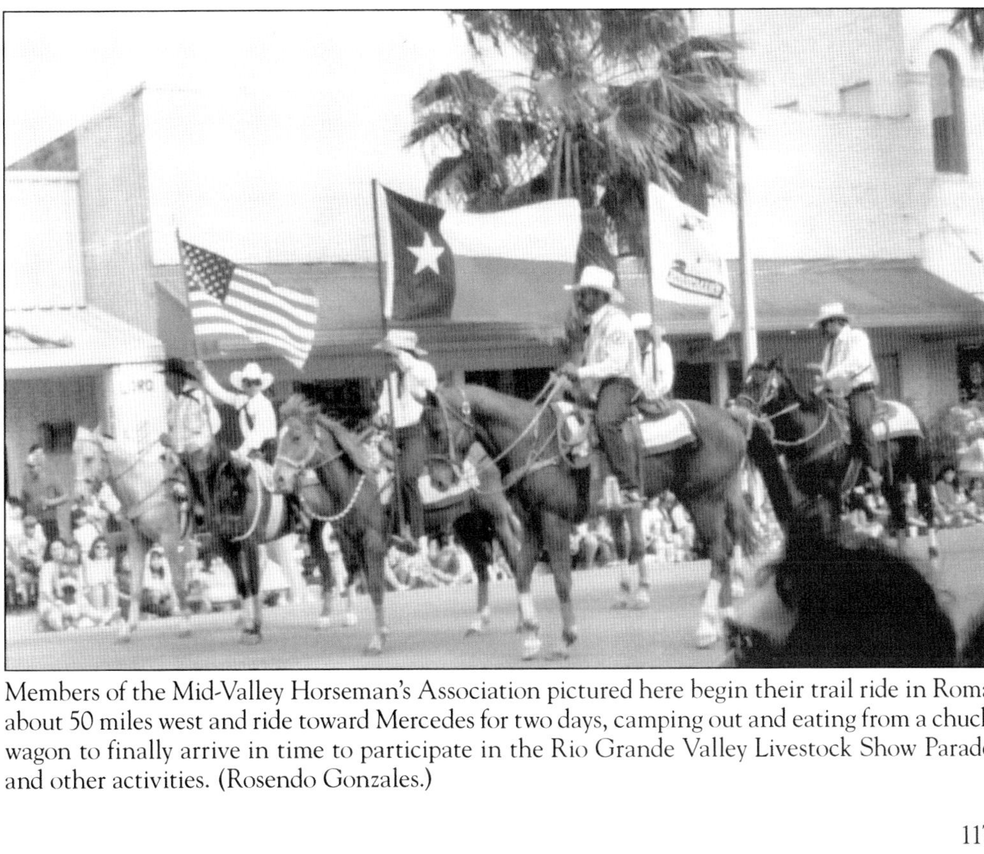

Members of the Mid-Valley Horseman's Association pictured here begin their trail ride in Roma about 50 miles west and ride toward Mercedes for two days, camping out and eating from a chuck wagon to finally arrive in time to participate in the Rio Grande Valley Livestock Show Parade and other activities. (Rosendo Gonzales.)

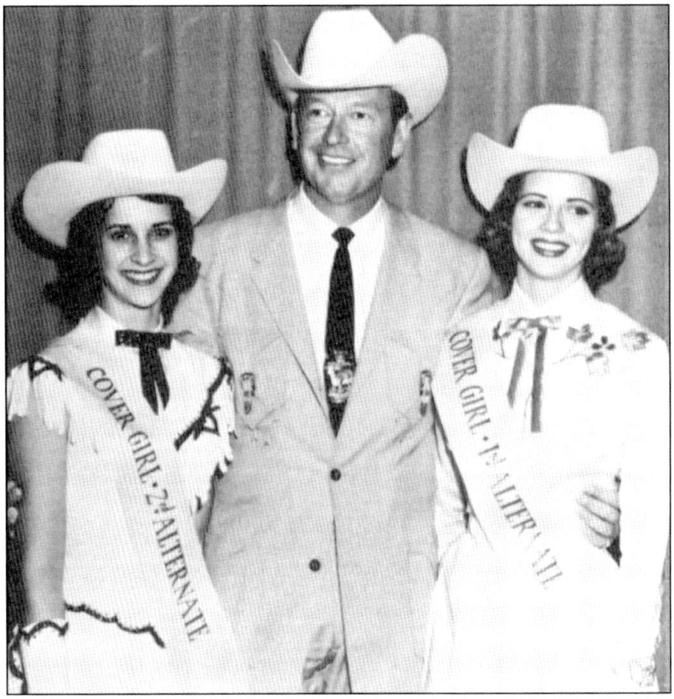

Singer, film actor, and songwriter Rex Allen (in the center) poses with 1962 cover girl alternates. At left is second alternate Sherrie Gallaway, and at right is first alternate Pam Knapp. Rex Allen, called the Arizona Cowboy, was well known for starring in 19 of Hollywood's Western movies with Buddy Ebsen and Slim Pickens as his sidekicks. (Mercedes ISD.)

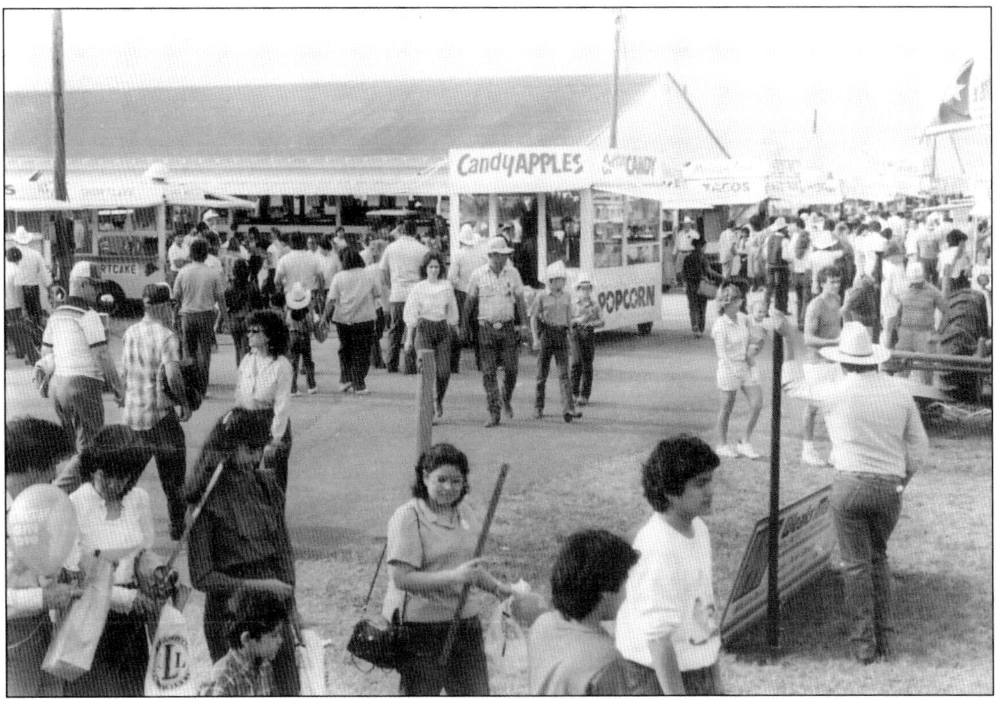

Enjoying the various food booths available at the Rio Grande Valley Livestock Show are many show visitors. Thousands of local visitors as well as visitors from other states and even other countries visit the Rio Grande Valley Livestock Show every year. It is considered one of the Top Ten Shows in Texas and recently draws close to 200,000 visitors annually. (Rio Grande Valley Livestock Show Museum.)

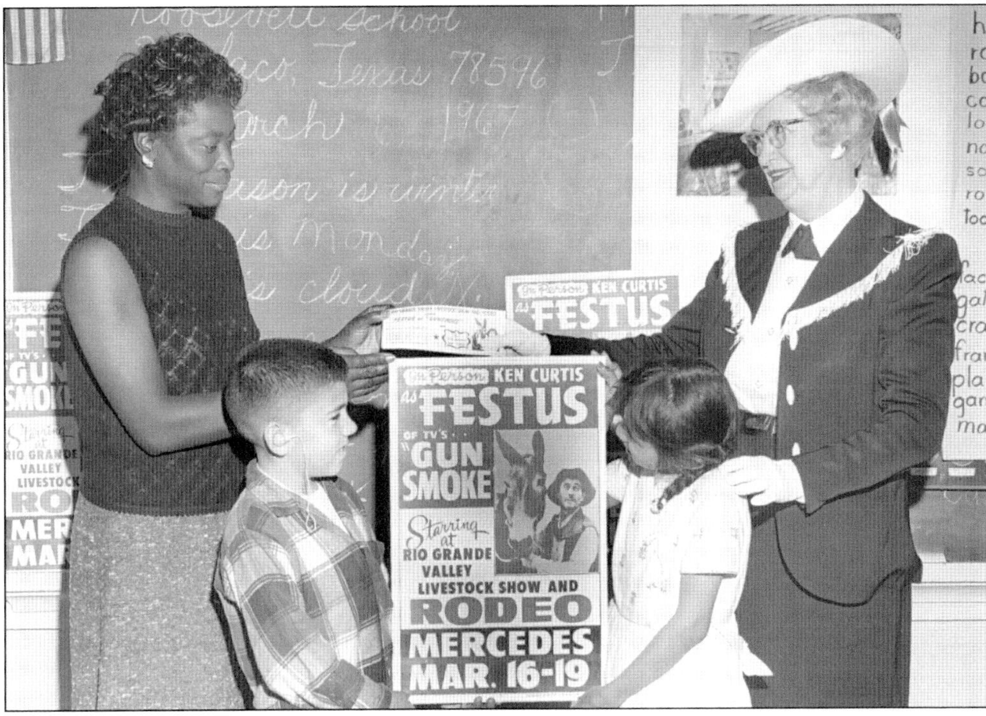

Parthenia Archer (left) receives two free rodeo tickets from show director Frances Cooper to see movie star Ken Curtis, who starred as Festus in the television show *Gunsmoke* and was featured at the 1967 Rio Grande Valley Livestock Show. Two unidentified children help hold up the poster announcing the event. (Weslaco Museum.)

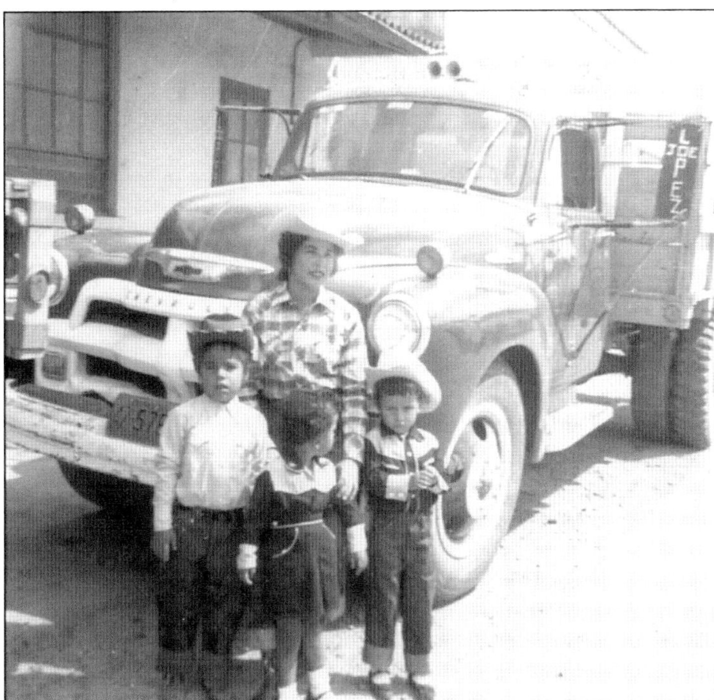

In this 1961 photograph, María Buenrostro (center back) prepares to take these children to the Rio Grande Valley Livestock Show. Children are, from left to right, Nátiz Buenrostro, Yolanda Jilpas, and Guadalupe Jilpas. Their activities include visiting the children's barnyard, the arts and crafts exhibits, the show animal pens, the rodeo, the midway carnival, antique farm equipment exhibit, a magician show, and enjoying live music. (Vito Buenrostro.)

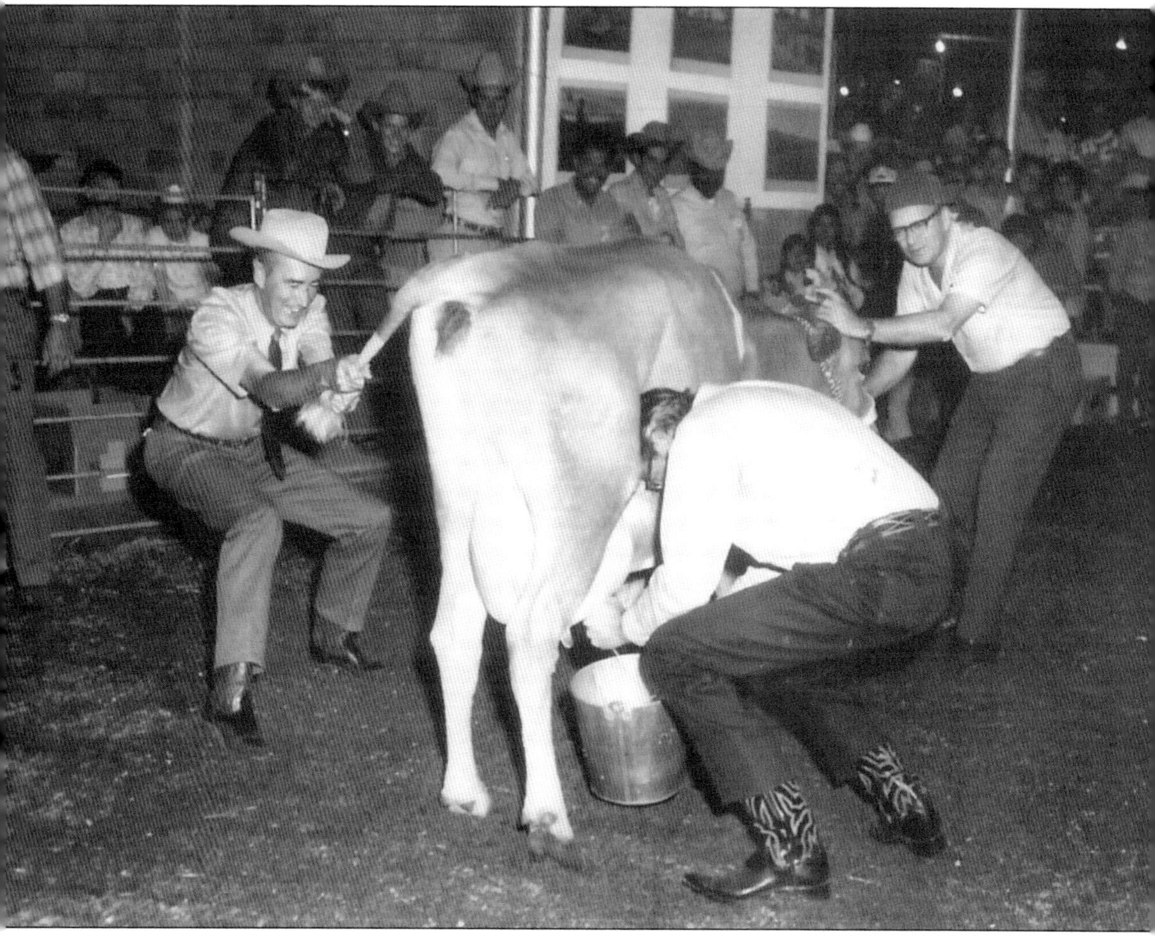

Charles "Charlie" Rankin, a popular Rio Grande Valley radio and television personality who was considered the "voice of agriculture" in the Valley for many years for his informative noon radio programs, takes part in a "wild" cow-milking contest during the 1971 Rio Grande Valley Livestock Show. From left to right, the competitors are Bob McDonald of KRGV holding the cow's tail, Rankin milking the cow, and Burt Johnson of KRIO holding the cow's head. Rankin was declared the winner. Rankin attended Texas A&M University after two years in the US Navy on an aircraft carrier during World War II. While at the university, he was instrumental in establishing the National Intercollegiate Rodeo Association, serving as its first president in 1949. He was often invited to serve as a judge or an announcer at the Rio Grande Livestock Show and Rodeo in Mercedes. (Rio Grande Valley Livestock Show Museum.)

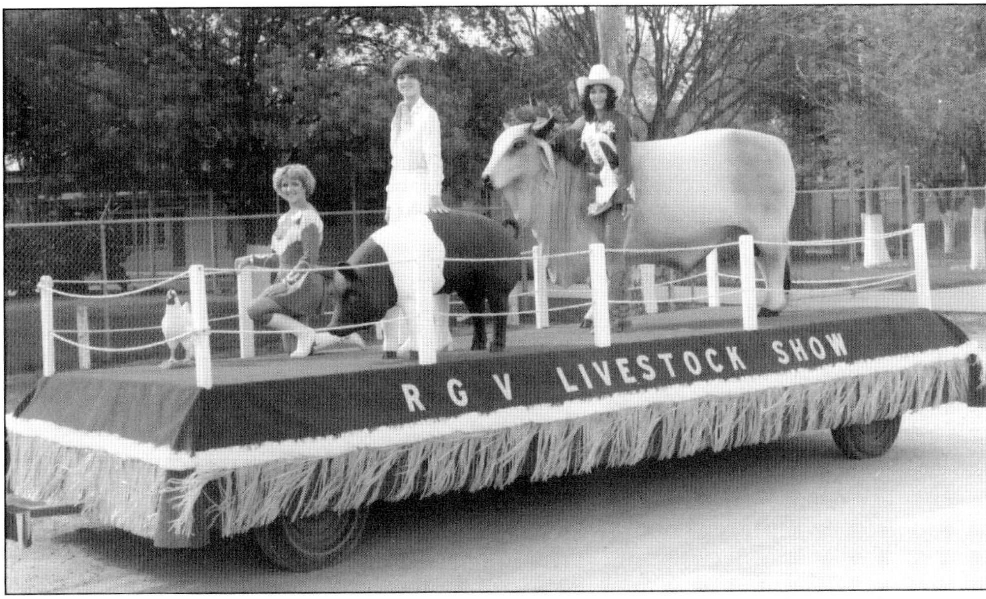

The Rio Grande Valley Livestock Show cover girl parade float every year features the winning cover girl and the first and second alternates. The parade is the opening event every March that kicks off the livestock show. The young ladies posing here are 1986 cover girl Claudette Smith and unidentified alternates. (Rio Grande Valley Livestock Show Museum.)

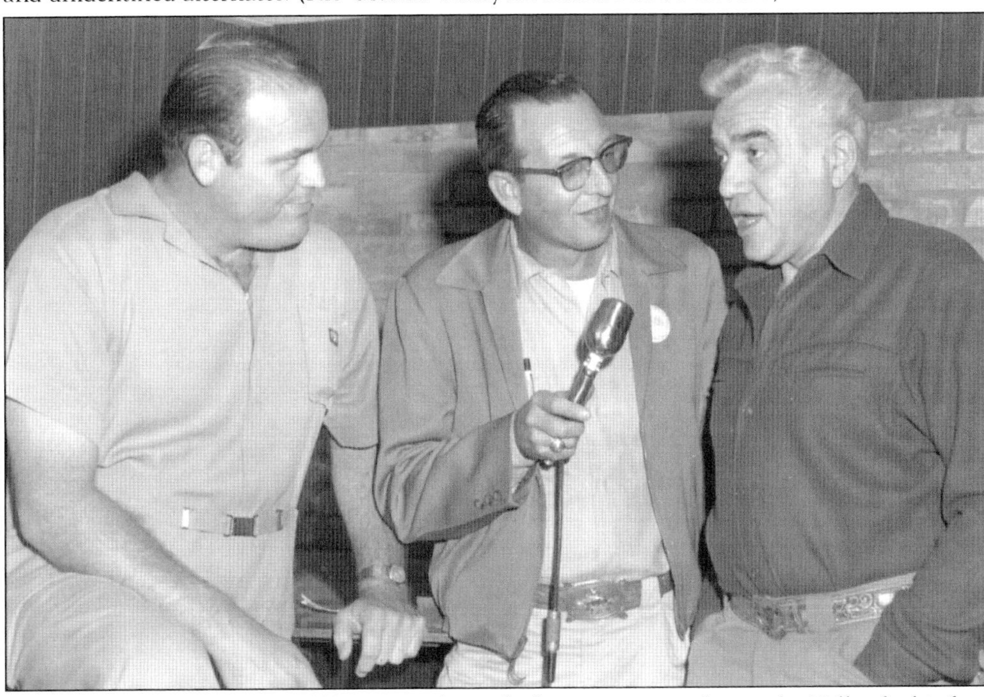

Charles "Charlie" Rankin, well-known radio and television personality in the Valley for his farm bureau talk shows, interviews Lorne Green and Ben Cartwright of the television show *Bonanza*. The two stars were featured guests of the Rio Grande Valley Livestock Show in 1973. The show often brought big name stars, including Gene Autry, Lynn Anderson, Johnny Rodríguez, Dwight Yoakum, and many others. (Rio Grande Valley Livestock Show Museum.)

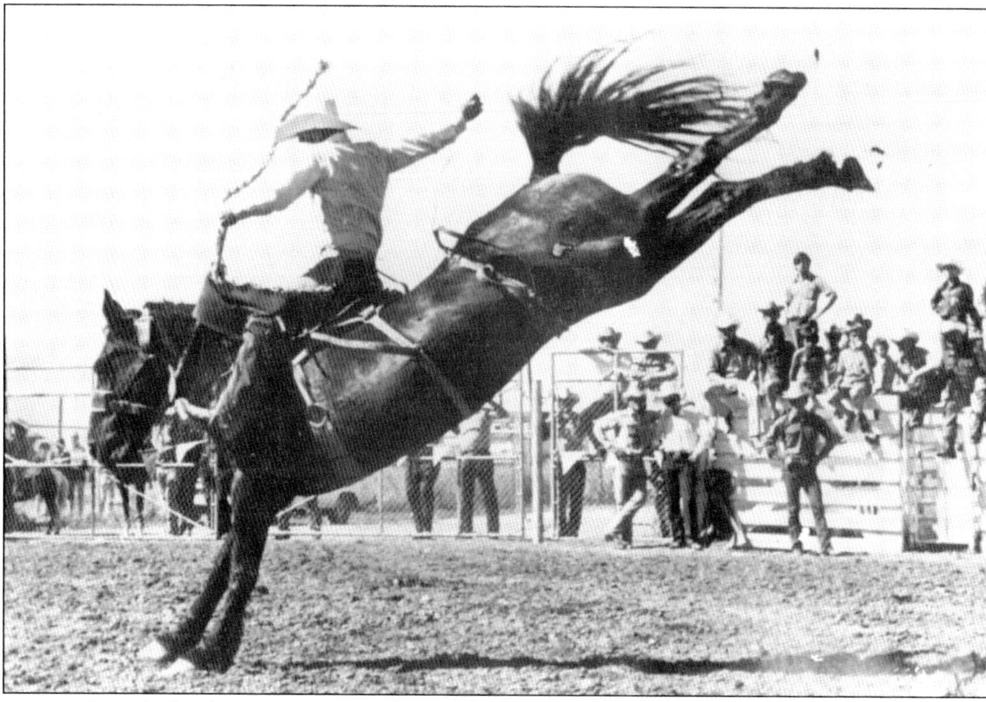

An unidentified rider competes in the saddle-bronc riding event at the Rio Grande Valley Livestock Show and Rodeo in 1959. In saddle-bronc riding, the rider holds a braided line with only one hand and attempts to stay on for at least eight seconds. Scores range from zero to 100 with 50 points depending on the horse's bucking moves and 50 depending on the rider's skill. (Rio Grande Valley Livestock Show Museum.)

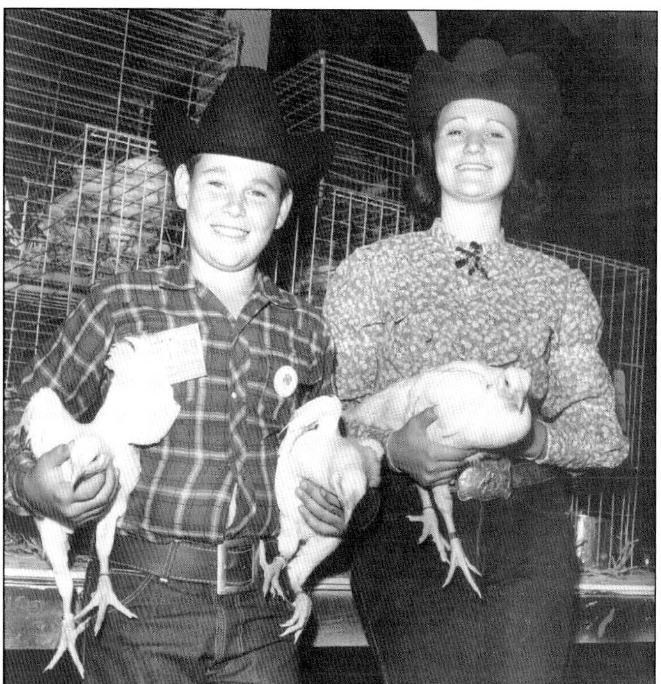

Taken at the fryer pens at the Rio Grande Livestock Show in 1965, this photograph shows Steven Dollery (left) and his sister Stephanie Dollery, 4-H members and children of James Dollery. James Dollery was an agriculture teacher at Mercedes High School and head sponsor of the FFA club in the 1950s and 1960s. (Weslaco Museum.)

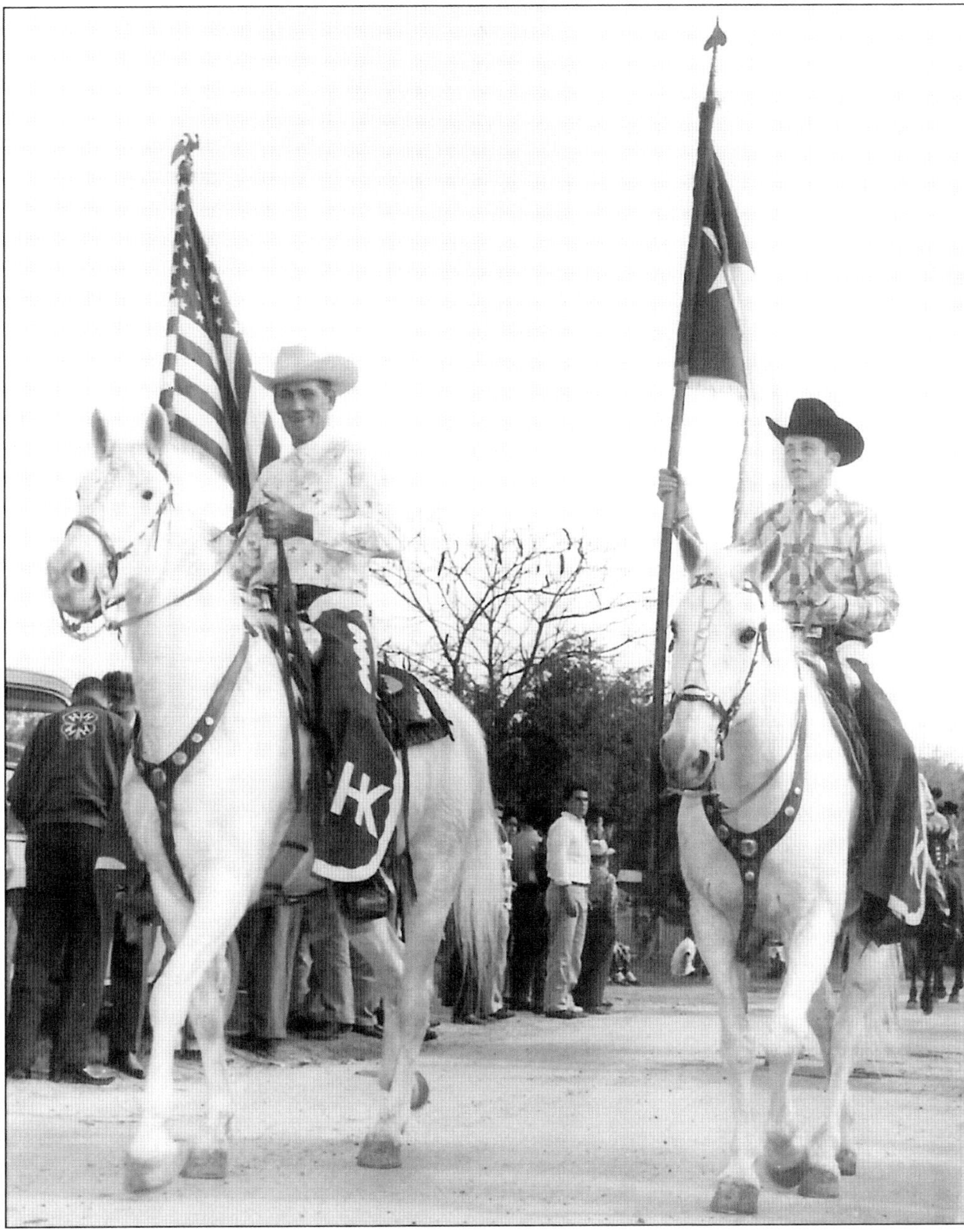

Leading the 1971 Rio Grande Valley Livestock Show Parade are two unidentified men wearing chaps with the famous HK brand of the 825,000-acre King Ranch. The HK brand was one of two official brands registered in 1859 for the King Ranch. The letters were the initials of Henrietta King, wife of King Ranch founder Richard King. In 1869, the Running W brand was registered and it remains the official brand today. The King Ranch is well known for developing the Santa Gertrudis cattle breed now recognized as a superior beef cattle breed. In its horse breeding efforts, the King Ranch has produced 1946 US Triple Crown winner Assault and 1950 Kentucky Derby winner Middleground. A King Ranch Quarter Horse named Wimpy was the very first registered horse of the American Quarter Horse Association in 1940, receiving the designation "P-1." (Rio Grande Valley Livestock Show Museum.)

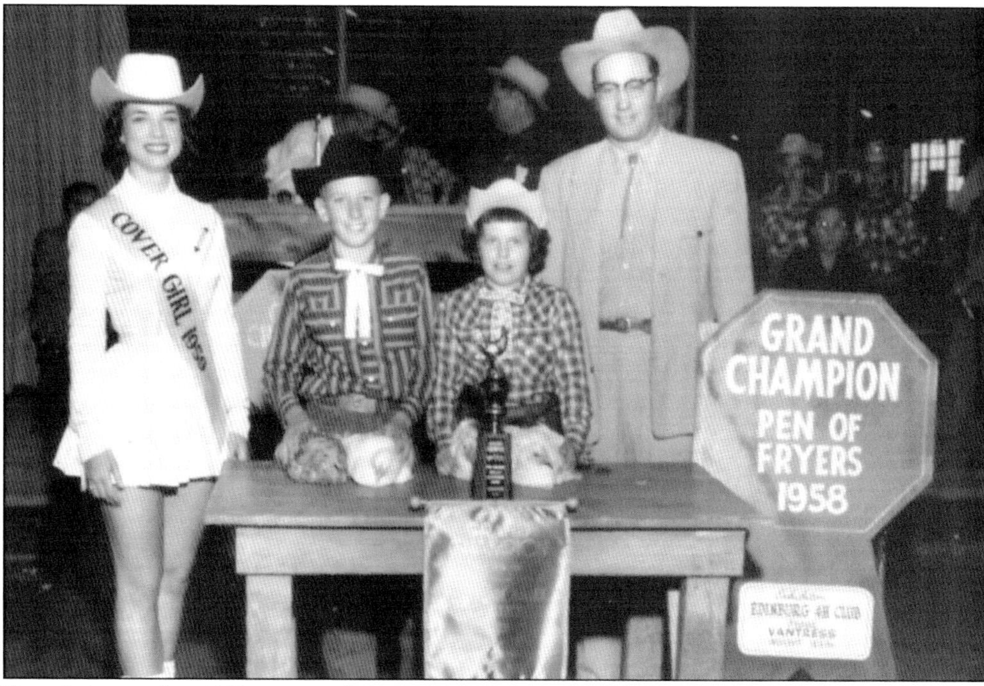

From left to right, 1959 cover girl Ann Watson poses in this photograph with Al Martin and Sherry Tripp, 4-H participants, and their "Grand Champion Pen of Fryers" at the 1958 Rio Grande Valley Livestock Show, as well as Dr. Joseph Townsend of Texas A&M University, who served as a judge at the event. (Rio Grande Valley Livestock Show Museum.)

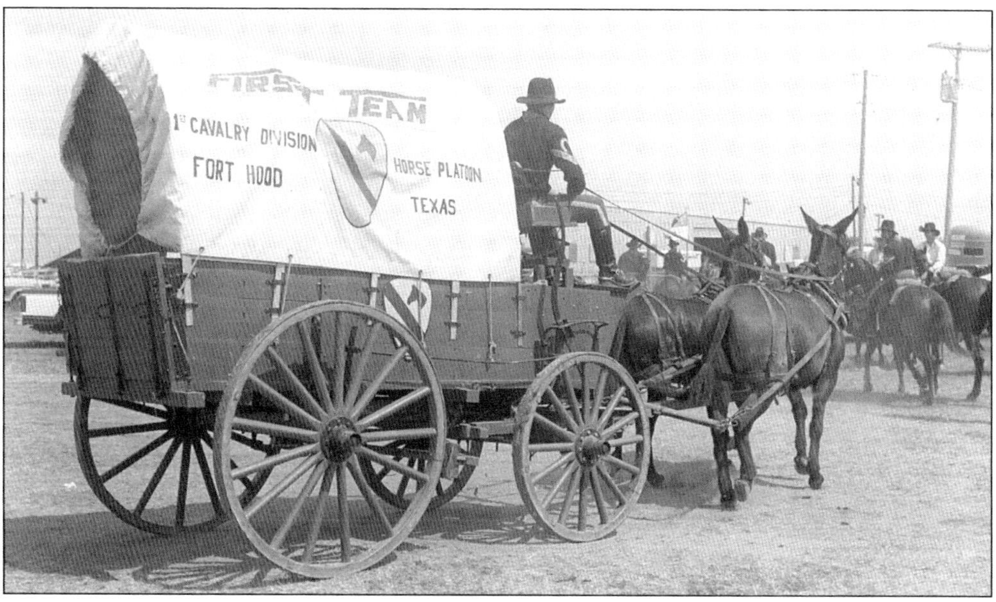

The Studebaker military escort wagon in this photograph is part of the 1st Cavalry Division from Fort Hood, Texas. The group formed in 1972 under the direction of Maj. Gen. James C. Smith and represents an 1870 era "horse soldier" troop wearing standard issue Civil War Union uniforms. They perform mounted drills and weapons demonstrations and were featured guest performers at the 1973 Rio Grande Valley Livestock Show. (Rio Grande Valley Livestock Show Museum.)

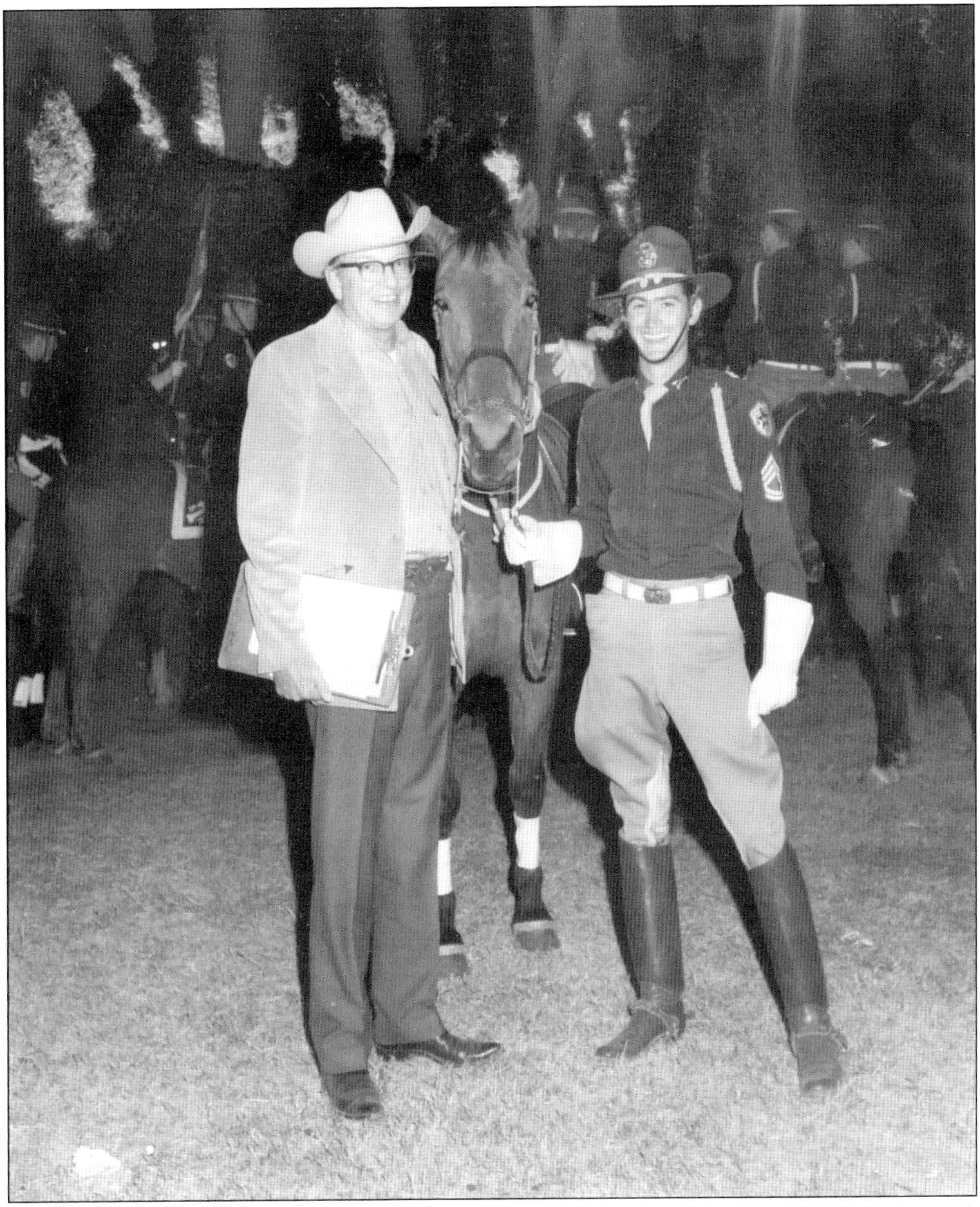

Charles "Charlie" Rankin (left) poses with an unidentified member of the Texas A&M University's Parson's Mounted Cavalry, a ceremonial horse cavalry unit founded in 1974 to preserve traditions of the Texas A&M Cavalry of the 1920s and 1930s. The Cavalry is part of the Corps of Cadets, which was established in 1876 as a student military organization. Texas A&M University is one of six US colleges classified as a senior military college. The Corpsman shown here with Rankin is wearing "senior boots," brown leather boots to the knees worn only by Texas A&M seniors. Parson's Mounted Cavalry represents the university at parades, agricultural fairs, livestock shows, and equestrian events in Texas. The group performed military maneuvers on horseback at the 1975 Rio Grande Valley Livestock Show. (Rio Grande Valley Livestock Show Museum.)

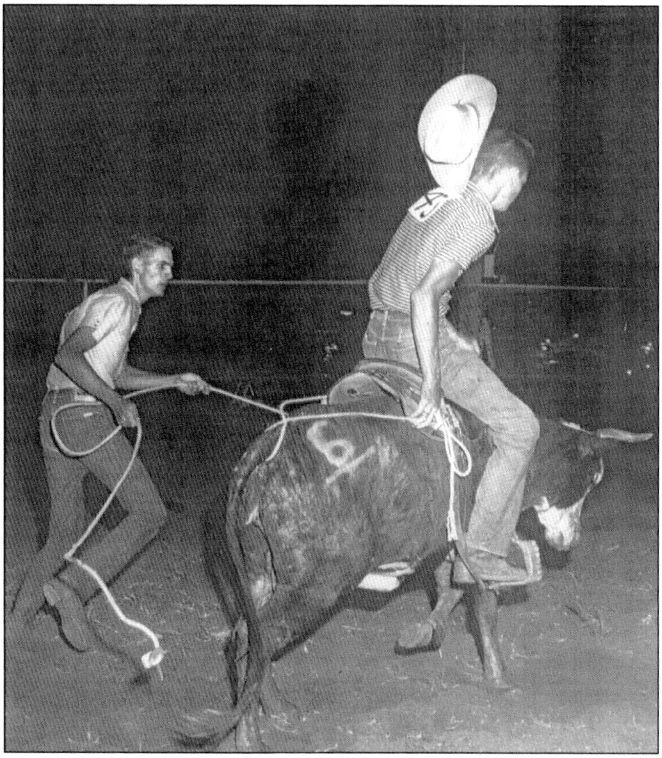

Vincent Neuhaus, left, and Earl Neuhaus, mounted, participate in a steer-riding event at the Rio Grande Valley Livestock Show in 1964. Both attended Texas A&M University in College Station, Texas. Both own several successful farm equipment businesses although in different cities, and Earl also has served as president of the Rio Grande Valley Livestock Show. (Rio Grande Valley Livestock Show Museum.)

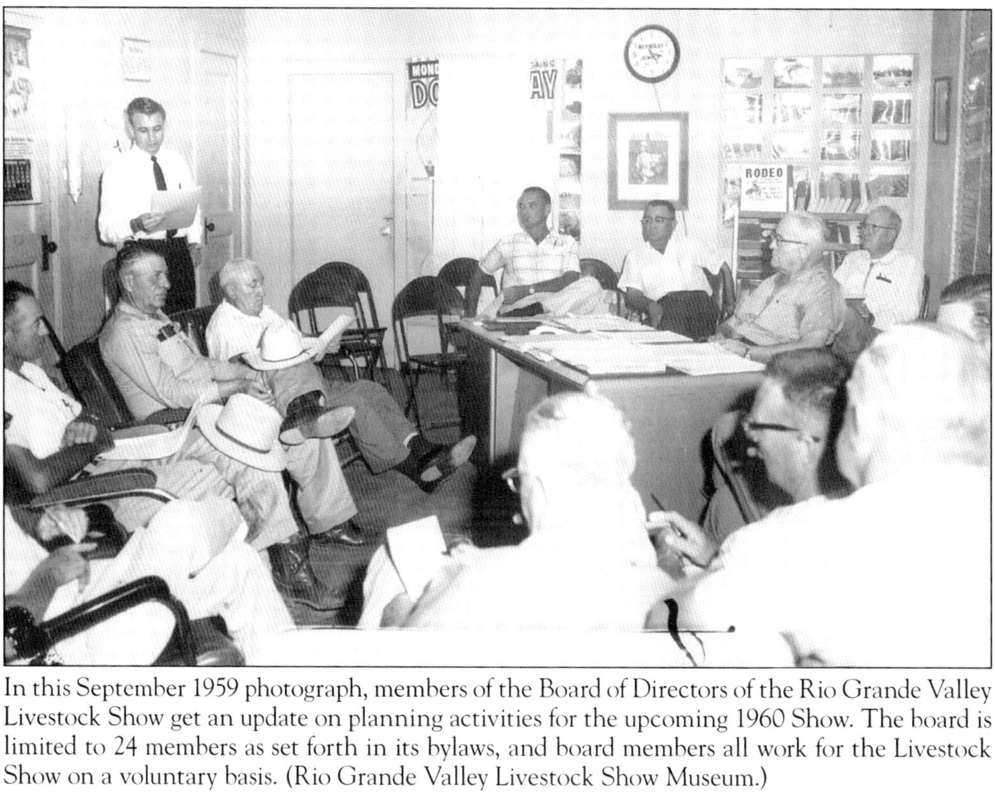

In this September 1959 photograph, members of the Board of Directors of the Rio Grande Valley Livestock Show get an update on planning activities for the upcoming 1960 Show. The board is limited to 24 members as set forth in its bylaws, and board members all work for the Livestock Show on a voluntary basis. (Rio Grande Valley Livestock Show Museum.)

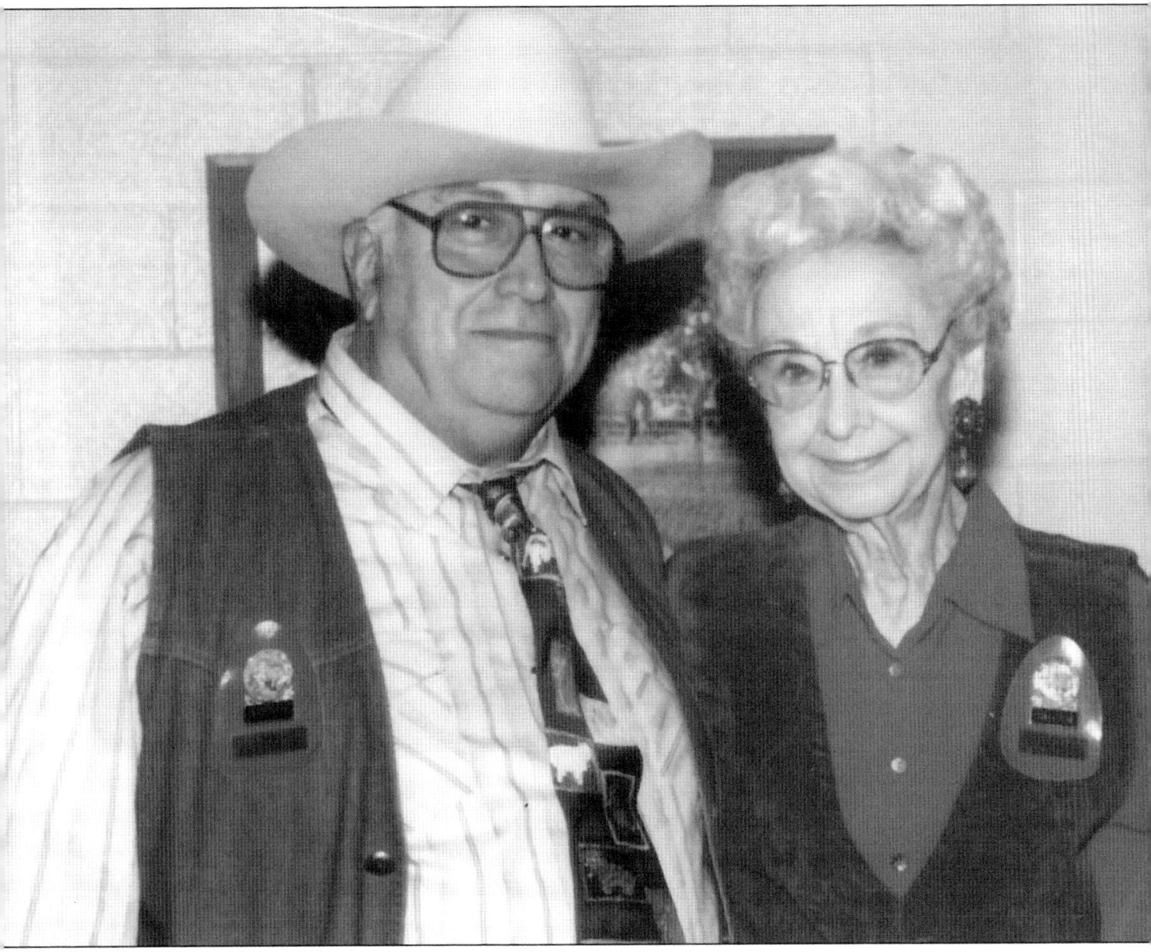

Pictured recently are Dario "D.V." Guerra (left), president emeritus of the Rio Grande Valley Livestock Show, and grande dame Frances Richmond Cooper, show director. Guerra is the owner of the D.V. Guerra Ranch in Edinburg and is a longtime volunteer with the livestock show. Cooper first went to work for the Rio Grande Valley Livestock Show in December 1954 as secretary to the manager. In 1959, she became show manager and remained in that position until she retired in 1986. Upon her retirement, she served on the board of directors as a volunteer until her death in 2009. She always declared she loved best the awards she received from the Texas FFA and the 4-H clubs. The Texas Association of Fairs and Events, in which she served 13 years as executive secretary, awarded her with its lifetime achievement award in 2002. In 2004, the International Association of Fairs and Expositions presented her with the prestigious Heritage Award for promoting not only the Rio Grande Valley Livestock Show but also fairs across the United States. (Rio Grande Valley Livestock Show Museum.)